Architecture byTeam

Architecture byTeam

A New Concept for the Practice of Architecture
by William Wayne Caudill
Caudill Rowlett Scott

VNR VAN NOSTRAND REINHOLD COMPANY   *New York   Cincinnati   Toronto   London   Melbourne*

Van Nostrand Reinhold Company Regional Offices:
New York Cincinnati Chicago Millbrae Dallas

Van Nostrand Reinhold Company International Offices:
London Toronto Melbourne

Copyright © 1971 by Litton Educational Publishing, Inc.

Library of Congress Catalog Card Number: 75-157696

Manufactured in the United States of America

Published by Van Nostrand Reinhold Company
450 West 33rd Street, New York, N.Y. 10001

Published simultaneously in Canada by Van Nostrand Reinhold Ltd.

15 14 13 12 11 10 9 8 7 6 5 4 3 2 1

Foreword

The end of the modern revolution in architectural *design* had just about been reached by the time of the mid-forties, and the era of the modern revolution in architectural *practice* had begun. Few realized what was happening at the time. All of the great modern masters, Mies, Wright, Gropius, Corbusier were alive and well and active. But architects, generally, were ill-prepared for coping with the great demands and necessities of the post-war building boom.

Of the prophets of the time, one of the earliest was Bill Caudill. He would readily admit that his vision of the future certainly did not encompass all that eventually came to pass. But he knew things were going to happen in architecture, and he expected to master them. Together with his earliest partner, John Rowlett, Caudill set out to conquer this world of change. Through the years, they never gave up the quest. And Wallie Scott, who joined with the others to make up the firm of Caudill Rowlett Scott, and Willie Pena who became a partner soon after, and Tom Bullock and all of the others who came later have never faltered in the quest either.

From its founding, Caudill Rowlett Scott was organized for growth, for change, for improvement of architecture and its practice. The concept of team architecture came early. As Bill Caudill, never one to pull his punches, now puts it, "The prima donnas have had their day. Now the architect is a team." The day of the single building for a single client by a single architect was coming to an end. In the future would come a group of buildings for a corporate client done by an architect team. To Caudill, a team is not the same thing as a committee, "A number of people polling their opinions and voting their prejudices." Rather, a team is composed of, "A group of specialists solving problems in an atmosphere where the opinions of each are respected, but the highest value is placed on the opinions of a specialist within his specialty."

According to the Caudill view, and that of CRS, the makeup and member-bership of a given team must vary considerably from that of another. In architecture, each team must have capabilities in three major areas: management, design and technology. Beyond that, each team must be matched to its task. A small team for a small problem, a large team for one that is more complex. A team of only architects sometimes, or of engineers. An interdisciplinary team composed of architects, engineers, planners, behavioral scientists, computer experts, construction managers, building-type consultants, systems experts for the large complex problems of urbanization—housing, transportation or the like.

Over the years, Bill Caudill and the others in CRS have nurtured the team concept and developed it. They have been responsive to growth and change and have generated both. They have built a large national organization with offices in Houston, New York and Los Angeles, with more to come. They pioneered what they call "squatters teams," groups who go into a client's offices for days or weeks at a time, to program and design right at the scene of the action. They incorporated the firm almost twenty years ago to enhance the benefits to their employees and to prepare for expansion. They spawned specialized functions prolifically and organized them into going concerns—organizations like their Computing Research Systems Corporation, their interiors and graphics division and their management planning group.

Much of what Bill Caudill and CRS have accomplished over the years has been quite controversial, if not downright revolutionary. Who ever heard of an architectural firm with a computer software company as a subsidiary?

But the controversy has proved a challenge to the firm, the revolution a way of life. Of late, the firm has been reorganized again, under a corporate umbrella called CRS Design Associates, Inc. which owns all of the subsidiary operations. Some will be shocked to hear members of the firm casually mention that this step will eventually allow the firm to go public if that should seem desirable.

The controversy, the change, the philosophy of Bill Caudill and CRS, as well as the concept and practice of architecture by team, are the subjects of this book. It is a very personal account by one of the great individualist members of the architectural profession, but an individual who chose to apply his talents and energies to team practice. Anyone who has any interest at all in architecture and its practice should find what the author has to say here both provocative and informative.

William Dudley Hunt, Jr., FAIA

Washington, D.C.
February 1971

Preface

The day of the prima donna approach to designing buildings has passed.

The new way is by team. Almost any team can produce mere shelter, but to produce buildings which possess architecture takes a new kind of team—one sensitive to human needs and values. The idea of architecture by team has three underlying, secondary ideas: (1) The team is a genius, (2) the client/user is a member of the team, and (3) the team is an ever-expanding unit, not limited to the design profession.

Let there be no misunderstanding what this book is all about. It isn't a survey of the field. Or a textbook. Or a scholarly piece of research. It started out to be that, but my advisors at Rice University, where I hold the William Ward Watkin Chair, read a chapter or two of the original manuscript and said that I should quit trying to play professor and "play it as it is—be a practitioner." One of them remarked, "Bill, CRS is more team-oriented than any firm we know. Make the book personal and CRS." I took his advice.

"Architecture by Team" is written primarily for the enlightened layman—for people who serve on building committees, for school board members, governmental officials, corporate officers, and others who are interested in designing and constructing new facilities. It is aimed at the users, too—those too-often forgotten people. The book also will be useful to members of developer teams which finance, design, and construct buildings. Hopefully, too, the design/building professional will be able to interpolate the CRS experiences with his own and profit accordingly.

What is Architecture? Any God-fearing, convention-going, dues-paying architect would never dream of saying out loud, not to mention putting in a book, what he thinks architecture is. I got caught. Since the title has the omnipotent word "architecture" in it, I had to devote at least a section to it. Unquestionably I will be a target for architectural theologians. So be it.

The title "Architecture by Team" also got me in hot water with some of the key people of the team I played on—the CRS team. I made the mistake of bringing in some of my teammates to criticize and advise. And what criticisms they had to offer! It took me five months to take out some of the big chunks of verbosity they wanted removed, and even longer to put back in some bigger chunks they thought should be included. My first reaction was to tell them, "Go to hell, I'll write the book myself." But the title had me in a corner.

My teammates Steve Kliment and Tom Bullock were particularly active in this butchering of the original manuscript. But I'm grateful to them. We have a better book. I also owe never-dying thanks to Ann Mohler and Jan Talbot, who have tried to keep my grammar clean. I owe, too, a big thanks to Jeff Corbin, who helped with the format and jacket design.

Of course, the greatest thanks should be to the CRS team. Without those wonderful colleagues of mine, I would have had nothing to write about.

Houston, Texas
March 1971

William W. Caudill

Contents

SECTION NINE: THE TEAM AND BUILDING SYSTEMS

Section

1

Background: Team Concept at CRS

For most architects "we" is the most difficult word in the English language. Architects seem to be innately "I" people. For this architect, however, "we" is easy to say. I can't say "I have designed over 700 buildings." But I can say "We have designed over 700 buildings." This "we" is Caudill Rowlett Scott—CRS—architects, planners, engineers. Although we have scores of registered architects and registered engineers on our team, it includes people in a lot of other professions, people such as behavioral scientists, hospital consultants, construction managers, computer programming experts, construction systems consultants, educational facilities specialists, and accountants. Through the quarter century of CRS' practice we have learned that we had to form a big interdisciplinary team to cope with the problems of urbanization. We believe in architecture by team.

1

CRS spirit of cooperation came early

Unless architects develop team consciousness, the profession has only a slim chance of survival. Those architects who still believe that the complex building groups of today can be designed by one man working alone are deluding themselves. And tomorrow? Architects must develop the art of collaboration to a high level of sophistication.

Our own team came into being in 1944, on the Coronado Ferry off San Diego, to be exact. While in the Navy, John M. Rowlett and I conceived the idea of forming a firm, although we must have considered the prospect while we were both teaching at Texas A & M University before World War II.

We both wanted to design schools, although it took us over two years of practice before we had the opportunity to do one—having followed the usual architects' pattern of beginning with small houses. Our interest in schools stemmed from the fact that Rowlett had graduated from the University of Texas with a degree in education as well as in architecture, and that at age twenty-six I had written a little book, "Space for Teaching," on how to design a schoolhouse. I had never actually designed a schoolhouse, but who cared? In those years they weren't building them anyway. At any rate, Rowlett and I were a team (of sorts) from the beginning.

I have always been committed to the team concept, whether playing short-stop for the Southside Bombers back in Durant, Oklahoma, when I was a kid, or tooting the trombone as a teenager in Oklahoma City in a series of dance bands with such exotic names as "The Derby Domes" and the "Seven Melody Gushers." The art of collaboration came early.

This photo of John Rowlett, left, and the author was taken on CRS Founder's Day—March 1, 1946. Rowlett was still in the Navy, and had to borrow the photographer's jacket to wear over his uniform. The drawings on the walls didn't belong to us, either. We had no jobs and no prospects of jobs—but we each had $500 to gamble on the future.

2

We doubled in size—from two to four

John and I started our fledgling firm over a grocery store on Guadalupe Street in Austin, Texas, on March 1, 1946. Two years later, we moved our office to College Station over the drugstore at Northgate. Six months later (the rent came due) we moved over the Southside Grocery, not a glorious or improved setting, since the Austin location had also been over a grocery business. (There must have been some sort of hereditary pull involved since both my father and my grandfather were in the grocery business, and I had served as a foodstore flunky during my high school and college days.)

The first office in Austin was operated as a team in its most simple form. All the work was done by the two of us. Fortunately, Caudill and Rowlett jobs were quite small, so we did not have to go outside the firm to get engineering consultation. Rowlett was good, more experienced than I, in production. I thought I was better in design. (I'm sure he thought otherwise.) Those were the days, of course, when models were not "in." But renderings were. Big renderings. I recall Rowlett's making a six-foot by four-foot rendering in oil, while I served as the master's helper. There was never a rendering like that one before, and there has been none since.

"Great Scott! I thought you were Channel 11, CBS." We have many other folklore stories about our Houston office. Since only the 40′ x 40′ entrance tower can be seen from the street, people get various impressions. At least three or four architects who have seen it from the road say it looks like a church. Some people have referred to it as a drive-in movie. One lady who drove up to the building saw only the entrance lobby and couldn't understand why such a small building needed so much parking. A New Yorker, whom we wanted to impress, drove up to the tower in a taxicab. The taxi driver, not wishing to offend us, said, "It sure is a small building, but I guess they get a lot of work done."

My dad and his dad before him had grocery stores. I worked in grocery stores on Saturdays and summers while in junior high school, high school, and during part of my college days. I was sick of the grocery business. Yet our first offices in Austin and in College Station were over grocery stores. I remember one time as a checker I got rattled, put the nickel in a paper sack, and tried to cram the bread into the cash register.

Here's the Southside Grocery in College Station, Texas, where CRS had offices on the second floor (having previously had offices over a grocery in Austin and a drugstore in College Station). It was from this address that William M. Pena wrote to a prestigious Manhattan furniture designer asking him to change our address "from over the Southside Grocery to Box 308, College Station, Texas, because the butcher is getting our mail."

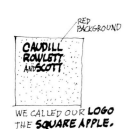

RED BACKGROUND

CAUDILL ROWLETT AND SCOTT

WE CALLED OUR **LOGO** THE **SQUARE APPLE**.

C R

WE HAD A **PRIMITIVE**, BUT EFFECTIVE TEAM — A **BACK-TO-BACK** SITUATION. WE KNEW WHAT THE OTHER WAS DOING WITHOUT LOOKING.

Rowlett and I had a good two-man team going, a back-to-back situation. He could be doing the plans while I was doing the elevations, and we would end with a coordinated set of drawings. We were tuned in; each knew what the other was doing without looking. We had a primitive but effective team.

Wallie E. Scott joined our partnership in 1949, and we became Caudill Rowlett and Scott. William M. Pena joined the following year. Bless Pena, he insisted on keeping the firm's name short. With four partners our team became more complicated, if not more sophisticated. During this period, while we officed over the Southside Grocery, I recall Pena's writing a letter to a prestigious Manhattan furniture company asking that our address be changed "from over the Southside Grocery to Box 308, College Station, Texas, because the butcher is getting our mail."

Our firm name was changed to Caudill Rowlett and Scott in 1949, when this picture was taken. Reading from left are Caudill, Scott, Rowlett, and the fourth partner, William Pena, who suggested we stop adding names to the CRS string as we took on new partners. The sawhorses were "borrowed" from Texas A & M University.

Here are the first four partners again, in a photo taken twenty-one years later. What a rat race it must have been! This shot was taken in the new CRS office building, located in no proximity whatever to a grocery store, but on a densely wooded plot hugging the banks of Houston's Buffalo Bayou.

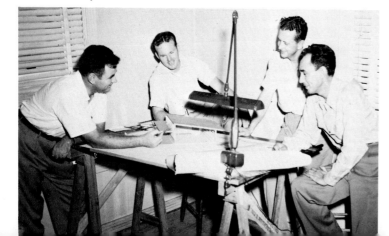

3
We weathered rough storms of practice

Before a young firm can design a building, it has to get one to design. The getting in those early years was tough. Invariably when all four of us were busy day and night trying to get a job out, we neglected to get one *in,* and without promoting new work we generally ended up dusting off projectless drafting boards with nothing else to do but borrow money from the bank and curse the "establishment" that was busy.

During one of these depression periods, Scott and Pena, fortunately both bachelors at the time, took home no pay for two months. Rowlett wasn't overly impressed with this sacrificial act, for he and his family had to live for six months on government unemployment compensation. As for me, I was teaching at Texas A & M, commuting the 100 miles to work, but receiving regular checks—and hot criticisms from a few practitioners who felt that their state taxes were paying my salary so I could be their competition.

In those days competition was rough and we had some heartbreaking experiences. I recall the time in 1953 when the school board in Manor, Texas, wrote us, "The majority of the board members was favorable to your firm, but one or two preferred others. To keep harmony we put the names of eight firms in a hat and drew. The name of another firm was drawn."

But the four of us wanted to eat. All the team effort in the world would not have saved that one.

So much for hearts and flowers. The point is that no matter how small the firm, there must be someone involved in the business of getting jobs,

BINGO!

NO JOBS

WE **LOST,** BUT WHAT A WAY TO RUN A BUSINESS

7

TAKE 4 PEOPLE, PULLING AGAINST EACH OTHER GETTING NOWHERE.

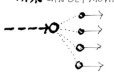

PUT THE SAME 4 PEOPLE IN A **TEAM** SITUATION PULLING TOGETHER, WITH A COMMON GOAL AND A COOPERATIVE ATTITUDE; THEN THE **TASK** CAN GET MOVING.

whether knocking on doors, filling out questionnaires, or going to interviews. Good times did finally come for us. We went along our professional way merrily and with some degree of success after the unemployment drought.

It was my childhood friend John F. Y. Stambaugh who warned us back in 1950 that we could no longer operate as four self-minded dilettantes. John was a team man—he had played third base with me in school and played his virtuoso tenor sax with me in those dance bands. "You remind me of four kids in four separate canoes gliding beautifully about in four different directions on a smooth lake," he charged. (He could have been more charitable and said four prima donnas, which we really thought we were. Members of our "team" had not yet learned to say "we.")

Stambaugh posed this question, "What will happen when the water gets rough?" And it did. We had many storms. Thanks to the counseling of Stambaugh, who has given us management and financial advice from the very beginning of the firm, we tied our canoes together legally and organizationally and were able to weather the storms. He also helped us to create a team dedicated to common goals stemming from a common philosophy—not just a firm of individuals sharing a common office. John taught us to say "we."

4

Our areas of specialization changed

After the psychological shock of switching from "I" to "we," each of us decided in which areas to specialize. Our areas of specialization then and now are two different things. Pena chose to do specifications and interior design (an unlikely combination). But he did quite well at both, especially in his work with color. In fact, he became nationally known for his work in ridding schools of "schoolhouse brown." Today he has given up color, and would not touch specifications with a ten-foot pole, not to mention trying to compete with the computer in retrieval and dissemination of the construction data so necessary for efficient specifications writing. As it turned out, his great strength is in building programming, as a nationally prominent speaker and writer, and in including programmers as important members of the team. He's a team man to the core.

Scott was the best we had on design development and production during the first six years of CRS. He has a keen analytical mind, and he knew how to put the pieces together. At the time, however, we thought he had little talent for getting along with clients, and would have hidden him in the closet during client visits if we thought we could have gotten away with it. Now Scott has developed his great talent to communicate (latent and untapped during those early years) with potential clients. Not all of our people have developed like Scott. We have some who still use the team to carry them.

SYMBIOSIS

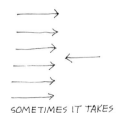

SOMETIMES IT TAKES THIS TO BE A LEADER.

Twenty-five years of team practice have changed Rowlett and Caudill as well. Rowlett used to play the role of Mr. Inside Man, bred to work but too compassionate to make fellow workers do the same. I was Mr. Outside Man—and the firm's SOB, the cracker of the whip. More recently Rowlett has capitalized on his apparent shyness. He is disarmingly aggressive; better than I with outside matters, such as making friends for CRS and dealing with prospective clients. This is good. Team members should not be alike, they should complement one another—Jack Spratt fashion. If two think alike, we don't need one of them.

S.O.B.

EVERY FIRM NEEDS ONE

5

A book was our promotion tool

My little book "Space for Teaching" turned out to be a good job getter. It was largely responsible for our first school job in Blackwell, Oklahoma. And it got us a job, almost without an interview, in Albany, Texas. In 1950 we received a call from Robert Nail, secretary of the school board, saying they were interviewing architects for a job, and that at least three of them had referred to the book. He said, "I'm curious to know about the guy who wrote the book. Would you be interested in coming to Albany to talk with the Board about it?" Would we! That night, after driving over 300 miles for the interview, we got the job. That $500,000 school was inconceivably big at the time. The fact that I had written the book and Rowlett had been educated to talk the lingo of educators helped us break into the school field. We were specially equipped.

This is the first CRS-designed school, in Blackwell, Oklahoma, made famous by a story written in *Colliers* magazine by Walter McQuade, now an editor of *Fortune.* Behind the grill are the "outdoor toilets." We told the school board that if we could use outdoor corridors, we could give them to extra classrooms. They needed the space. Legally this was a Caudill and Rowlett school because Scott had not yet obtained his license in Oklahoma—the Texas and Oklahoma architectural registration boards were fussing—but both Scott and Pena played very strong parts in designing this school. Scott and I made up the first squatters where we "lived in the school board room for a week." Design was started in 1948. Philip A. Welber was the associate architect, our first.

Of course the book didn't always work in landing jobs. During one of our many business droughts after our firm got started, we mailed the book ahead before an interview—it was about the only evidence that we knew how to design a schoolhouse. When we arrived for the interview, however, the president of the school board acknowledged receipt of the book, gave me a cold once-over, and said, "I'm sorry your father could not have come." We didn't get that job, but I did go out and buy a hat, to give the impression of age and experience.

"Space for Teaching" was recognized in 1952 by the Royal Institute of British Architects as "the most generally useful school design studies in existence"; and leading United States educators, including Dr. Walter D. Cocking, considered it one of the strongest forces to revolutionize schoolhouses in America. What the little book did, besides help put us into business, was give us a specialty. CRS became nationally known school specialists—without having done too many schools. Ten years later we had a hard time convincing people we could do anything else.

The Albany School, shown in a November 1951 photo, was a "finger plan" to end all finger plans. We stretched the concept to its elastic limits, and had classroom wings stretching all over the plains of West Texas. The photo shows the wood egg crate ceiling, which reflects a mixture of natural and electric light, a pioneering effort in the luminous ceiling.

6
CRS growth was inevitable

CRS is committed to growth. To keep the people we want to keep and to do the things we want to do, we simply have to grow. It has been a natural thing for us. When we felt that an engineer was important to team operation we brought in an engineer. When we thought we needed a planner to help us with outside spaces as in the case of the high school in San Angelo, Texas, we added a planner to our team. We acquired interior

11

The first six CRS partners posed for this photo in 1956 in Oklahoma City. From left to right are Caudill, Rowlett, Scott, Bullock, Nye, and Pena.

THE TEAM GREW.

designers and graphics designers as we needed them. It was not a deliberate plan on our part to get big—at least not in the beginning. We grew because we had to. It is another story today. We are growing because we want to. We believe in the expanded team.

In May 1952, we brought in Bill Perry, the first nonarchitect, nonengineer, type. Bill taught us that making a profit is no sin, contrary to our artist-like upbringing in various schools of architecture. The little schoolhouses we were destined to do were profitable. They allowed us to expand the partner ship. After Caudill, Rowlett, Scott, and Pena came Thomas A. Bullock. Like Pena and Scott, he was a student of Rowlett's and mine. Tom later became our boss. After Bullock there was Charles Lawrence who was made a partner in 1956 and whom I rank among the nation's top designers. In the same year Edward F. Nye was made a partner and today as a structural engineer he is our most experienced technologist. Then in 1961 C. Herbert Paseur was brought into the partnership, and in October 1965, he took over from Bullock the responsibilities as the chief administrator of the firm. All eight of these men have served on the CRS Board of Directors. We shared common goals but we thought differently. And that was our strength. Today we have even greater diversities and the resulting greater strengths. We believe there is strength in numbers, provided the people can be brought together in team action. If not, numbers mean nothing, except to gum things up.

In 1955 we were confronted with the importance of being big, which we were not. We were trying to get a big housing job out of our Oklahoma City office, which we had established in 1952 (the same year we moved our office from over the College Station grocery store to a first-floor situation in Bryan, Texas. Progress!).

By this time we realized that we had to present a big team if we were to get any big jobs. For instance, our Oklahoma office, run by John Rowlett and Tom Bullock, wasn't much of an office—only three little rooms and just a few young college kids on the drafting boards. When out of the blue we received a letter that a group from the Air Force would visit our Oklahoma City office to see if we were qualified (and large enough, was the implication) to do a housing project for the Air Force Base in Enid, Oklahoma, Tom Bullock got very concerned about how we could impress the Air Force. When the momentous day arrived for the visitation, Bullock had all the college kids in neckties. Athough he denies this, I distinctly recall that he had some of the kids' friends sitting around, dummies to make us appear bigger than we really were. Bullock also maneuvered the visitors through the office so many different ways that we were convinced they got vertigo and thought they were in a large office. Subterfuge, yes— but our team got the job, and our break into housing.

Here, in a photo taken in 1955 in Oklahoma City, are Tom Bullock, manager of that office, and Herb Paseur, his chief designer. Paseur later became both Bullock's and my boss.

13

7

Bullock led the CRS team between August 1957 and October 1965

The year 1957 was one of drastic change for CRS. At the time we had forty-two people including the eight partners. That year Tom Bullock took over the leadership from me. That year CRS invaded the East Coast, giving us three essentially self-contained offices—Bryan, Oklahoma City, and Corning, New York. That year we started planning the move of our Bryan office to Houston—Tom's idea. And, even more important, in 1957 we changed to a corporate form of organization.

Actually it was a combination partnership/corporation; we retained the partnership for two reasons: We felt the profession looked down on the corporations as something deadening to creativity, even bordering on unethical; and most state laws permitted architectural practice only through partnerships of specific individuals.

In July of 1957 CRS Design, Inc. was superimposed upon the partnership. There were tax advantages and managerial benefits for operating an expanded CRS team. Interestingly enough, in 1968 we gave serious consideration to returning to a pure form of partnership, again for tax advantage. So there are no cut and dried answers.

But going the corporation route did more than save us a few bucks—it strengthened the team concept by giving us a broader base of ownership. We were forced to work together.

Oklahoma City's Bettes Building, designed by CRS in 1955, was our first office building, and it was designed to house the CRS Oklahoma City team. It was this office in which Tom Bullock gave the Air Force vertigo with his whirlwind tour of our facilities.

Ten years after our move to Houston, we completed our own office building. It sits on a four-acre site on the Buffalo Bayou not far from downtown Houston.

15

CRS Design, Inc. also provided a device for giving everyone in CRS long-range security and profit sharing through the Deferred Compensation Trust, which set aside profits. Another thing the corporation did was dull the hard line between partners and nonpartners, making us a more cohesive group. In the summer of 1958, under Bullock's leadership, we approved and initiated a ten-year program to strengthen CRS through diversified practice by a unified team.

The plan was based on the assumption that we would grow. It established a full-time research program; a full-time public relations-promotional program for liaison with publicational, governmental, and educational fields and completed CRS projects; CRS with metropolitan planning growth; professional advisory group from within and outside of CRS to create a broader base of experience and operation; an improved Associate-Partner Plan; a financial program to encourage growth; a system of sabbatical leave for professional improvement. It intensified action of the existing CRS program: (a) multioffice engineering and planning growth, (b) development in new areas of management and planning for total CRS, and (c) development of experienced professional depth in the individual. It organized a CRS-sponsored conference on community-educational planning. To a certain degree every one of these has been achieved although it has taken twelve years instead of ten.

As a part of the plan, and through Bullock's insistence, in late 1958 we pulled up roots (which were very dear to my family and me) in the College Station-Bryan area and moved to Houston. Of twenty-seven CRS families we left only one in Bryan when we moved. But the move was a shock for all of us, and even more of a shock to some Houston architects who one Monday morning discovered that "this CRS bunch" was the largest firm in the city.

In 1959 Bullock set in motion a plan for creating a "team of teams" which would bring together through strong centralized management—MPC/Management Planning Center—the three basically self-contained firms. This unification was a major part of the ten-year plan. A slump was largely the cause of this change from a decentralized organization to a centralized organization. When one office had work, another might have nothing to do. But there was another even more threatening reason: qualitatively one office was getting behind another—a five-year lag. MPC made us more integrated. There began an interchange of personnel. Specific tasks demanded specific task teams, one of which might consist of representatives of each of the three offices. As an example, in the Corning office we had a steady flow of talent from both Oklahoma City and Houston working in concert on projects which were managed from the Corning office.

CRS became one team. Tom Bullock must be credited for this. His charisma, his complete dedication to the team concept, his sensitivity to co-workers, his humor, and his leadership helped weld the ever-growing firm together and give it a feeling of unified smallness.

8

We examined the team concept

At the same time we were making the 1958 ten-year plan, we began to have doubts about the team concept and wanted to reinforce our beliefs in it. We asked each key man at CRS to answer the following questions: Do you honestly believe and practice: that CRS must *grow* to produce a better architecture; that CRS growth depends on individual growth;

that to grow, CRS must have outstanding leaders in the profession; that the multioffice condition must have unity; that the team concept encompasses all CRS personnel; that the team concept requires a highly developed communication system which is not only good in itself, but, even more important, develops a good communicative attitude; that to instill confidence in our clients and with our firm, strong leadership must prevail; that CRS should move in any direction if there is an outstanding opportunity to make a contribution; that the success of the team depends on the individual's trying to encourage and inspire other team members?

The results of this inventory of team belief served to reinforce the team concept.

9

Paseur took over leadership in 1965

Following the unwritten policy of an open-end firm, Bullock requested in 1965 that someone else take over. Herb Paseur was elected, and assumed his duties as managing director in October 1965.

Paseur believes that management is an art and a science: "It can be creative, inspired, dull, stylized, heavy-handed, superficial. The art of management is a talent which can be developed; the science of management can be taught. Therefore aptitude for management varies. As for me, I have no philosophy of management—only ideas and convictions."

Paseur contends that management theories can be stylized—new ideas developed by the theorist every few years. "However," he adds, "good

CAUDILL → BULLOCK → PASEUR → ?

THERE IS AN UNWRITTEN POLICY OF AN **OPEN-END** FIRM TO HAND OFF THE LEADERSHIP.

managers have a natural style which is applied consistently. Management is the trigger mechanism of the firm or project which makes things happen in a controlled manner. It sets goals, monitors and controls progress and evaluates results." Paseur, although long away from the designer's drafting board, still has the designer's attitude—that creativity relies on freedom of action within few controls. He believes that good management motivates by inspiration rather than fear; that it creates change which in turn changes management; and that the control of this cycle is the important measure of management.

"Management," according to Paseur, "is a delicate balance between permissiveness and authoritarian control." He has found that a chaotic situation is easier for management to solve than a stratified, hardened problem. He says he'll take chaos anytime because it is easily changed.

"I like to think," Paseur points out, "that my job is to create the proper environment to allow people to perform their tasks with the least interference. If these people then create architecture, then I had a hand in the doing."

Paseur's reputation for getting things done with minimum fuss goes beyond the firm he leads. The Houston Chapter of the American Institute of Architects elected him president for 1972, the year the national convention is to be held in Houston.

Paseur, like Bullock, came up through the firm from the bottom. I recall visiting the Oklahoma City office when Tom Bullock pointed to a young man at a drafting board. He said, "Be nice to that guy; we want to keep him." Keep him we did. Ten years later Paseur became our boss. I'm glad I was nice to him in the early days.

It was a different team—an evolved team—when Herb took it over. Herb was confronted with how best to manage a large group of highly educated, creative people. He found it was more like running a university. Where Bullock and I could get things done either by an authoritative approach or using the Machiavellian touch, Paseur could not get by with such tactics. He had to rely on persuasion, not dictation. His position required a quiet, strong leadership. He was fully qualified.

In 1970, with approximately 240 people on the total CRS team, Paseur helped to cause another major organizational change. CRS is like an enormous heart which contracts and expands in regular cycles. First the organization form was centralized; then decentralized; then centralized; and under Paseur, the change was back to a decentralized form.

Paseur was primarily responsible for the creation of the first affiliate company, CRS2, officially called Computing Research Systems Corporation. CRS' computer department had been a hard-line, fast-riding outfit developing new ways to adapt the computer to architecture practice. Our young, aggressive computer enthusiasts were making speeches all over the country, plugging the use of computers at architects/researchers conferences and had developed saleable software. So the CRS Board of Directors decided to put them in business for themselves, serving other architectural firms and institutions concerned with building programs. They were in operation July 1969.

Some of us old timers were shocked when we read the first "ad" that appeared in the *Wall Street Journal* aimed at the professional service market. We had been brought up to believe that advertising was a professional sin. Of course our computer boys were operating within ethical boundaries since CRS2 is not an architectural firm.

Expanding team size, changing characteristics of practice, quality control, and desire for increased profits were the underlying reasons for changing from a departmental organization (in corporate terminology) to a divisional organization. Paseur, in a memo to the CRS staff dated 27 February 1970, stated, "The divisional organization will decentralize management and control and will make our organization more responsive to profit and quality of our projects. A division will be fairly autonomous and will be responsible for its own day-to-day operation including income and expenses."

By July of that year, after Paseur's assistant, John Focke, had led a group in completing a computer system for accounting and management information, and after plans had been completed for development of management procedures for job budgeting and divisional profit planning (each division was a profit center), the new organizational change went into effect. But not without pain.

Some of us thought the change would balkanize the total team. Others argued that "profit centers" were unfair to those on the tail end of the business (it is easier to make a profit in the early stages than in the later wrapping-up period). Others had completely opposite views and were enthusiastic about new opportunities for individual development, about the possibilities of creating small specialized teams, and breaking up bigness into more humanistic groups which would result from decentralization.

The 1970 organizational change created these divisions: (1) Construction Documents; (2) Engineering; (3) Health Facilities; (4) Houston; (5) New York; (6) Interiors and Graphics; (7) Management Planning Services; (8) Central Services Group.

10

CRS organizes for the future

The Board of Directors, Caudill Rowlett Scott, Inc., in November 1970 set up an umbrella organization under which the original firm and CRS2, plus future affiliates, would operate. The mission of this holding company, called CRS Design Associates, Inc., was to create, by developing within and through acquisitions, a family of firms, all working together toward solving the large, complex problems of environmental design. The Board felt that such a move would also strengthen each individual firm—the team-of-teams idea.

Herb Paseur was relieved of his duties of managing CRS, Inc., and was elected President and Chief Executive Officer of the new corporation. Tom Bullock was elected Chairman of the Board.

Early in 1971, a third corporation was added to CRS Design Associates, with the goal of offering construction management services. Charles Thomsen was chosen to head this new venture.

In January 1971, CRS spawned another division: CRS Los Angeles. Paul Kennon, Tom Hooker, and Truitt Garrison were selected to head the West Coast operation. In October 1970 we sent a squatters team to Los Angeles to design the interior-space which we leased in the Bradbury Building on Third and Broadway in the thick of the downtown area. Obtaining offices in this historical, seventy-five-year-young building reminded me of two other pioneering efforts: We bought a hundred-year-old farmhouse on Sing Sing Road near Corning, New York, to be used as an office when CRS "invaded the East"; then when we moved to Manhattan, we set up shop on the sixth floor in the old Grand Central Building. Despite our computerized tendencies, we are a sentimental lot.

A Chicago based operation is also contemplated.

I suppose from the very beginning, without realizing it, CRS was committed to growth. Deep down we are expansionists.

11
We had difficulty conditioning our people to the CRS way of practice

Throughout the years we continuously recruited, trained and integrated talent and experience to strengthen the team. But not without trouble—particularly the integration part. Conditioning these newcomers to play on our team has been difficult. Integrating the first partners was no exception. During the first five years of "marriage" (there was no honeymoon) we came close to a split-up at least three times.

Out of the smoke of early inter-friction came this maxim: "A new man joining the CRS team must first be a good guy and, second, know his stuff." And it is a proven fact. Every time we have violated this rule we have plunged into trouble.

Even though there are all kinds of difficulties integrating new people into the team, it is worth the effort. Mavericks like Frank Lawyer, Phil Williams, Joe Thomas, Charles Thomsen, Norman Hoover, Paul Kennon, John Focke,

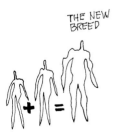

THE NEW BREED

and Carl Landow "kicked to beat hell" at first, causing all kinds of internal disturbance; but when they started pulling in the right direction, CRS began to move faster and with more confidence.

The CRS personnel fire department has been active every year of its existence. We anticipate many more fires. There is a natural tendency for teams to reject new people. But without a constant flow of new blood, teams are destined to fall by the wayside. Also without a deeply rooted belief in the team concept, there is no hope of survival.

12
"Process first" pays off

Throughout CRS' history, services have been as important as buildings. It was process over product the day we opened our office. Perhaps herein lie both strengths and weaknesses. There have been many cases in which children and teachers have loved our schools, but competition juries have not. And the reason was that the students and teachers had a better understanding of the buildings—what the schoolhouses were supposed to do and why they were designed the way they were. This is understandable because the users were involved in the process. The jurors were not. And it is difficult to separate product from process. This accent on process has unquestionably affected the character of our buildings. Of greater importance, it has generated and stimulated the team concept—more lasting than styles.

Although we have few "masterpieces" to show for our efforts, if we had it to do over again we would do just what we have done—accent services.

For one thing it has taught us teamwork. For another, the accent on services prepares us for the next twenty-five years, particularly the next decade.

It is a good bet that the current interest in conservation and pollution control will lead to the public's demanding better buildings, better neighborhoods, better downtown areas, and better everything else that contributes to a functional, beautiful environment. And when this pressure is exerted the architect will not be allowed to hide in some corner and work alone. He will have to team up with a lot of other professionals. And the users too.

CRS' main contribution to the profession has been in the programming aspect of architectural practice and in our acceptance of the premise that better buildings result when the client/users are on the planning team. This has led us to the development of new methods of serving our clients and new ways for team communication such as analysis cards, the squatters, the user/architect clinics, and computerized cost controls. Of particular significance are our planning management services to large cities such as Minneapolis (1964) and Baltimore (1969)—where no design was involved —and to state governments such as New Jersey, where we had a contract in 1968 to raise the planning of higher-education facilities to a more sophisticated level using computers.

In CRS during the last five years, the planning management services (nonbuilding services) have been on the increase. I see no slacking off, in CRS or in other similar firms. In these days we are becoming more involved not only in studying the function, but also in finding better ways to manage the function. It is most interesting to see how management consultants are getting into the practice of architecture and architects are getting into management. Users are demanding that the two disciplines come together.

Ever-increasing expanded services—a pattern CRS has had for its first twenty-five years—is a promise in the next twenty-five years. The evolving form of CRS—as an internal work/management production tool—through involvement with outside consultants, manufacturers, and builders also prepares us for the future. The real team of the future will include client/user, developer, financier, building, manufacturer, and others.

13

CRS is a future outfit

THE CRS TREE SYMBOL WAS ACCIDENTLY CREATED DURING A **SEMINAR.** IT IS MORE OF A PHILOSOPHY THAN LOGO.

←THE 3 ROOTS REPRESENT THE THREE DEEPLY ROOTED BELIEFS OF THE CRS TEAM— (1) THE PROBLEM SOLVING APPROACH, (2) THE TEAM CONCEPT, AND (3) THE HUMAN-ISM OF THE PHYSICAL EN-VIRONMENT. THE TRUNK IS **ARCHITECTURE.** THE LIMBS ARE THE CHAR-ACTERISTICS OF CRS DESIGNED BUILDINGS SUCH AS (A) FLUID SPACE, (B) EN-VIRONMENTAL CONTROLS, (C) STRUCTURAL ORDER, (D) THE UMBRELLA IDEA, AND (E) INDIGENOUS TO THE REGION.

Our commitment to the premise that a total team is needed to do total architecture made us grow. We are a growth outfit. We have to grow to do the kind and size of projects we want to do, and to keep the talent we have helped to develop.

In running the firm now, Herb Paseur is faced with new problems directing hundreds of people and hundreds of projects. The logistics problem alone seems impossible at times. New techniques and new attitudes must be developed to allow us to operate on a higher plane of sophistication.

Our growth is symbolized in our logo—the CRS tree—which developed as the result of an in-depth discussion we had during a CRS design seminar held at my home one February evening in 1960. I had been pleading with our people to make clear statements as to what the CRS team really believed. "Where are our roots?" I kept asking. After much discussion we decided that we had three main roots: Belief that buildings should have human values, belief in problem-solving methods, and belief in the team concept. Then we listed nine limbs which characterized our products.

26

Frank Lawyer later translated our verbiage into a simple outlined tree, roots and all.

To keep the CRS tree growing and healthy, we try to infuse new talent at regular intervals, to bring in new blood at a leadership level. This new breed of hard-hitting, sharp young men, such men as Terry Tengler, James Falick, James Thomas, Michael Trower, Jeff Corbin, Robert Mattox, Ott Luther, Bob Walters, Bill Steely, Jack DeBartolo, Joe Griffin, James Hughes, Bob Reed, Jonathan King, Jim Cagley, Steve Kliment, and many others too numerous to name, bring about changes—and fast. This is the way it should be.

TOGETHER
WE CAN DO A BETTER JOB
THAN
WE CAN
SEPARATELY

Children are clients. This was a concept the CRS team had from the very beginning. In the early fifties we insisted upon working with teachers and children. We still do. This "traditional" classroom can be completely thrown open with three other classrooms, permitting team teaching in one large, loft-type space. This elementary school in New York City was occupied in the fall of 1966.

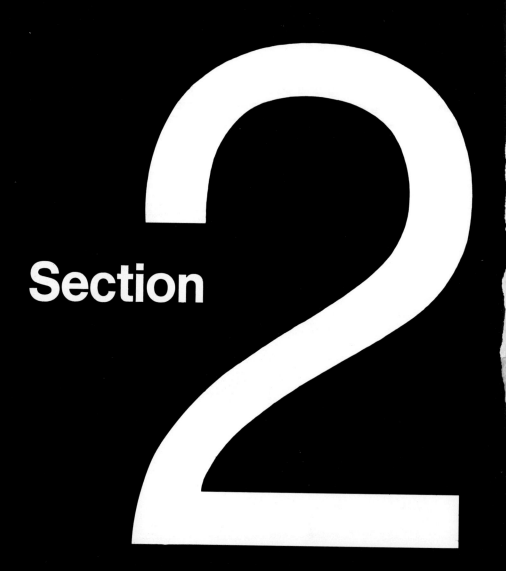

Section

The Prima Donna is Dead

Saying that the building industry is in for a change is like saying "Ho-hum, it may rain one of these days." Now if someone comes along and says, "By three o'clock this afternoon it will be raining cats and dogs," then we take a little notice. If he says, "We'll have a fifty-year flood on our hands!" We start tossing sandbags—taking immediate action. So I cry, "Flood!" The building industry is not only in for a big change—the change has already started. The users are getting into the act. Architects, engineers, builders, and manufacturers must change their attitudes and their ways of doing things so that they can meet the change. So must architectural critics and writers—particularly those who have yet to discover that the prima donna is dead.

14

The prima donnas have had their day

The world—including this practitioner—owes much to the great masters of architecture who reigned during the first part of this century. Frank Lloyd Wright, Le Corbusier, and Mies van der Rohe were my idols. Walter Gropius, Richard Neutra, and Alvar Aalto were also my gods, down the mountain a piece from Olympus. There was a third, a lower, level of younger architects who, had they lived in another era, might well have taken the place of the greater deities. But the third level of architects have not a chance in this day. Nor will they.

When we consider the problems facing this country and other nations which must rebuild old cities and build new ones just to keep pace with current demands; when we consider the war on poverty and the necessity of providing architecture for all people; the need is obvious for large interdisciplinary teams which attack problems from all directions at once. Giant projects require giant teams—not prima donnas.

There must be a major onslaught by teams of many disciplines.

Isolated effort by an independent architect working alone will not do the job.

The so-called "great man" approach must give way to the great team approach.

From now on the great architects will be on great interdisciplinary teams.

Not long ago my partners and I met in the Houston CRS office with a group of architects from Chicago about a possible association. We wanted

WE NEED A NEW DEFINITION OF **GREAT ARCHITECTURE.** NO LONGER CAN EXAMPLES BE LIMITED TO MONUMENTS AND PERSONAL EXPRESSIONS OF THE PRIMA DONNAS. MORE FITTING TO THIS DAY OF **SOCIAL CHANGE, GREAT** BUILDINGS MUST DO **GREAT** GOOD FOR A **GREAT** NUMBER OF PEOPLE.

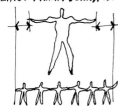

NO MATTER HOW BIG THE GENIUS **PRIMA DONNA** IS: HE CANNOT COVER THE AREAS NECESSARY TO SOLVE THE COMPLEX PROBLEMS OF URBANIZATION. IT TAKES A **TEAM.**

to set the right climate for discussion so we spent the first part of the meeting expounding on the merits of creating architecture by team. We argued that:

- Buildings are becoming too complex for one person to design.
- Building projects are becoming increasingly large.
- Therefore they must be designed by teams.

I was particularly active in selling the team concept to our Chicago visitors. I pointed out in no uncertain terms that today is the day of the team, and the so-called great masters will be replaced by the great teams. And I added, being always alert to a chance to brag, that we hope the CRS team someday will be a great team. I tried to clinch the argument by this: "There is not a prima donna among us."

(The resolution of this statement, unfortunately, was somewhat dimmed, to put it mildly, by a perfectly timed knock at the door of our closed meeting room. It was my secretary, who interrupted the meeting, entered the roomful of coffee drinkers and announced, "Mr. Caudill, here is your tea. I hope it is the right color." For receiving such preferential treatment, my face turned the wrong color.)

The prima donnas have had their day. Now the architect is a team.

THE ARCHITECT IS A TEAM

15

Team action is difficult to understand

Although the idea of the prima donna is dear to the hearts of many professional architects today, it is still more dear to those who write about architecture in the mass media—not to mention the professional press. The hero is still on his pedestal in the eyes of the architectural historian and the newspaper fine arts-architecture critic. The temple builders are still considered the rightful newsmakers, the headliners; and writers continue to cater to these little architectural gods.

One of the reasons, of course, is that the team is difficult to understand, and even more difficult to pinpoint in written copy. This is why sportswriters tend toward the hero and goat bit. Many times in CRS we have had to squelch hero-seeking reporters prepared to write an entire story crediting only one member of the firm. We have had to insist that stories be rewritten, that credits be revised when based solely on one of the principals and unfairly ignoring the work of other key people and associated firms.

A **TEAM** IS HARD TO EXPLAIN.

There is always more than one leader working on the jobs we do today. There has been an increasing number of jobs in CRS that Caudill, or Rowlett, or Scott, had little to do with. Caudill Rowlett Scott (note no commas and no "and") is now more a logo than a logical name; the three of us simply got there first.

Not long ago I read a newspaper account of the opening of a public building in which the architect was given quite a spread. If quoted correctly, within two short paragraphs the architect said, "I did this," or "I did that," six times, and "my building" twice.

PERSONAL EXPRESSION IS FINE HANGING IN A FRAME.

Yet did he really do the building? Didn't he get just a little help? Did he program the needs of the client by himself? Did he draw every line? Make every engineering calculation? Specify the cement, aggregate, and texture of concrete? Estimate the cost? Nurse the building through construction? There is no denying that it is a good building. But the architect had a great amount of help doing it. It is my guess that at least forty people were involved. And did the building belong to him? Really!

16

The team is seldom credited

THE WRITER HAS A HARD TIME EXPLAINING THE TEAM TO THE PUBLIC.

IT IS EASIER TO GIVE **CREDIT** TO ONE MAN.

Let's assume we can forgive the mass media writers for their sin of omission in failing to credit the team. What of the writers of books on architecture?

It appears to me that most writers have deliberately played down the increasingly important role of the team during the last decade or so. They cling, apparently, to the notion of the master; they seem to look at a building as a piece of sculpture created by a single artist—as a masterpiece signed by one man.

Take the classic architectural book of our time, Giedion's "Space, Time and Architecture," unquestionably the most profound, influential book of the last three decades. Yet in a late edition, the word "team" was never mentioned. Giedion does give credit in a few places to the partnership idea. Whereas most other architectural historians talk about "Sullivan's Chicago auditorium," Giedion refers to it as "their auditorium," thereby giving Adler equal credit with Sullivan. Giedion also referred to other famous partnerships, giving credit to both Walter Gropius and Marcel Breuer for some of their projects; to both Burnham and Root for some of theirs; and to both Holabird and Roche for several of theirs. Although Giedion tried very hard to give Raymond Hood full credit for designing Rockefeller Center, three firms were actually involved. The world "firm" was mentioned only once—in a footnote. Giedion simply could not accept the team idea of creating architecture. He is quoted as saying that the environment of the large firm crushes the creative impulse of the young architect. He could not have been more wrong.

Consider Peter Blake's "The Master Builders," a fine treatise on Le Corbusier, Mies van der Rohe, and Frank Lloyd Wright. The word "team" goes without mention in the book, even in his closing remarks about the future aspects of architectural practice. Rather, Blake indicates only that the future of architecture depends on the individual. I can't argue that— but I say that the great architect will have to be on a team.

Consider "Team 10 Primer," a little book comparable to Le Corbusier's "Towards A New Architecture." It is understandable why Corbusier ignored team. Despite the title, if one reads "Team 10 Primer" hoping to learn something about the effectiveness of team action, he will be disappointed. This book makes students probe more deeply, and forces those of us who are practitioners to reexamine and rethink our beliefs. The team in this case implies a sharing of philosophies so that each member of the team can better understand his own individual work. That is not the "team" as I see it. It is true that sharing philosophies and goals is important to team action, but there still must be action.

In Robin Boyd's "The Puzzle Of Architecture," first published in 1965, a book heralded as the best work on developments in the profession since the turn of the century, team was hardly mentioned, yet during the last two or three decades there has been an increasing emphasis on team in the practice of architecture. Throughout the book Boyd gives Sullivan full credit, and neglects Adler, who deserved a few roses himself. In his first discussion of Lever House, Boyd mentioned only Gordon Bunshaft, who, he thought, has done a good job. Only in a later mention of Lever

House (as resembling a little United Nations' slab sitting on a square doughnut, a rather uncomplimentary comment at best,) did Boyd deign to mention Messrs. Skidmore, Owings, and Merrill. A most obvious omission in Boyd's book is that in praising Walter Gropius for his great contribution to architecture, Boyd never credits him as the leading proponent of the team concept—as the man who invented the architectural team.

17

Few writers credit team action

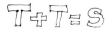

WE NEED NEW **THEORIES** PLUS **TEAMWORK** TO **SOLVE** THE COMPLEX PROBLEMS OF URBANIZATION.

Now let's consider another case, Christian Norberg-Schultz's "Intentions in Architecture," a book deep in theory, and one of my favorites. Norberg-Schultz is one of the few theoreticians who seems convinced that in this day teamwork is absolutely necessary. Although I would like to see Norberg-Schultz make even firmer statements concerning the team concept, the book is a commitment to team action, and includes theory which will be useful to the team.

One more case, this one closer to home: "Architecture of America," by John Burchard and Albert Bush-Brown. This marks the first time CRS work was mentioned in a hardback history. Burchard, my mentor at MIT, might have been plugging for his former student. Nevertheless, when he and his co-author discussed the San Angelo High School in West Texas, they gave me the credit, with no mention of the team effort by the firm. They talked about "his" pioneering work, and referred to this project as "his school," flattering—but inaccurate. A lot of us got in on the pioneering work, and it wasn't "my" school, either by ownership or authorship. Rather,

Because of a divided school board, Central High School in San Angelo, Texas, shown above, was a battle from start to finish—from site selection to moving in. Had it not been for Frank Pool, President of the Board, I do not think this school would have been built. As it turned out, visitors from all over the world come to see this thirteen-building high school campus. The group participation process which produced the school was rough, but the product is highly successful.

it resulted from team effort involving many CRS people and the student and teacher clients, particularly Frank Pool, the president of the school board, and G. B. Wadzeck, superintendent of schools. If certain people on the CRS team could have been singled out, Frank Lawyer, Dave Yarbrough, Bob Walters, Earl Merrill, Dave Bullen, and Ed Nye should have been mentioned. All played strong roles in the conceptual design and design development. I will say that when things went wrong, I got the lashes—and have the scars to prove it!

In this 500-page book, the authors devoted only four or five pages to discussion of the team, a slight but well-developed discussion. They pointed out that the large architectural firm practicing on a nationwide basis is uniquely American, but not accepted by the majority of those in the profession. The general opinion is that the large firm "could never do much in the way of innovation or . . . could never be capable of distinction." The authors are right. Until 1960 the large firms had a bad name.

Things have changed, attitudes particularly. Team now is not such a nasty word. Teams can—and do—make radical innovations. A giant team was required to put the first man on the moon—a most creative effort. That was no one-man show. We have quite a few "moon" projects to do right here on this earth. That is why some of the space-age firms are getting into the architectural business.

18

Architectural training was anti-team

Architects of my generation were taught in school to exert individualism, to ape the actions of the great masters (prima donnas all), and we responded by wanting to become prima donnas ourselves. I even wanted a cape like the one Wright wore.

The truth is that we were also trained to bully, to tell our clients what they should have. And I thought what they should have was "me." My own design. My current taste. My convictions, if not prejudices. I greatly admired the famous architectural hero who had the courage to tell the client to go to hell if that client had the audacity to interfere with his forms—or complain that his roof was leaking.

But the implications of training for the profession went even deeper than the "great man" concept.

Before 1960, students were taught that there was a certain stigma about the big architectural firm, that they were somehow tainted with commercialism and design incompetence. I recall no complaints, however, about the technological competence of the big firm, or its ability to serve clients from the standpoint of construction economy and practicality. "Meeting the budget" was never mentioned by my professors.

Littleness was goodness. When I first began to teach in 1939, I did my share of downgrading the big firm. As an instructor at Texas A & M, I made it my villain. "Watch out," I would tell my students. "When a firm gets over thirty people, have nothing to do with it." My reasoning was that when a firm got that big, it became a "plan factory," stifling creativity and deterring professional growth. I would have my fledglings see for themselves how right I was by pointing to the architectural banality produced by the large, established firms. At one time, I even theorized that there was an inverse correlation between the number of employees in a firm and that firm's performance quality. I had a pretty good case. The best buildings were generally the smallest buildings—done by the smallest firms.

WE WERE TAUGHT TO WORSHIP THE GREAT PRIMA DONNAS.

WE WERE TAUGHT TO LOOK DOWN AT THE CLIENT.

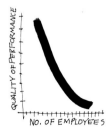

THE POPULAR NOTION THAT LITTLENESS IS GOODNESS IS SIMPLY **UNTRUE**.

I didn't realize it at the time, but I received considerable psychological comfort in believing that the small firms were the best. I could tell my students—and even more important, tell myself—that at any time I could "hang out my shingle" and be on equal footing, if not more so, with those larger, older firms. I completely discounted their experience in design and construction, and, even worse, gave very little thought to serving the client. I was more interested in serving myself. The professional aspect meant nothing to me. The amateur looked better than the pro. The dilettante professor looked better still, doing no architectural work, and therefore beyond the reach of criticism while he criticized the work of others.

This is a view of an elementary school in Charlottesville, Virginia, designed by Stainback and Scribner, Architects, with the CRS team. The underlying idea—the children are the client—generated the playshed from which the photo is taken.

As a young professor, I was as antiestablishment as the students are today. But my line was "Never trust a firm over thirty."

Architectural education is changing. And just wait until the current crop of students assumes leadership in the profession. It will be very hard for these wonderfully social-minded students of today to play two roles—that of society's benefactor and that of prima donna.

19

Team participation requires a mature attitude

John Rowlett and I designed mostly small homes and a few apartments during the first two and three years of our practice. I recall most vividly the time when we had just finished the preliminary plans for a house for a professor at Texas A & M. John had taken the lead on this one. We were both rather proud of the skillful way we designed this house and how we had cleverly manipulated our client so he finally came around to seeing things our way.

The morning after preliminary plans had been approved I was in the little College Station bank, trying to borrow money to meet expenses. The girl at the front desk seated me on a bench to wait until my banker was ready to see me. While waiting, I could hear my banker talking with another customer. Every word of their conversation came through. The customer turned out to be our client, who was trying to borrow money to put on his house which we had designed! Naturally my interest ran high. So I turned my radar on the conversation so as not to miss a word. I didn't.

IF THE **CLIENT** THINKS IT IS HIS IDEA, THE ARCHITECT'S "SELLING THE JOB" IS DONE.

Our client, when asked what the house was going to be like, did a fine job of explaining it. I was proud. We were good teachers. Then the banker asked him who designed it. His answer was something like this. "Well, I designed it, but I got a couple of young architectural profs to draw it up." I was mortified! After all the work John and I did, particularly John, who "poured his soul out on the drafting board," this credit-snatching buzzard would not give us the honors for our masterpiece. In fact he did not even mention our names. What a terrible thing to happen to two brilliant young architects on their way to taking Wright's and Corbusier's places. When I told John of our client's terrible behavior, he was as upset as I. If we did not need that building to show off our great talent, we would have told our client to kiss our feet. But wisely we kept quiet, until now.

We have matured considerably since then. Today CRS goes far out of the way to get the client to believe ideas are his, as they often are. We now consider the client as part of our team. And if he thinks the prime concepts are his, all the better. When he moves in, he'll see that the building works. Who cares where the good ideas come from, just so they are there.

20

The architect can't go it alone

"THE TROUBLE WITH ARCHITECTS IS THAT THEY HIRE ARCHITECTS" OR "BIRDS OF A FEATHER FLOCK TOGETHER."

I know from years of practice that it takes all kinds of people to solve the architectural-sociological complexities. Certainly architects can't do it alone. Architect Ernie Kump said years ago, "The trouble with architects is that they hire other architects." He was way ahead of the times. The well-established architectural firms have relatively few architects. But they are all after the same thing—to produce buildings which have architecture. People on these teams should not be alike.

Many architects have not the slightest notion of programming, cost controls, performance specifications, and other areas of sophisticated practice. Many conceptual designers have neither talent nor patience to get into the nasty nitty gritty of architectural detailing. But someone has to. Conceptual design goes just so far. Someone must be responsible for putting the pieces together. And putting the pieces together has great fascination for some of the other professionals. The way those pieces are put together very often determines whether the building is just a good building or a great one—whether architecture is created.

Producing a great building or even just a good building is not a one-man effort. Either the architectural critics and historians don't recognize this or they simply don't know how a building design is put together from the concept to the refinement of details. I suspect that they single out only one or two people for ease of writing, not from ignorance of the architectural process. At least I'll give them that much credit.

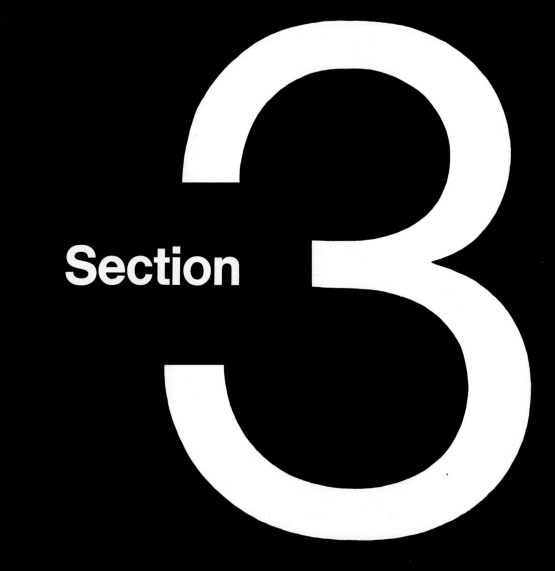

Section 3

What is Architecture?

To understand architecture by team one must first know what is meant by architecture—a term for which every architect and every layman has a different definition.

For the purpose of this book, accept my definition of architecture. Discard it later, if you insist, but accept it as a clarifying catalyst for better understanding of architecture by team.

21

Architecture means many things to many people

Various definitions of architecture range from the highly exclusive designation of a few masterpieces scattered through the world to everything built by man. I say that neither polarity of opinion is correct. What is architecture for one person may not be for another.

Consider my definition:

Architecture is an aura which emanates from the man-made environment, evokes emotional response in the individual who experiences it, fulfills both physical and psychological needs, transcends mere shelter, and reflects the extent of man's development.

Architecture sends signals. The individual who experiences architecture receives the signals. Architecture is the soul of space. It cannot be seen, but it is there. Architecture vivifies inanimate form. Form and space transmit. A person receives. A sensitive person perceives the soul and feels the life. Without people, there could be no architecture.

Because architecture evokes emotions in people, it is an intensely personal experience. A building may have the aura of architecture for one person, and not for another. It may transmit strong messages to one person, who is capable of receiving the messages, and be devoid of any message whatsoever when another person, a person of different values, experiences, and feelings, is involved. Thus, the same building may be *architecture* to one person, and mere *structure* to another.

ARCHITECTURE IS AN AURA—EMANATING FROM BUILDINGS, FULFILLING CERTAIN BASIC NEEDS RELATING TO HUMAN VALUES AND CREATING AN **UPLIFTING EXPERIENCE.**

ARCHITECTURE IS A **PERSONAL** EXPERIENCE RELATING TO BUILDINGS AND THEIR SPACES.

22

Sponsors of architecture must understand the architectural experience

In the quest for the aura that is architecture, there are two things which those who sponsor architecture must know:

First, they must know that every individual has the right to experience architecture, just as he has the right and the need to experience painting,

Learning spaces must possess that aura which is architecture. This is a high school in Winona, Minnesota, which CRS designed in 1965, with Eckert and Carlson.

sculpture, music, and the dance. But the responsibility relating to architecture is greater, for one can escape poor painting, smash a sorry piece of sculpture, turn off inferior music, or walk out on a bad ballet. But it is most difficult to escape the physical environment from which architecture may or may not radiate. If the environment is devoid of architecture, people get hurt. Architecture is a birthright.

Second, we must realize that although the experience of architecture is a highly personal matter, almost *no* architecture can be created for one person alone; that so-called "private architecture" is rare, that almost *all* architecture, regardless of the matter of "private" ownership, is truly in the public domain.

To demonstrate the fact that most architecture is in the public domain, the homeowner in suburbia "owns" the view of the new "Old English" manor across the street—it is "his" to view with favor or with distaste, "his" to sense the aura of architecture and appreciate it, or (as is far more likely in the case of the "Old English" house) "his" to abhor the sham. Similarly the businessman commuting to his office "owns" the building-scape through which he travels, and is uplifted or depressed by what he sees. The housewife "owns" her shopping center with "her" stores, and is influenced by what she sees and feels there. So most man-made environment, whether created for the sole use of one person, or for use by thousands, lies in the public domain. The building may belong to a single person, but the architecture belongs to everyone.

Is there such a thing as private architecture, which relates to one person alone? Yes—but only rarely.

One must look at architecture from within—take a very personal point of view. Try to put yourself in this story that follows.

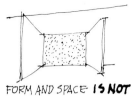

FORM AND SPACE **IS NOT** ARCHITECTURE.

ARCHITECTURE OCCURS ONLY WHEN THERE IS A PERSON TO **EXPERIENCE** IT.

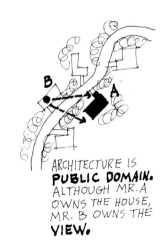

ARCHITECTURE IS **PUBLIC DOMAIN.** ALTHOUGH MR. A OWNS THE HOUSE, MR. B OWNS THE **VIEW.**

23

A man creates his private architecture

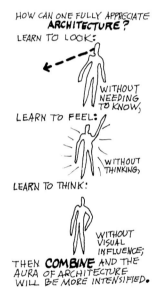

HOW CAN ONE FULLY APPRECIATE **ARCHITECTURE?**
LEARN TO LOOK:
WITHOUT NEEDING TO KNOW;
LEARN TO FEEL:
WITHOUT THINKING;
LEARN TO THINK:
WITHOUT VISUAL INFLUENCE;
THEN **COMBINE** AND THE AURA OF ARCHITECTURE WILL BE MORE INTENSIFIED.

A friend of mine wanted to convert his garage into a den—a hideaway. He wanted a place to listen to his classical music, a place in which to escape the distractions of his wife's television, his son's rock and roll tapes.

My friend, who happened to be an engineer, not an architect, knew he wanted visual privacy, audio privacy to keep out extraneous street noise, the proper sonic setting, the right air conditioning and mood lighting. He felt he could solve these problems, and was confident his den, nee garage, would function as he had hoped.

But there was another consideration. The man had an aesthetic problem. He realized that in addition to a place which provided the proper physical environment, he wanted his hideaway to be a pleasant space, an inspirational space. Whether he realized it or not, he wanted architecture. One would think, since he was not an architect, that the job of creating space and form from which architecture would radiate would be too difficult for him to handle. Not for my friend. He had all the confidence in the world that he could solve the problems of physical and emotional shelter.

At this point the man knew he liked soft stuff on the floor, that he liked fine, warm woods with rich tones on the walls. He liked special lighting effects to provide the visual setting for his music. He wanted an intimacy about the space. He wanted the room to be in psychological contrast to the other rooms in the house. He wanted a certain magic—that "plus" something that lifts the spirits. He wanted "his architecture" to go with "his" music.

Here we have one of those rare cases—private architecture. The music lover had to answer to no needs but his own. He cared not whether his wife and son were pleased with the finished product, whether his neighbors might like it, whether his friends might like it. He could lock them out and he had the right to do so. His quest was for his very own, private architecture. He got it.

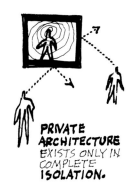

PRIVATE ARCHITECTURE EXISTS ONLY IN COMPLETE ISOLATION.

His finished den was all he had hoped for. There was privacy. There was space conditioning to give him the best musical sound. And the best lighting and ventilation in his terms. And there was an aura which evoked pleasing emotions within him. The den did radiate the aura that is architecture—for him.

24

Architecture for the public carries social obligation

Now let's say one of the nation's best authorities on architecture comes into the man's den. He thinks it's terrible, reeking of banality. So what! It doesn't matter. The space has architecture to the music lover/engineer. He owns the place. He owns the view. And it is hidden from the public. It is private architecture, pure and simple.

We may draw a parallel between my friend and his music room, which answers his own set of physical and emotional needs, and a project completed by the highly individualistic architect to whom architecture is merely a tool for his own self-projection. Such an architect may fulfill every aspect, physical and aesthetic, to endow the building with qualities which result in the aura of architecture for him. If the building evokes no similar response in its users, or in those who view it in passing, the architect has then failed to produce architecture, except on a unilateral basis—his own. He neglected his responsibility to the public. He did the building for himself. He treated it like a painting or a piece of sculpture—to please himself first. Both my friend with the den, then, and the architect who created architecture answering only to his personal set of emotional needs have produced an architecture which is private, not to be shared with others.

Most rooms, buildings, and spaces must answer to the needs of many people. It is the responsibility of the architectural team to know that their work should transmit the aura that is architecture to all people, present and future, who will come into contact with its work. In the architectural sense, almost every building is public domain.

The people must have their architecture. Laredo, Texas, with a large percentage of the population in low-income groups, takes care of its plain people. Laredo has a strong belief in education and insists on building schools which possess the aura of architecture. J. W. Nixon Senior High School (right) was designed by CRS in 1963 with A. A. Leyendecker.

25

Many people must help create architecture

Accepting that almost all buildings and their spaces are public in nature, it behooves the architect to remember that he is designing not for his own self-expression, but to create the aura of architecture for his client, for the immediate and future users of the building, for those who live in the area of the building, and for those who will view it in passing.

How may architecture be created? How may a building be instilled with the aura of architecture, so that the aura is experienced by the maximum number of people? Very simple. Bring a lot of people—especially the users of the building—into the planning.

Architecture gives life to a building, but architecture is a personal experience. So buildings without people have no architecture. The Amarillo Civic Center, which CRS designed with Hannon and Daniel in 1966, exemplifies how important it is that public buildings possess the aura of architecture. Planners of buildings used by many people have great responsibility—because there are so many people to be pleased.

It has been our experience in CRS that if many people—owner, users, and professionals—with diverse sets of emotional and physical needs, and different reactions, are involved in the planning of a building from its very inception, it is more likely that architecture will result and will satisfy many people. This is particularly true with user participation.

Since architecture is a personal experience relating to human values, personal involvement, and a certain degree of "ownership," architecture has a better chance of occurring when the "experiencers" are involved in planning. The more the better.

It stands to reason that when a man wants architecture in his own house he should have a hand in its planning. If it is desirable for teachers and students to experience architecture in their schools (and most education leaders agree that learning is accelerated when learning spaces have amenities as well as efficiency) then it stands to reason, too, that it would be best to have the teachers and students "get into the act" of planning and work with the professionals. So it goes with churches, with hospitals, with housing The plural approach will result in a different product from the singular approach; the traditional expression of one man gives way to team expression. To think what this expression will be in years to come is most exciting.

Some junior high school students, named to work with a CRS team in planning for their new school building, confessed that they "hated the cafeteria" and would rather duck off to the corner drugstore, to lounge in its leatherette booths and consume their sandwiches. They were right. I went with them. The drugstore *was* better. We did something about it. Result: the new "lunchroom" was designed more like a drugstore, and it became the social center of the school. Architecture emerged partly because the kids were involved in the planning, but mostly because real needs were discovered during programming. What might have been mere structure was elevated to architecture.

A psychologist working with architects and a student committee vetoed the preliminary concepts for a new girls' college dormitory. The architects wanted three-girl suites, sharing a common bath and living-study area. But the psychologist's special training gave him the know-how to tell the architect and the student-planners that three was an unworkable number. This numerical arrangement invariably resulted in pairing two of the girls against the one, and increasing the conflict of personalities during the school year. Result: suites were devised for either two girls or four girls, and the resulting structure had a far better chance of succeeding.

An English teacher in Tyler, Texas, a member of a faculty building committee for a new gymnasium, made this off-the-cuff remark: "Wouldn't it be nice if we could have an indoor play court as nice as an outdoor one?"

This all-glass gymnasium which CRS designed for St. Joseph's Academy, Brownsville, Texas, in 1955, is the successor to one which we did at Tyler in 1954.

This triggered a chain reaction of discussion which led to the construction of an all-glass gymnasium which had the aura of architecture for almost everyone. The conservative East Texas school board would never have "bought" the design had it not had such a strong concept behind it. Glass breakage? The country's first all-glass gym would have had a perfect record for the first year of operation were it not for a coach who threw a baseball to test the "nonbreakable" glass.

26

Public appreciation of architecture should be put on a personal level

Personal architecture should be cherished, not condemned, by architects. An appreciation of personal architecture places the layman in a better position to appreciate public architecture. And if he senses the values of architecture, personal or public, architects' jobs will be much easier—because public architecture is still a personal experience. Sensitivity to architecture should be nurtured—everywhere.

The middle-aged adult of this day was given a healthy start toward music appreciation when his parents bought their first Victrola. Later, radio added to his development process. Now his children, with records, tapes, cassettes, electronic video recorders, and educational television have even better opportunities for music appreciation.

There is a way to popularize architecture, and the first step is to personalize it. Most people do not experience architecture except when they get out of their personal orbit (be it in the slums or in a brand new subdivision),

CHILDREN SHOULD BE TAUGHT EARLY THE EFFECTS OF MAN-MADE FORMS AND THE DEFINED SPACES -- AND THE IMPORTANCE OF ARCHITECTURE.

visit a museum, use a public library, or go to a theater. If they are lucky they may have a neighborhood school which radiates architecture. In every city there are isolated examples of excellent buildings and spaces. Sometimes it's a church; sometimes it's a concert hall, or a skillfully designed shopping center.

Consider "private" places. Most dwelling places are mere shelter, without the *plus,* the aura of architecture; however, some people manage to create architecture in private spaces within their own homes and offices by personalizing certain rooms which are "theirs."

There is another point: it is healthy when people get excited about architecture. Shortly after World War II, when the modern movement was beginning to take hold and the simple Miesian-type house caused raised eyebrows, if not outright neighborhood arguments, this sign was posted by a home owner in front of his new modern house:

"I don't like your house either."

My own first little house was referred to as "a hamburger stand" and some early CRS schools were called "chicken houses." Maybe the barbs stung a bit, but at least people were getting stirred up about architecture. When architecture is put on a personal basis, it is easier to get excited. (My partners and I fought back the name-calling with, "Children should have as much right to good lighting and ventilation as chickens.")

No one can question the seriousness of personal architecture. My friend who designed his own den was deadly serious. The homeowner who put up the flippant sign was nevertheless serious about his architecture. Even the critics who called our early schools "chicken houses" were serious. But I respected the opinions of the users—the children and teachers—far more. I shall never forget what a first grader told John Rowlett when asked how she liked her new school. The little girl said, "I wish I lived here." Or what a third grader said to William Pena when Pena was trying to evaluate performance of lighting in a third-grade classroom. The redhead said, "It's like springtime here in the wintertime" (there was ice and snow on the ground). To understand what those two kids were talking about is to understand architecture.

Children are most sensitive to their environment—probably more so than adults. To children architecture is a very personal experience. This early-fifties CRS-designed school in Port Arthur, Texas, reflects the concept that "the real clients are the students, not the school board members." Yet it was built most economically, substantially less than its monumental predecessors. Architect J. Earl Neff was our associate on this project.

27

Architecture is a measure of people

Architecture gives life to a building, and enriches life for the users of the building. The term "users" should be taken in the broad sense. Each morning on my way to work, I pass a beautiful building which makes me feel good, and it bolsters my spirits. Even if I never enter the building, I am still a "user" of that building.

Since architecture is an everyday experience, for all people, buildings become excellent yardsticks for measuring the values of the people whom they serve.

Buildings tattle on people. They reveal secrets. I live in a contemporary house. The dining room has a 6'9" ceiling. The living room which adjoins has a 36' ceiling. My house says: "I like contrast."

My neighbor has a symmetrical house, which looks something like Georgian—except the garage wing has to have expensive drapes to match the bedroom wing opposite. I think it's awful. He thinks my house is worse. As one can look at a man's house and tell about the man, so one can look at a city and learn about its people.

A visitor in Houston will see the Jesse H. Jones Hall for the Performing Arts, and experiencing the dynamic space flow of the grand lobby, realize that Houstonians care about things above mere subsistence. The visitor will see the Tenneco Building, and its fine detailing of quality materials, and realize that Houston commerce places value on things above mere money. He will see the Dome Stadium and, feeling its new space-scale,

SOCIETY MUST HAVE THE **DESIRE** FOR ARCHITECTURE. AND IT MUST DEMAND THAT **PLUS** SOMETHING.

Will people-spaces have the *plus* something as does
Houston's Jesse H. Jones Hall for the Performing Arts?
Note the Lippold sculpture.

realize that Houston boasts men whose planning is not bound to the prosaic.

However, if the visitor carried on the tour, he would also see pseudo-historical facades covering thousands of new apartment houses. Pure sham. He will see overdressed mansions, dingy all-weather carpets on motel driveways and seas of trailer houses. He will see the slums of the Fifth Ward, the dirt and decay of buildings which once possessed architecture, and he will wonder if Houston cares about its poor.

Here is sculptor Richard Lippold, who joined the CRS team for the design of Houston's Jones Hall for the Performing Arts. Lippold's sculpture "Gemini II" dominates the 66' lobby of the Hall. Others who collaborated on the total team are Walter P. Moore, Consulting Engineers, structural engineer; Bernard Johnson Engineers, Inc., mechanical-electrical engineers; Bolt, Beranek and Newman, Inc., acoustical consultants; George C. Izenour, theater design engineering consultant.

All these bits of Houston's architectural (and nonarchitectural) fabric give the visitor a clue to what people are like in Houston—their commitments, how they live, what they love, and the extent of their social consciousness.

28

We need more good buildings and some great ones

The great building, a Mies high rise, a Pietro Belluschi church, stands out like a lily in a cesspool in the polluted environment in which most of us live. The great buildings are needed to restore life in a dead environment. But the environment also needs simple buildings, noncompetitive in the visual sense, which quietly rebuild and restore the urban scene. Great

The spaces and forms of the Claremont College Science Center, designed by CRS in 1965, are for all students and faculty to experience. After serving as an understudy to Charles Lawrence, Norman Hoover came into his own as design leader for this project. Everett L. Tozier was our associate architect.

and just good buildings are needed. Architectural teams which design great buildings play no small part in bettering all people, even if their buildings are a relatively small part of the totality of man-made environment.

Like a single stove, an architectural masterpiece warms its environs and at the same time encourages the creation of other good buildings. The architectural pacesetters are warranted even at the risk of dominating the visual environment.

29
What's in the future?

The simple fact is that today's architects have very little influence on the total environment. Architect-designed buildings average about 25% in volume dollars. The architect may have even less influence tomorrow if he fails to join the team. If today there are far too few buildings which possess architecture, tomorrow may be worse, and will be if architects lose out.

Amenities may be sacrificed for expediencies and economies. But this need not be.

The future depends upon two things:

• Whether the public will develop appreciation for architecture so that architecture is a necessity of life, not merely a luxury.
• Whether the profession of architecture will meet the challenge of creating architecture when providing for rapid population growth.

ARCHITECTURE IS NOT EVERYTHING—THE TOTAL PHYSICAL ENVIRONMENT—AS ARCHITECTS LIKE TO BELIEVE. IT IS SOMETHING SPECIAL. IT IS THE PLUS SOMETHING THAT CAUSES A MERE ROOM, OR A BUILDING, OR A NEIGHBORHOOD TO RADIATE AN AURA WHICH GIVES A PERSON A BENEFICIAL STIMULUS.

TOO MANY BUILDINGS HAVE A NEGATIVE REACTION ON PEOPLE.

INTERDISCIPLINARY TEAMS ARE NEEDED TO DISCOVER NEW WAYS TO HELP CREATE ARCHITECTURE BY DESIGNING FORMS AND SPACES MORE APPROPRIATE FOR THE NEEDS OF PEOPLE,

RESULTING IN POSITIVE REACTION.

By the year 2000, only a long-range plan away, this country will need to nearly double its facilities. With few insignificant exceptions, most people will live in cities. Polluted air, polluted views, and constant exposure to visual chaos may lead toward deterioration of the spirit and body.

If today's cities are chaos, tomorrow's may be worse.

Multiply the dirt.

Multiply the pollution.

Multiply the visual disorder.

Multiply the traffic of people and their machines moving about.

Multiply the problems of cities without offering bold solutions; then the future will carry the aggravated complexity and confusion which will strangle any therapeutic effects architecture might have. If architects simply continue to have as little influence on the total physical environment as they have today, the future is glum. In this country, during the building boom of the fifties and sixties, there were not enough architects to go around—fewer than one architect to every 6,000 people. England, on the other hand, had one architect for every 2500 people, with over 80% of buildings designed by architects.

America's schools of architecture must immediately quadruple their output if the nation is to find solutions to the many complex problems of urbanization.

The city dweller's escape to the country must be stopped. There will be no place to run. There will have to be ways to get places. If traffic is un-

EVERY **COMPLEX** PROBLEM

CAN BE BROKEN INTO A NUMBER OF RELATIVELY **SIMPLE** PROBLEMS; HOWEVER, ALL ARE INTERRELATED.

bearable now, it will soon be worse. We can get to the moon—but how will we get to our offices?

30
Who's responsible?

One would think the development of a public architectural consciousness is the responsibility of architects and architectural educators. Not so. There are too few architects and too few architectural educators. There must be other sponsors.

The builders—entrepreneurs in industry, insurance companies which finance buildings, government officials and other decision makers—must want architecture.

The nonarchitects who sponsor architecture are crucially important—as people who can convince other people that architecture should be valued with law, medicine, even theology. The more the better. When architecture is popularized, then there will be a fight against visual pollution as there is against air pollution, and we may have an effective, beautiful environment. It's a public responsibility.

Sponsors of architecture must join architects and a concerned public to ask the following questions: Will there be architecture in transportation systems? Will there be architecture in housing megaforms? Will there be architecture in play spaces? In learning spaces? In worship spaces?

Will there be that aura which emanates from man-made environment and reflects the extent of man's development?

ARCHITECTURE IS MORE THAN SHELTER. IT CONCERNS THAT + SOMETHING.

IT IS THAT **PLUS** THAT CAUSES A DOOR KNOB OR A CITY TO **RADIATE** AN AURA.

Section 4

Why the Team?

What can a team do that one architect alone cannot? For one thing, a team can do more—and do more in less time. But quite apart from the aspect of quantity and efficiency, two questions arise:

First, can a team produce a better building? Second, can a team create spaces which radiate the aura which is architecture? The answer to both questions, our experience has shown, is an emphatic yes—provided that competent professionals can learn to work together with a common goal—the express purpose of creating architecture. When really experienced pros get together on a high level of professional interchange, things begin to happen. New thoughts are generated; ideas flow. The excitement of creative interchange and interaction not only helps solve the complex problems of planning and construction, but, more important, enhances the likelihood that architecture will emerge.

31

What is a team?

A team is an association of people who share common goals, who are willing to cooperate, and who can communicate with each other.

An architectural team exists when the prime goal is to create architecture.

The character of an architectural team is omnidirectional, certainly not linear. In other words, an architectural team is not like a mile relay team which operates in linear characteristic—with the handoff in a straight line. It is more like a basketball team, requiring a high degree of interaction from all directions. This is a situation in which everybody is there at the same time, ready to make the most of his special talents when called upon. It is bouncing off ideas, and profiting through interaction. It is transmitting and receiving encouragement. It is the complement of talent and experience. It is the interplay of different minds to zero in on a problem. It is well-defined, and perfected procedures, but also the ad lib. It is problem solving by group, but by a group that has been trained to work together.

32

A team is not a committee

Periodically throughout our practice we've been bombed by such triteness as "The camel must have been designed by a committee." So let me say at the outset: A team is not a committee.

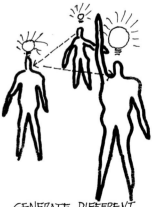

AN ARCHITECTURAL TEAM IS NOT SO MUCH LIKE A MILE RELAY TEAM WITH LINEAR CHARACTERISTICS --

IT IS LIKE A BASKETBALL TEAM REQUIRING A HIGH DEGREE OF INTERACTION FROM ALL DIRECTIONS.

THOUGHTS BOUNCING AROUND FROM PERSON TO PERSON.

GENERATE DIFFERENT AND MORE DEVELOPED IDEAS.

This 1950 photo of the CRS squatters team for the Colorado College Science Building exemplifies the fusion of diversified talents. Reading from left to right are Joe Thomas, mechanical and electrical engineer, Bill Lacy, designer, the C of CRS, Dave Yarbrough, technologist, Frank Lawyer, senior designer, and Herb Paseur, project manager. The Olin Hall of Science was strictly a team effort. Ed Nye, structural engineer, participated in the squatters by phone. He could not be two places at once. Together this team did a better job than any of us could have done separately.

One of the most important aspects of team action is that interchange and interaction generate new ideas which bounce from one person to another in the refinement process and build up into a form-giving concept. Above, left to right, are Bud Luther, Gilbert Moore, Emaly Shuman, and Bill Wright during a 1968 CRS squatters related to planning state colleges of Maryland.

A committee connotes a temporary arrangement consisting of a do-all-the-work chairman surrounded spasmodically by a half-dozen drones who wish they were not there in the first place. Committee action generally relates to pooling opinions and voting prejudices. Team action concerns solving problems by a group of specialized professionals each of whose opinions are valued, but more so when matters fall within his areas of specialization.

Committees are appointed. Teams are developed and sometimes it takes years. It took me ten years simply to learn how to communicate with

Charles Lawrence, for example. Yet we both came from the same kind of background; both had similar education; and both of us are designer types. Admittedly there is an age difference, but I'm not that much older to cause a communication gap.

Some members of our firm after a decade of service still have difficulties playing on a team. Communication can be the hang-up. Generally it is because the person does not fully appreciate the talents of other people on the team, or because others do not think as he does. Our experience has taught us that these differences create strength in team action. We've learned to capitalize on them.

A team is built on dependency. A committe is not. When a committee becomes a team, the members—every one of them—have learned to work together as a group of specialists, and depend upon each other.

TO BE ON A TEAM IS NOT ALWAYS EASY. QUITE OFTEN, ONE FEELS "OUT OF IT" AND LONESOME.

THERE WILL ALWAYS BE **IN-FIGHTING.** EVERY KEY PERSON IN CRS, INCLUDING CAUDILL, AT ONE TIME OR ANOTHER EITHER THREATENS TO QUIT OR IS CONSIDERED AS A CANDIDATE FOR RESIGNATION. TEAM IS TOUGH.

33
One man alone cannot design the complex structures of today

Architecture is too important to be the responsibility of one man, no matter whose name may appear as sole credit for a given project. In fact, a building is only rarely the work of one man alone—be it a small dwelling or a massive urban development.

In a sense, all architects are on a team—even the single-minded prima donna who fancies himself the sole creator of "his" building with but little thought for the opinions of the users of that building.

ARCHITECTURE IS TOO IMPORTANT

TO BE BOUND TO THE ANACHRONISM OF ONE MAN'S EXPRESSION.

Yet every architect, prima donna or not, consults the client before the demands of the project are programmed. So, in actuality, the client is part of the team—a poor team, nevertheless, a team. Once programmed, is the project, no matter how small, within the complete grasp of the architect? Never. He calls in other architects on his staff, outside specialists in structure, in heating and cooling, plus consultants in many fields—from kitchen people who know how best to dispose of dirty dishes to psychologists who specialize in architectural space. No doubt about it, the architect has help. It is still a team situation.

Take the so-called one-man firm.

The architect has a client. To get started, he and his client talk land, talk function, talk money, and talk form—what the project is going to look like. The architect doesn't like the client to tell him what it should look like, but that is generally what happens. Preliminary discussions end. The lone architect takes off from there. Now if everything goes right, when the architect brings his schematics back to the client, he will have a design tailored to the land, the program, and the pocketbook. But if things don't go right? What then? It is going to cost too much money! What then? The client had a different kind of heating and air conditioning system in mind! Now what? There is a landscape problem that just now shows up. And where are the special lighting effects? The lone architect is beginning to discover that he won't be able to go it alone. So he calls in outside help.

If the lone architect is an anachronism, the small firm is not. There is a place for the small firm, particularly the firm which specializes in a specific building type (such as houses or shopping centers) and has the capacity to collaborate with other firms. There is, however, no place for the "miniature" firm, the firm which attempts to do many types of buildings, without sufficient experience or professional specialization in any particular architectural field.

34

What can a team do that one man cannot do alone?

Obviously a team can do more—and do more in less time. Our experience has shown that, first, a team can produce a better building, and second, a team has a better chance to create spaces which radiate the aura which is architecture.

The creation of a team for the task at hand—from the very beginning of a project—forestalls problems along the course of completing the project.

Consider the air conditioning and heating engineer who is called in only after the schematic design is complete. His frustration is understandable—when he discovers that the schematics require miles of ductwork and that the huge blowers are apparently intended to be hidden in one small broom closet. One of our engineers said, "What you expect me to do is like hiding a tractor in a fruit jar," when confronted with the problem of an undersized mechanical room. He pleaded to be brought in earlier so he could have his say.

An interdisciplinary approach, involving people concerned with a wide range of specialties, results in more efficacious planning and smoother progress. An involved client who has participated on the team generally is a more satisfied client. It's a CRS policy to bring him in early and keep him with us throughout the project.

INVOLVEMENT IN
TEAM ACTION

CREATES A NEW
DYNAMIC DIMENSION
OF ABILITY AND
UNDERSTANDING.

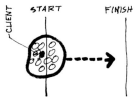

THE INTERDISCIPLINARY
APPROACH--TEAM ACTION--
SUGGESTS EARLY PARTICIPATION.

Equally important is the mystique of group interaction among client and professionals, inexperienced and experienced, specialist and generalist, and the benefits to all concerned. Team action brings forth in each member a new dynamic dimension of ability, of understanding, and of willingness to work toward the common goal: the creation of buildings and spaces which consistently surpass those by the lone architect who, after the solitary formation of his design, calls in his team of consultants only when he encounters a problem which he alone cannot solve.

When members of the team have the opportunity to share their ideas from the very beginning—not after the fact of the preliminary design—their ideas are honed and resolved. When members of the team are involved only after the design is set, they merely hack away at the design and decimate the embryonic architectural product bit by bit, so that a piecemeal reworking is necessary—until the product is, ultimately, after major surgery, restored to an imperfect whole.

35
Teamwork stimulates ideas

One of the beauties of team interchange is that when an idea emerges, it is batted about like a shuttlecock.

The idea may have come from the novice, or from the experienced designer. It may have come from the structural engineer. Possibly the client prefaced his suggestion with "What if . . ." and thereby changed the entire concept of the problem with an idea which even he was beginning to verbalize for the first time. Group action takes hold rather suddenly. The team members grasp the "idea." They debate underlying thought which shapes the forms and spaces and vivifies a formerly static session, and instills into a plan the stuff of which enduring architecture is made.

We benefit from mixing insiders with outsiders. We have found that the outsider with fresh views either will contribute or will stimulate "insiders" to rethink the problem and make a fresh contribution.

An idea may have been submitted by a psychologist, who merely tossed it out as a teaser, as was the case in the design of the CRS office building when consultant Dr. Thomas E. Lasswell said, "If you really want to mix up the total team, why don't you have gang toilets? Let the brass use the same 'head' as the other men—no officers' country."

Group discussions generate and develop ideas, like the time a Tyler, Texas, junior high school English teacher said, "Wouldn't it be nice to have an indoor play court that is as good as an outdoor play court?" Before that seemingly insignificant idea stopped bouncing around the conference room, the United States had its first all-glass gymnasium in the making.

I recall the time CRS was associated with Perkins and Will to design a high school in Norman, Oklahoma. An English visitor, Antony Part, who later was knighted by the Queen, came through Perkins and Will's Chicago office and we were discussing the school with him. Out of the blue he said, "You seem to have an excessively large hall here. Why don't you make it slightly larger and use it as a social center?" Without knowing it at the time, Sir Antony created the first social center in an American high school.

In the Bryan CRS office we invited Herb LaGrone, an Austin, Texas, junior high school principal at the time, to bring us up to date on forward edu-

MIX THE HARD-NOSE PROS WITH THE ROOKIES —

THE UNDER-STUDY IDEA.

Here is Norman High School, which uses the idea of an enlarged corridor as a social center. The idea was conceived in 1961 by England's Sir Antony Part, a visitor to the Perkins and Will/CRS project team.

cation thinking relating to these "tweeners." For some reason our discussions drifted from progressive education to "why have doors in schools?" LaGrone, now Dean of Education, Texas Christian University, could see no reason why. So the next school we designed, the A&M Consolidated High School, had no doors, pioneering the way for the open plan in the United States. Herb, as an outsider, helped us "bust the classroom box wide open."

The greatest outside force which helped CRS to shape its schoolhouses was Dr. Walter D. Cocking, editor/educator/inspirer without peer. Walter had the challenging personality which scrapes away pretense and the superfluous. He would say such things as, "You have what appears to be a good schoolhouse. But what I think is irrelevant. The only real important matter is: 'What will the children think of their building?' "

And another time Walter shook us when he said, "Why do we need schoolhouses anyway? Education should be integrated with the community. Let the classrooms be in the community—in the stores, in the churches, in the factories, in the museums, and in government buildings." The result was a classroom in the Brazos County Courthouse. It was never used because it was not the users' idea. The idea of community-integrated schools was spelled out in detail in CRS Investigation No. 11, "In Education the Most Important Number Is One" (1964), a booklet dedicated to Walter. Some of his ideas were way ahead of the times and are only now beginning to take hold, such as the classrooms on the street supervised by Manhattan Community College.

If teamwork helps give more definite, more sophisticated form to the idea, or causes a diversion which creates a better idea, certainly that's a good argument for team action. Good ideas are hard to come by.

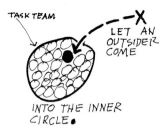

TASK TEAM

LET AN
OUTSIDER
COME

INTO THE INNER
CIRCLE.

Children were the ultimate client in the systems-built
open plan Birch Elementary School at Merrick, L.I., New
York. The school was designed and built in thirteen months.

36
Many may share the credit

At least ten people in CRS feel that the idea of combining the curvilinear form with the rectilinear cage of the Jones Hall for the Performing Arts, Houston, was their own individually conceived proposal. Eight or more CRS people honestly believe that they were individually responsible for starting the nation on its trend toward "open planning" in schoolhouses.

Six or seven people on the architect/client team which designed Harvard's Larsen Hall have the satisfaction that they individually conceived the "two first floors" idea which made it possible to maximize ground floor space and keep the height of the tower within zoning limits.

The jury that awarded Jones Hall a top national prize said, "This theater combines dignity and gaiety in and under a classically disciplined structure. Good theater—good architecture—good fun, it is black tie all the way." Each of at least ten people in CRS secretly feels that curvilinear form within the rectilinear cage is "his idea." This is the way it should be.

There was deep client involvement in planning Larsen Hall, Harvard University. A faculty committee under the leadership of Professor Bob Anderson worked continuously with the CRS team during both the programming stage and the squatters. We set up an office in the Faculty Club, drafting boards and all. It was decided early by the group that the "new building should wear Harvard tweed of the original brick buildings." The large windows are the "water holes" where the intellectual giants commune on current problems of education. Lower photo is a view from a water hole—faculty/student lounge.

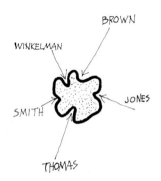

BROWN
WINKELMAN
SMITH
JONES
THOMAS

WHOSE IDEA? IT IS HARD TO TELL. MANY PEOPLE WITH MANY **POINTS OF VIEW** PARTICIPATED IN ITS FORMATION.

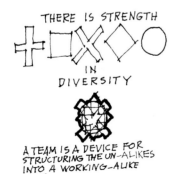

THERE IS STRENGTH IN DIVERSITY

A TEAM IS A DEVICE FOR STRUCTURING THE UN-ALIKES INTO A WORKING-ALIKE UNIT.

But whose idea was responsible?

The person who introduced it? Who timidly suggested it as the English teacher did—or boldly tossed out to stimulate the discussion and get the reactions of others, as the psychologist did? Or the biology professor who dubbed the peripheral service core an "exoskeleton"?

The idea belonged to its originator.

But it also is the property of those who modified it, amended it, enlarged upon it, argued against it, and to all those who somehow managed to enhance its worth by refining and purifying it, and lifting it into a vivid idea with meaning valid for all concerned.

37
The team firm lasts longer

Like the diversity of opinion which adds team strength, the team becomes even stronger and has more lasting power if there is diversity in the ages of its members and if it has an open-ended policy regarding leadership.

There is a distinct difference between a team firm of 100 employees and the one-man firm of 100 employees. The team outfit has a much better chance of long life, for one thing. When the "great man" dies, so does his firm, unless there is another "great man" standing in the wings ready to take over. Generally there is not. The majority of architectural firms fold shortly after the death of the principal partner. That's why the name Caudill, Rowlett and Scott has been changed to Caudill Rowlett Scott and is being gradually changed to CRS. We are a long-range outfit and the day is not too far ahead when Mr. Caudill, Mr. Rowlett and even "young" Mr. Scott are put out to pasture. In fact, on my fiftieth birthday I was given a piece of green carpet labeled "Caudill's Pasture," a reminder—if not a gentle threat—that youth will be moving in. It should. It is.

However, many in CRS still treasure the old names and the "old" partners. Tom Bullock, for example, dearly loves to line up Caudill, Rowlett and Scott—in that order—on those rare occasions we are together to show us off. He then steps back and says, "There you are. Those are the original founders." I know when we die he would like to send all three of us to a taxidermist, have us stuffed, and put on display in the lobby.

"HAVE US STUFFED AND PUT US IN THE LOBBY!"

A long-range team calls for continuous flow of new blood—at the bottom to let in new young talent, and at the top to dissolve the crust so this tender talent can rise to the leadership level. With such an open-endedness, the firm (total team) has a continuous renewal which perpetuates its life. Its life does not depend upon one man.

Historically CRS has changed its top leadership about every eight years—a deliberate attempt to give the younger and more energetic leaders the opportunity to inject vitality into the bloodstream of the firm. Not only has there been added new vigor during the handoff and during the following years of operation, but such a move gives added life insurance. There is a continuous mixing of the young and old at the leadership level. Herb Paseur, the current General Manager—the man responsible for day-to-day operation—was made a partner six years after he was hired as a draftsman for CRS and was selected to the top leadership position only four years later. Paseur's predecessor, Tom Bullock, took over the total operation of the firm's three offices when he was around thirty-five years old, five years after he was made a partner.

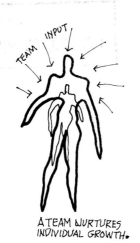

A TEAM NURTURES
INDIVIDUAL GROWTH.

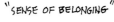

"SENSE OF BELONGING"

What happened to Mr. Caudill, Mr. Rowlett, Mr. Scott, and Mr. Pena, the first partners? Put out to pasture? Certainly not. They serve as advisors and teachers to the new crop of leaders. They developed their own specialties. And they are on the firing line of practice so that the clients can benefit by their many years of accumulated know-how. In team action there is no rest for those who "got there first." Every man must pull his load, regardless of age. In this profession longevity seems to be the key to success. The old have a great chance to contribute. And the young have the opportunity to lead. Young leadership not only brings vigor to the team as a whole, but it appears to extend the professional life of the old hands. There is constant renewal. The risk of the team's splitting is lessened when there are both the young and the old at the leadership level—a mixture of enthusiasm and experience.

Team environment is a great climate for the professional development of the young leader. The team offers professional vitality through stimulation and friendly competition.

One case in point was that of a brilliant student of mine who after graduation joined a small firm as its "chief designer"—in fact, its only designer. He had a free hand to do anything he wanted to do. After two years of "satisfied" practice, he brought his work back for my evaluation. All I could say was, "My, you've regressed!" He had been operating in professional isolation. No competition. No one to question his philosophy. No one to irritate his self-satisfaction and to stimulate professional growth. He needed "old hands" around. There was no one there to look after him.

One of the strongest arguments for the team is that it gives the individual a sense of belonging. It is important to every member of the team to see that every other member of the team grows and develops to his maximum capacity. For good reasons: The individual's professional development adds to team growth and longevity. As the individual grows, so grows the team.

38

Team efficiency can be equated with quality performance

It has been our experience these past twenty-five years that team efficiency and quality performance go hand in hand. And we are betting that it will be even more true the next twenty-five years—the only years that really count.

THE GENERALIST

THE SPECIALIST

Take the case of our national award-winning buildings—the fifty or so that were judged by the profession as being very good. With but few exceptions, each building was conceptualized during what we refer to as the CRS squatters—an on-the-spot, uninterrupted block-of-time (usually one week), team-effort design and programming session. No phones to bother us, no interruptions to speak of, and no disruptive breaks. The squatters represent the highest order of efficient operation during the most critical period of the design sequence. There is no doubt about it—CRS' best buildings have been designed during squatters. History substantiates this. Our future plans call for better methods of increased team efficiency which we are convinced leads to higher quality performance.

THE TEAM

Another lesson from CRS history: A team can be creative. A look-back at our best buildings proves that our maxim "together we can do a better

With William E. Blurock Associates, the CRS team—with Frank Lawyer taking the design lead—conceptualized and developed an entire campus in Cypress, California. The view is of the second-level piazza and the library. A true commuter college, cars occupy the first level, the idea being to separate vehicular and pedestrian traffic. This is an example of a plural situation: The project is a group of buildings, the client is a corporate body, and the architect is a team made up of professionals from two different firms.

job than we can separately" would be more accurate if it were: "Together we can do not only a better job than we can separately but with the team we can produce a more innovative product."

39
Architects find in-depth specialties

A few years ago any self-respecting architect honestly believed he could do everything. Specialization was a nasty word. Today it is something else. Every man is a specialist.

That's the reason for having a team. It's a group of specialists. A team must be composed of different talents united in purpose and organized to perform together with efficiency. Each member of a team must specialize in something—do something different and better than someone else. It is a straight case for specialization.

It took Willie Pena about ten years to find "his place" on the team. He went from specifications, to color, to project management, to running the drafting room, and finally to programming. What kind of an architect is Pena? There is no question: he is an architectural analyst, one of the best in the country.

Pena believes that "it is only by first seeking out the problem and defining it that a valid solution can be developed." His and John Focke's expression "problem seeking" is as much a part of the architectural nomenclature as CRS' squatters. When asked, "Why problem seeking?" Pena replies, "Design is problem solving; programming is problem seeking." He strongly advocates the client/user's involvement in the process. He believes that although the programming process is essentially analytical, there is room for intuition, but reminds us that "intuitive insight must be based on knowledge and experience." Pena was the first person I heard talk about the necessity to distinguish "wants from needs." He says, "A wants-versus-needs situation occurs whenever the client defines his problems in terms of architectural solutions (form and space) rather than functional requirements." He concludes, "The architectural team's job, then, is to determine those assumptions upon which the client based his solution and to evaluate these." Sometimes accused of being too elementary, Pena continually stresses the bases of programming. He lists five steps in problem seeking: (1) establish goals; (2) collect, organize, and analyze *facts;* (3) uncover and test programmatic *concepts;* (4) determine the real *needs;* and state the *problem.* Pena adds, "Architectural practice is no different from any other process. You can't solve the problem unless you know what it is."

But even in that area of specialization, Pena finds that programming is becoming too general and needs subdividing. Accordingly he spends most of his time in his capacity of "The Professor of CRS" training others to be experts in more specific areas of programming such as in schools, in office buildings, and in hospitals.

And the greatest compliment that Pena can receive is that some of his trainees are becoming better in-depth specialists than their teacher. So grows the team.

William Pena, "The Professor of CRS," is continuously training his understudies.

40

The team surpasses the one-man approach

In the twenties Le Corbusier pleaded for a "new architecture." He got it—a one-man effort. He made his contribution most significant and timely. But now his "new" is old. His forms are tired, inappropriate for this day.

His one-man approach is outmoded. Corbu knew this before he died and had already begun to convert to a more comprehensive way of solving the complex problems of urbanization. He started to recognize the need for team effort. He had begun to discard painting for the computer as a source of inspiration. Yet most architects still use the original Corbu approach—formal + singular—to architectural practice. They still like to paint or sculpt. There is nothing wrong with this. Such skills are invaluable to the designer. But to say that a specialist in computer programming or experts in the administrative aspects of building systems must be good painters and sculptors is ridiculous.

The difference between the 1920s approach still in use and the team approach predicted for the 1970s is basically the difference between the singular and the plural.

Compare the how-it-was with the how-it-is.

THEN:
The project was a single building.
The client was a single person.
The architect was a one-man designer.

Frank Lawyer is shown discussing some ideas during the 1960 squatters for the Colorado College Science Building. Herb Paseur, then the project manager, is silhouetted on the right. A thirty-member faculty committee led by Dr. Will Wright served as the client/users. We considered each a member of the total planning team.

NOW:
The project is a group of buildings.
The client is a corporate body.
The architect is a team.

The design of a small house could be classified as a singular situation—a single building for a single client by a single architect. Today, firms rarely do simple, single buildings on the scale of little houses or small churches. If they do, they do them in bunches. Then the singular becomes the plural.

In looking toward the future, firms are having to reaxamine their thinking and reshuffle their personnel to cope with the larger, more complex projects. They are having to think plural.

41

The challenge of the team is creation of a new architecture

Urbanization demands team action, and big teams. Just what kind of forms will emerge through team action remains to be seen. Combining the team and the systems approach at a high level of sophistication will give the majority of people buildings which radiate the aura which is architecture—a citizen's right.

Will a new kind of architectural expression develop when individual professionals learn to work in a situation of group dynamics? When architects finally learn that they are not self-sufficient, capable of doing everything in the splendid isolation of the nineteenth-century genius? When they accept the fact that they must work not only with other architects, but with other specialists in the fringe disciplines—including the manufacturers and contractors? When architects learn to perform in interdisciplinary teams, what will their buildings and spaces be like?

No one really knows.

All we know is that buildings will be different—hopefully, much better. The process is the product in one sense. The team process, being a relatively new way of doing things, will inevitably result in new forms.

A team may not be able to produce a great symphony (although no one has proved it can't), but it now appears most probable that teams can create great examples of architecture which surpass those produced by the "masters." The new master-teams will be recognized for their creative collaboration and organic synthesis of forms and spaces. There will be not only unity of purpose, but oneness of operation as well. The master-team, the team united in common effort, can accomplish almost anything—even the creation of a new "new architecture."

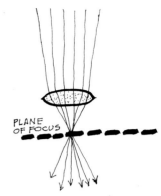

PLANE OF FOCUS

A TEAM IS LIKE A MAGNIFYING GLASS WHICH **FOCUSES** THE SUN'S RAYS INTO ONE PENETRATING FORCE.

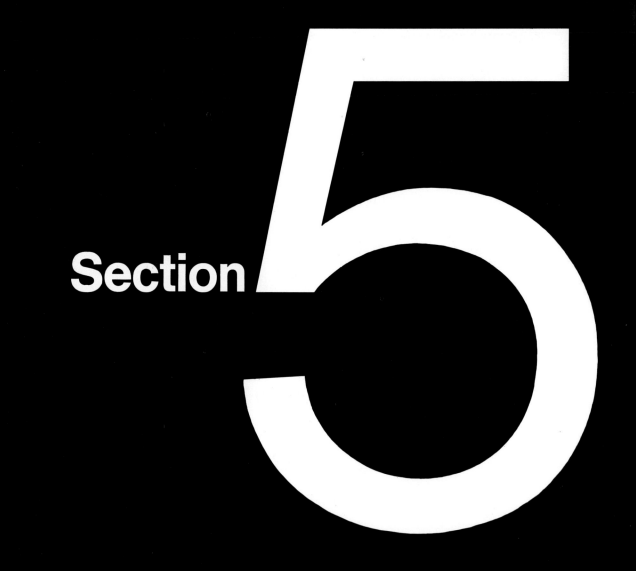

Section 5

Two Theories
on Team Action

Two theories contributed to architecture by team in CRS. These are sometimes referred to as the triad theories since one concerns three aspects of product while the other concerns three aspects of process. The product theory measures function/form/economy and concerns the integration of these three qualities. The process theory and its resulting troika plan assure coordination of management, design, and technology—three components of architectural practice. These two theories reinforce the team concept.

42

Two theories reinforce CRS team concept

Two theories have stemmed from CRS' deeply rooted belief in the team concept. One concerns product. The other process. Each concerns three distinctly separate, but interrelated integrated components. These theories are:

OF PRODUCT
Architecture has a better chance of emerging from man-made environment when the environment has been created by team, using an omnidirectional approach which expresses product in terms of function, form, and economy—the three determinants considered simultaneously, each developed to the greatest magnitude, and brought into unified equilibrium.

OF PROCESS
Since every architectural task requires three kinds of thinking/action relating to management, design, and technology, the task can best be done by a team led by a troika of manager, designer, and technologist.

Each of these triad theories has resulted in reinforcing the team concept of practice.

From the product theory we have a yardstick for measuring performance of product at any stage of development (be it a feasibility report or a finished building). Such a yardstick is a valuable team tool.

From the process theory we have a device which, superimposed over the constantly changing organization structure, helps assure a balanced problem-solving approach in which each of the three components of architectural practice is given serious consideration.

The following chapters discuss both theories and their derivatives.

43

The product theory dates to the early days of the firm

Before 1950 we argued (and we still do) that if an architectural firm's goal is to produce buildings and spaces which radiate architecture, then there must be agreement among the team members on the principles or laws which govern architecture. We had a triad theory relating to product. The product was a schoolhouse. In a book published in 1954, "Toward Better School Design," it was reported that we believed "the good school plant (is) based on three planning factors so inextricably fused that they form a kind of trinity, a three-in-one consideration." We listed education (function), environment (form), and economy (no change there) as these considerations. The theory then was basically the same as it is now. We've found no reason to change. In fact, history gives the trinity, or triad, of planning factors even more validity.

As we have said, architecture has been defined as an aura which emanates from man-made environment, evokes emotional response in the individual who experiences it, fulfills both physical and psychological needs, transcends mere shelter, and reflects the extent of man's development.

From the very beginning in CRS we have found that the product theory is a natural law which seems to govern whether or not architecture emerges from form and space. In one case when as young, inexperienced architects

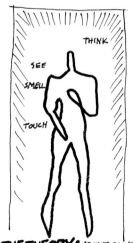

THINK
SEE
SMELL
TOUCH

THE THEORY: ARCHITECTURE EMERGES FROM FORM AND SPACE WHEN **FUNCTION, FORM,** AND **ECONOMY** ARE BROUGHT TOGETHER IN A STATE OF INTEGRATED, EQUILIBRATED UNITY.

we were reluctant to say "no" to our client, we got into hot water and so did he, financially, because his house cost too much money. For this particular person many years went by before that house began to radiate architecture to him. His wife, however, liked it from the beginning; she wasn't concerned with the final price tag.

At about the same period we designed and helped to build another house in which the wife was the chief complainer—with good reasons. I shall never forget the day she met me at the airport, (the project was 300 miles away) and drove me straight to her new home. She had me stand on the public sidewalk, told her husband to get in the shower, her son to stand by the lavatory, and her daughter to sit on the john—so I could witness "the daily family bathroom drama" as everyone else did who walked or drove past the house. We had really goofed. We had specified a translucent glass wall which clearly revealed the forms behind it at night. No matter how economical the house was or how beautifully proportioned the forms were, to that woman there was no architecture because the house did not function properly.

$$\underrightarrow{EC} \; \underrightarrow{FO} \; \underrightarrow{FU}$$
"FORM FOLLOWS FUNCTION"

To some of the townspeople the first CRS school looked "like a horse barn." It made no difference how much of a bargain they got on the construction market, or how well the building functioned as an educational tool, it still did not have what it takes to generate architecture—for them. But to the teachers and children the school had architecture—beautiful, logical forms and spaces which were conducive to learning, creating the aura that is architecture.

$$\underrightarrow{FO} \; \underrightarrow{FU} \; \underrightarrow{EC}$$
"LOWER COST THE BETTER"

Early in the game we became convinced that architecture had a better chance to emerge when function, form, and economy were considered simultaneously and each developed to its greatest magnitude, culminating in a kind of equilibrium which results in complete integration of these three.

$$\underrightarrow{FU} \; \underrightarrow{EC} \; \underrightarrow{FO}$$
"FUNCTION FOLLOWS FORM"

NONE OF THESE AXIOMS WILL DO. THERE IS NO SEQUENCE. THE **ARCHITECTURAL APPROACH** IS NOT LINEAR, BUT OMNIDIRECTIONAL.

95

44

Team action requires accepted laws

ARCHITECTURE IS RELATED
TO SPATIAL AND FORMAL
ORDER CREATED BY
THE INTEGRATION OF
FUNCTION, FORM, AND
ECONOMY WHICH IN
ONENESS PROMOTE
THE DIGNITY OF MAN.

THE APPROACH IS
OMNI-DIRECTIONAL

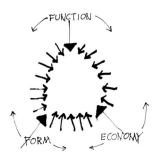

WITH MANY DICIPLINES
CONVERGING ON THE
PROBLEM FROM MANY
DIRECTIONS.

The triad theory of product states that it is a team making use of an omnidirectional approach that can best integrate function, form, and economy. In a sense this is a law governing architecture. Architecture is more likely to occur and to reach more people when an interdisciplinary team of experts (in contrast to one individual) plans the physical environment. Most certainly the product or products will reflect more points of view, thereby increasing the chances that architectural phenomena will occur more often for more people. When the users are called in to help in planning the chances are even greater, because architecture relates to human values, and human values relate to personal participation in the design process. That is why teachers and students should be brought in on planning schools, why nurses and patients should be members of the team that plans hospitals. Users' involvement in the determination of spaces and forms greatly increases the chances of the emergence of architecture.

Accordingly there has always been need for theory relating to principles and laws which all the planning participants of the team can understand and can use effectively in the design approach. The product theory does it for us. It is reasonable to think that such a theory not only can be easily applied by the team, but must be so basic in application that it is universally applicable to almost any form or space, or adaptable to any of the fast-changing periods of architectural development.

The triad theory of product has been tried in many diverse projects and proven workable by the CRS team during most of its twenty-five years of practice.

This little elementary school in San Angelo, Texas, designed by Don Goss and the CRS team, exemplifies the interrelationship of function, form, and economy. In essence it's a circle under a square. The circular plan was dictated by function and cost. The mortarboard hat provides shade from the west Texas sun. So function, form, and economy are one. This schoolhouse has that oneness.

FUNCTION

IS THE **DO** -- THE WAY PEOPLE AND THINGS MOVE TO DO THE TASKS THEY HAVE TO DO.

FORM

IS THE **BE** -- THE 'I-AM-WHAT-I-AM' AND THE WHAT WE SEE, THE PHYSICAL MANIFESTATION OF BOTH FUNCTION AND FORM.

ECONOMY

IS **MAXIMUM** EFFECT WITH **MINIMUM** MEANS RELATING TO BOTH FUNCTION AND FORM. ECONOMY CONVEYS AN ATTITUDE AND SPIRIT.

45

Meanings of the product triad must be tied down

Words like function, form, and economy are so common that they take on different meanings to different people. For the purpose of clarifying the triad theory relating to product, accept the following definitions:

Function is the do. Function is physical (at this point don't muddy the water by mixing emotional function with physical function). Think of function as the task—the biggest task as how a city works, or the smallest as how a doorknob works. Function also relates to the way people move about to do the jobs they have to do. If a building functions, it responds by making the job easier to do.

Function is the "do." For one thing, it concerns how people move about to conduct business. Here we see the users of the Carlsbad, New Mexico high school going about their task. The building, designed by the CRS team and Kern Smith, Associate Architects, in 1961, responds to function.

Form is the "what we see." Form is the promise of function and relates to economy. The above structure by the CRS team led by engineer Joe Thomas and architect Charles Lawrence houses the nuclear reactor at Texas A & M University. Designed in 1958, this is typical of contemporary structure in which engineering factors have greatly multiplied in response to new technology. Architectural form must reflect functional validity. This project was a joint venture of Convair, General Dynamics, and CRS.

Form is the be. Form relates to appearance—what we see. Form must say "I am something," and what that form tells the viewer depends upon the task it is supposed to do. Form reads with greater clarity if it has the simplicity of a single idea. Architectural form is shaped by reasons of *site* (a house on a mountain differs from a house on a prairie); of *task* (a factory reflects its manufacturing process); of *fashion* (people want architectural symbols to express their moment of time); and of *space* since form defines space.

Economy is means/effects. Maximum effect with minimum means—that is the essence. Economy in architectural terms implies that there is nothing

"LESS IS MORE"
MIES

99

AS **MIND, BODY, SPIRIT** RELATE TO MAN,

SO DO **FUNCTION, FORM, ECONOMY** RELATE TO A BUILDING

Visual economy quite often reflects monetary economy. This idea of "maximum effect with minimum means" is particularly true with the Maine South High School near Chicago, designed in 1961 by the CRS team in association with Erickson, Kristmann, Stillwaugh, Inc.

superfluous, yet nothing wanting. It is not frugality, but has a closer relationship to simplicity—elegance through restraint in the visual sense. Economy is not bareness, complete exclusion of amenities. Economy is "the most for the money."

Although the three words are distinctly different and the dictionary pulls them completely apart, nevertheless there is a very pronounced interrelationship when an architectural product is concerned.

Function is the validity of form.
Form responds to function.
Economy disciplines both function and form.

The three are one.

100

There is function of form, form of function, and the economy of both function and form. It is the architectural oneness we have talked about.

Form, for example, cannot be considered alone, at least not architectural form. Form must relate to both function and economy. Undisciplined forms, like pseudo facades, fake columns, ersatz arches, and false fronts sometimes stir the emotions, but eventually palliate the intellect. The aura that is architecture relates to both emotions and intellect.

Architecture is more likely to occur when the function, the form, and the economy of the product are clear and meaningful.

Architecture is more likely to occur when the function, form, and economy of the product are clear and meaningful. Shown is the Quincy (Massachusetts) Vocational-Technical High School, with Kenneth Parry and Associates as associate architects.

46

The triad theory of product is summarized

The following points relating to the triad theory of product are relevant:

(1) The theory is disarmingly simple. For centuries philosophers have been wrestling with the mind/body problem, only two inseparable variables; yet the problem is still unresolved. The function/form/economy problem is just as complicated, perhaps more.

(2) From the theory there stem two very practical design tools which architects and their interdisciplinary collaborators can use:

A team approach for solving problems during the architectural process.

A systematic evaluation—the function/form/economy yardstick—by team from conceptualization to completion.

(3) The key of the theory is integrated cooperation—bringing together function, form, and economy so that each element works for the other two in a mutually beneficial relationship.

(4) The scope of the theory covers everything from a doorknob to a city.

(5) The prime purpose of the omnidirectional approach deriving from the theory is introducing precision to the architectural process.

(6) The outstanding advantage of the evaluative device—the function/form/economy yardstick—which stems from the theory is that evaluations can be made at every stage of development. In other words the task team can apply the yardstick at any time, not waiting until the bids come in or until the users decide whether they like the product—the final and most accurate measurement.

(7) Since the theory requires an omnidirectional rather than a linear approach to problem solving, it is particularly adapted to team action.

(8) Time must be considered as a function of each of the elements of the triad.

In sum, where an architectural product—doorknob or city—is concerned, architecture has a better chance of emerging if it is produced by team, making use of an omnidirectional approach which expresses product in terms of function, form, and economy, considered simultaneously, developed to the greatest magnitude, and brought into equilibrium.

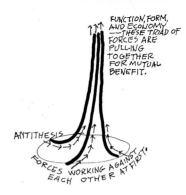

47

What is architectural oneness?

The integration of function, form, and economy leads to architectural oneness. Function alone has the promise of form and economy; form, the promise of function and economy; economy, the promise of function and form. Fulfillment of the three promises produces architectural oneness. And achieving this oneness enhances the chances of architecture.

The simple soda straw has the three-in-oneness. The soda straw has meaningful *form;* its *function* is of the highest magnitude of usefulness; it possesses both monetary and visual *economy.* And there is effective equilibrium of the three forces. The soda straw epitomizes the logic of design. It is pared to the very essentials, scaled and formed in just the proper manner for its job, beautiful in its simplicity. What a pump!

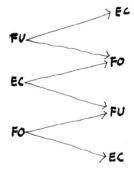

FUNCTION HAS THE PROMISE OF FORM AND ECONOMY.

ECONOMY HAS THE PROMISE OF FORM AND FUNCTION.

FORM HAS THE PROMISE OF FUNCTION AND ECONOMY.

WHEN THINKING **FUNCTION**
THINK FORM AND ECONOMY.

WHEN THINKING **FORM**
THINK FUNCTION AND ECONOMY.

WHEN THINKING **ECONOMY**
THINK FUNCTION AND FORM.

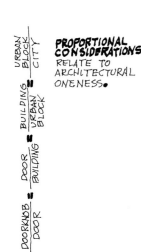

PROPORTIONAL CONSIDERATIONS RELATE TO ARCHITECTURAL ONENESS.

To understand the soda straw is to understand the triad of forces which act upon the total physical environment. Every human is affected by the forces of function, form, and economy, although the effects vary from day to day. The time consideration, therefore, must be superimposed over the triad, since human activities (function) change from day to day. An architectural form with a certain task to perform today may be required to do something else tomorrow. Time tells on function, form, and economy. So the oneness relates to time.

Let's jump from the soda straw to the doorknob, to bring us a little closer to architectural oneness. A good doorknob looks like what it does. It does what it looks like. And it looks—and does—with minimum means. A doorknob can possess the quality of architecture, or it can be without. If there is architecture in the doorknob, it must do its task well for the user, look attractive to the user, and feel good in the hand of the user. It must transmit that plus something which transcends mere "doorknob" to beautiful, functional architectural form, if it possesses architecture. And if it possesses architecture, the oneness of form, function, and economy will be there.

Now consider a door. A door can possess architecture, or it can be without. A lot depends upon whether there is oneness. It is a matter of where it is as much as what it is.

Consider a building. A building can possess architecture, or it can be without. If it does, there is oneness.

Consider an urban block. The block can possess architecture, or it can be without. If it does, there is oneness.

Consider the city. The city can possess architecture, or it can be without. If it does, there is oneness.

People who handle the doorknob, open the door, live or work in the building, walk down the city block, are necessarily concerned with how the entire city works, how it looks, how it feels, and how much it costs to live there. The city, in its entirety, is shaped by the forces of the triad and is affected by this oneness.

The doorknob, the door, the building, the urban block, the city—each may transmit architecture, or none may transmit architecture, depending upon the fusion and strength of the forces of function, form, and economy.

A bad city with a few good buildings is like bad steak sprinkled with good seasoning. Just as the steak is still bad steak, made a bit more palatable by seasoning, the city is still a bad city whose few good buildings merely help relieve scattered visual and functional inadequacies. Rarely does one clear and unified signal of architecture emanate from a city. But there are always isolated sparks.

An excellently designed doorknob helps only a little to improve a poorly designed door, but there is a spark.

An excellently designed door helps only a little to improve a poorly designed building, but there is a spark.

An excellently designed building helps only a little to improve a poorly designed urban block, but the spark helps.

An excellently designed urban block does little to improve a poorly planned city, but thank goodness for the aura that is architecture, if only in a small portion of the city.

Nevertheless the more small signals of architecture the better the chances are for a clear, strong signal. That's why the little things are important. The product triad theory, as proposed, serves the little things as well as the big things. The city, the largest element, and the doorknob, the smallest, are both germane to the three-in-one concept. We are back to architectural oneness—the big scale as well as the small scale.

In sum, architectural oneness is the fulfillment of the promises of function, form, and economy at any and all scales.

The triad theory of product relates to little things like study carrels (Stillwater High School, designed in 1958) and furniture. Philip A. Wilber was our associate architect.

Here is an example of "zero detailing." In the CRS home office we literally glued the glass to the concrete, eliminating window sash. In this case there was visual and monetary compatibility. "Little things" designed with care help create architecture.

48

The budget shapes form and function

Everyone knows that there must be a marriage of form and function. Most people forget that money more than likely decides what both form and function will be, even to the slightest detail. The budget—that great exorciser of frills—plays heavily in the triad theory relating to product.

Budgets help scrape off geegaws. Monetary limits help eliminate the non-essentials.

A case in point is the Harvard Graduate School of Education built in 1966. Frank Lawyer, now a vice president in CRS, Charles Lawrence, and I—heavily involved in this project along with our professor clients—wanted to have a building with great visual unity. We thought the best way to do this would be to make it of one exterior material—brick, that original Harvard brick that looks like tweeds the students wore. So we did. Even the soffits of the deeply recessed windows were designed to be brick. And it was somewhat of a trick to detail brickwork which would be used as ceilings.

Fortunately we ran out of money during the design development stage and these stalactite-like brick soffits were never constructed. Instead, the soffits were built of economical white stucco. That was all we could afford. In going the lower cost route, we got a much better building. The little white soffits gave life to what might well have turned out to be a dreary, monotonous exterior. Here is a case where budget forced us to go "lean and clean," and a better building resulted. So sometimes having to trim to meet the budget can be good.

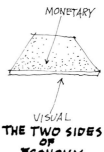

MONETARY

VISUAL

THE TWO SIDES OF ECONOMY

Larsen Hall, Harvard Graduate School of Education, felt the cost paring knife and profited by it. For one thing, we had to use plaster soffits in the deeply recessed windows insead of the brick "stalactite" as originally planned. Cost cutting simplified and gave an added sparkle to the white soffits that they would never have had if the budget were not limited.

Here is a case where trimming was disastrous: In 1955 in my home town of College Station, Texas, the children and teachers moved into what was recognized all over the world as one of the most radically designed schools —the A&M Consolidated High School designed by the CRS team. This school was the granddaddy of "the open plan." We had a terrible cost problem. We even left out partitions to cut cost. Since the school was in our own backyard, we were so anxious to obtain quality that we became too optimistic about cost. Bids were high, but we were able to whittle the costs down to get the schoolhouse under contract. The sad part—and it was very sad indeed—was that the school board decided to have the exterior walls cement-asbestos board instead of the marble we had specified. This decision was regretted for years to come. There was only $13,000 savings in using the high-maintenance cement-asbestos instead of the marble, and these savings were eaten up within three years because of breakage. We cut too much.

Most architects and engineers have been trained to work within monetary restrictions. They have been taught that "less is more," that they must "get rid of the superfluous," "make designs lean and clean," "get the most for your money." Economy connotes getting more for less.

Another example of the interrelationship of function, form, and economy is Jones Hall for the Performing Arts in Houston, designed in 1962. It is disarmingly simple in appearance, but is actually as complicated as a battleship, necessarily so to give it its multifunction, multiform aspects. The miles of cables, the thousands of pulleys, and the computerized controls to lower or raise ceilings and expand or contract the acoustic volume cost money. It was cheaper to build this one building than three separate buildings— one for concert, one for opera, and one for ballet, plays, and musicals. Yet the casual viewer, who does not see the hidden mechanism behind the

Had the budget included another $13,000, the exterior walls of this school could have been marble instead of cement-asbestos board. This internationally known school suffered from low-first-cost high-maintenance syndrome. The school board's decision to trade low first cost for high maintenance was most unwise. Cement-asbestos for marble. Another bad move the board made was authorizing enclosure of the open porch. This move not only destroyed the amenities but also robbed the students of precious shade and rain shelter area. The temptation to capture cheap space was just too great. This photo was made during the first month of school in 1955.

walls and ceilings, has the impression that Jones Hall is uncomplicated and was not costly. Nevertheless, Houston got a lot for its money.

Even by combining three buildings into one, we were confronted with a very limited budget. At one time, the "classic cage" was designed to be of bronze cladding. At the end of preliminary design, the budget said, "No, it's too expensive." Reluctantly, we decided on one material, travertine marble, for the cage as well as for the great curvilinear walls. This decision to cut cost could not have been a better one. This one material, as built, provides visual strength and elegant simplicity which could not have been achieved with two major materials. Here visual and monetary economy worked together.

There seems to be a psychological aspect of economy. In Roanoke, Virginia, in the late fifties, we had worked up a very simple and economical wall system using marble as both exterior and interior material. One of the school board members nearly blew his top when he heard our proposal. He said, "I don't give a hell whether it is cheaper or not. Marble looks too expensive." Unquestionably, he was responding to pressure about the high cost of school construction. After hearing about this, Herb Paseur retorted with an interoffice memo that went something like this: "Due to the complaint on Roanoke, we have devised a new sandwich wall material—1/8" Douglass fir plywood laminated on both sides of 1" thick marble. This will give us the economical utility of marble and the aesthetic quality of crating plywood." This what-looks-cheap is good has cropped up in times of both prosperity and depression. It is a curious thing, difficult to understand.

About 1950 in College Station, Texas, the Methodist Church converted a large attic into a little chapel. The preacher, a highly intelligent man, said, "Bill, why don't you put in some false beams to make it have more of an ecclesiastical atmosphere?" Appalled at the suggestion of such a thoughtless act I said, "My God, that's sacrilegious." Needless to say, he was more shocked than I. Fakery in a church!

There were many arguments among the members of the building committee. The chapel was finally built. Truth and integrity prevailed. No false beams! But, sadly enough, the argument was not won on the premise that there must be a marriage of function and form satisfying the intellect as well as the naked eye. It was won on the basis of the budget. Economy makes form honest.

49

Is there architectural perfection?

If the triad theory relating to product has validity, then when the magnitudes of function, form, and economy have reached the ultimate, and when these three forces are in perfect equilibrium, there should be architectural perfection.

Will this ever happen?

It hasn't happened yet.

What about the Taj Mahal? Is it perfect?

As far as magnificent form, yes. As a monument to love, and as a world attraction, it functions exceedingly well. But the Taj Mahal is not perfect. For one thing, it cost too much money and the masses rebelled. The construction of the magnificent structure drained the coffers of the kingdom. The building was a contributing factor to the downfall of the great Moguls.

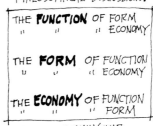

DEFINING THE FOLLOWING WOULD MAKE INTERESTING PHILOSOPHICAL DISCUSSIONS:

THE **FUNCTION** OF FORM
"   "   " ECONOMY

THE **FORM** OF FUNCTION
"   "   " ECONOMY

THE **ECONOMY** OF FUNCTION
"   "   " FORM

MOST CERTAINLY THE INTERRELATIONSHIP WOULD BE BROUGHT TO THE SURFACE.

What about the Parthenon? Is it perfect?

Unquestionably it is one of the masterpieces of the world. The asymmetrical plan of the building group gives excitement and functional logic. It sits majestically on the Acropolis, creating a near-perfect union of land, sky, and structure. It embodies the aspirations of the Greeks who used it, and epitomizes the spirit of the age. The Parthenon also exemplifies a remarkably sophisticated development in the use of prefabricated architectural components. But perfect? No, for the Parthenon got its builders into trouble because of the unforeseen enormity of construction costs. And why should stone joinery look like wood?

What about the Guggenheim Museum? Is it perfect?

It is a classic example of organic architecture; it permits an infinite variety of spatial experiences. And its composition successfully unifies the many complex curvilinear forms into visual singularity.

But the Guggenheim lacks the universal space which is necessary for the function of a museum. The building is not subservient to the art which it houses. And it is not a harmonious component of the neighborhood in which it is situated.

The Taj Mahal, the Parthenon, and the Guggenheim Museum are all great buildings, but none is perfect. Although perfection may never be reached, the quest for architectural excellence is far nearer realization when architects have high standards of measurement, as well as the innate determination for achievement of perfection.

This quest for perfection is what the product theory is all about.

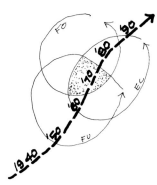

FUNCTION, FORM, AND ECONOMY—EACH HAS ITS OWN MOMENT OF **TIME.**

50

The product theory suggests a problem-solving architectural approach by team

If the triad theory of product is clearly understood by each member of the team, there will be a natural team approach to solving problems—much like setting up a tripod. Our experience has shown that it is very easy for a task team to look at the overall problem in terms of adjusting three legs

The design sequence requires continuous evaluation of what has been done and what needs to be done in terms of function, form, and economy. It's like setting up a tripod—trying to achieve a trilateral balance. To do this requires many of the "skull practices" of total team, including the users. Every sketch needs not only a functional and formal evaluation but also a price tag put on it. This 1960 photo, taken during CRS squatters for Olin Hall of Science, Colorado College, shows Frank Lawyer "line backing" me at a session with faculty. Our associate on this project was Carlisle B. Guy.

—function, form, and economy—to achieve the right kind of balance from early conceptual stages to and through detailed design development.

When the function leg is too long either the form and economy legs must be lengthened or the function leg must be shortened. Same for the other two. The design sequences call for periodic evaluation and constant adjustment of these three legs. Effective team play requires that systematic evaluation be communicated to all participating members so that proper adjustment can be made.

Let me illustrate: When the CRS team with our local associate, Max Lovett, planned a new high school in San Angelo, Texas, in 1955, we went through the usual programming procedures. We sat down with the school board, superintendent, principals, teachers, and even a few students, and listed what each user thought should go into this new school. They told us they wanted so many classrooms, so many labs, so many shops, offices of such and such a size, student activities rooms, an auditorium seating so many people, a basketball court with seats for so many spectators, a swimming pool, cafeteria, library and so on. That was simple enough. We came out with a list of spatial requirements necessary to make the school work as it should—at least as the people we talked with thought it should.

In other words we pulled out the *function* leg of the tripod. And with all the things they wanted, it went out full length.

Next we talked to the board, superintendent, operation and maintenance people, department heads and principals about what form the building should take, specifically the materials and kind of heating and electrical system which the school should have. "By all means let's have the best. We certainly want the floors to be marble and marble along the wainscoting. We want the best heating system and obviously we need plenty of foot-candles in all classes and labs. And air conditioning is a must." Every time they talked we heard the cash register ring.

So we pulled out the *form* leg of the tripod. It, too, went out full length.

Then after days of finding out what our clients wanted (quite distinctly different from what they needed) we finally got around to asking that most important question, "How much money do you want to spend?"

They told us. So we pulled out the *economy* leg of the tripod. Horrors! Where the function and form legs reached four feet, the economy leg was only six inches!

We had a most imbalanced situation. There were only two alternatives: modify the functional and formal desires, or spend more money. Naturally, the client preferred to do neither.

What actually happened was that our client did both—converted the "want list" into a more condensed "need list" and dug up some more money. This resulted in a trilateral balance among function, form, and economy.

This same kind of omnidirectional thinking was carried on throughout basic design and design development. There was a continuous adjustment of the tripod.

As it turned out, the building was very successful. San Angelo got the most for the money. And the United States got one of the pioneer secondary school buildings of the current modern education movement. A 12' model of it was exhibited in Moscow during one of the trade fairs. It also took a top AIA national award. The tripod was balanced. The product theory was put to practice.

HORRORS!
THE ECONOMY
LEG IS TOO
SHORT.

FUNCTION

FORM

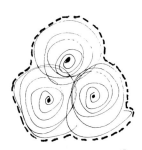

FULFILLMENT OF THE **3 PROMISES** OF FUNCTION, FORM, AND ECONOMY PRODUCES **ARCHITECTURAL ONENESS.**

51

Fruition of the process theory came in 1970

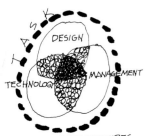

EVERY **TASK** REQUIRES 3 KINDS OF THINKING/ ACTION RELATING TO THE **DISCIPLINES OF ARCHITECTURAL PRACTICE.** TEAMWORK IS IN THE OVERLAP.

A **TROIKA**--3 MEN JOINTLY LEADING A GROUP-- CONSISTS OF A SPONSOR FOR EACH DISCIPLINE OF PRACTICE.

Process is defined here as a series of actions or procedures by people, implying input, as opposed to product or that which is something produced, which implies output.

In January 1970, CRS initiated the Troika Plan—a device superimposed over the corporate structure to assure a balanced problem-solving approach to give simultaneous and serious consideration to each of the three components of architectural practice—management, design, and technology.

This stemmed from the triad theory of process which states that every architectural task requires three kinds of thinking/action relating to management, design, and technology and can best be accomplished if the task is done by a team led by a troika (a triune leadership) consisting of a manager, a designer, and a technologist.

The Troika Plan evolved from criticisms by the firm's principals who felt that design and technology were taking a back seat to management. Tom Bullock expressed it well when he said, "All the excitement is in the front end of the business—computerized programming, job getting, publications, and building-type studies. What we need is something to bring excitement to the back end of the business (technology) and to bolster up the middle (design)." The Troika Plan has done just that.

The Troika Plan provides a task troika for every major project so that one specialist is responsible for effective management; another for quality design; and another for advanced technology. We wanted no one of these three neglected. In addition, the plan called for three highly experienced people at the director level, called the CRS Troika, to oversee the total task.

52

Components of the process theory are defined

The process theory, like the product theory, has three distinct but inter-related components. These are defined under the following headings:

Management is the act or art of managing, implying direction and control. Management concerns the judicious use of means to accomplish an end involving the smallest or largest task. A manager is a process-oriented specialist. He has a natural tendency toward functionalism. The manager group includes project managers, programmers, accountants, human behavior consultants, and building type consultants such as school specialists, community college specialists, university building specialists, office building specialists, civic center specialists, and housing specialists.

Design is the act or art of designing, implying artistic skills of composition, of creating architectural form, and of defining architectural space. Design, in addition to being related to things of architectural nature, concerns graphics, competition and exhibit panels, and formats of publications. A designer is a product-oriented specialist. He has a natural tendency toward formalism. The designer group includes the architectural designers, interior designers, landscape designers, graphics designers, planners, photographers, delineators, and model builders.

Technology is the act or art of employing means to achieve a practical purpose, implying applied science and engineering necessary for human

If it were not for Phil Williams' managerial talents (he is also a highly experienced planner) this dormitory group at Duke University, designed in 1964 with the Six Associates, would never have been built—at least this way. Phil had the task, with designer Frank Lawyer, to "invent a new Gothic that Duke could afford."

The talent of a great designer is needed on every building project where architecture is concerned. Frank Lawyer led the design team for the Cypress Junior College built in North Orange County, California. CRS was associated with William E. Blurock.

sustenance and comfort relating specifically to structure and environmental controls of land, space and architectural form, building systems, system building, and the technical aspects of any task. A technologist is a person interested in both product and process and concerned with "putting things together." The technologist group includes production architects, structural engineers, mechanical engineers, electrical engineers, civil engineers, design developers, systems specialists, estimators, specification writers, construction administrators, and production technicians. It should be mentioned here that there are occasions when one person plays two or even all three roles, but generally he is best qualified for only one.

By the time we put the Troika Plan into effect CRS had reached an enviable position in the profession. The quality level of our products had

What is architecture? This beautiful little school in New York City, P.S. 219, designed in 1962, certainly has it. And what do you see? Mostly structure. In a sense the technologist is the architect. Although Ed Nye is a structural engineer, he created a strong architectural effect through structure alone. By this example he is a poet.

always been comparatively high, although not consistently reaching the highest level. Frankly, our reputation had been made more on *process* than *product* at the time. In the area of sophisticated architectural programming and computer approach to architectural practice, this reputation particularly has been very widely recognized.

The input excelled the output.

The underlying idea behind the Troika Plan is to improve the output—all products, including everything from a technical report to plans for a new university—by further strengthening the process of doing things through an administrative structure which provides balanced leadership—manager, designer, technologist working together on each major task.

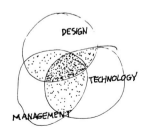

119

53

The Troika Plan forces better teamwork

Because of the Troika Plan, 1970 proved to be a great year for increasing the effectiveness of team action. The manager, the designer, and the technologist—three completely different types—were forced to work together. At first they did not like it.

ONE-MAN GANG
THIS KIND OF "TEAM" IS REALLY NOT A TEAM. IT IS A BIG GUY WITH SOME CADDIES.

The complaints are still ringing in the ears of those of us who helped put the plan in motion. A designer would say, "This project manager is driving me nuts. He puts the screws on everything I try to do in the name of cost control. Why can't this guy have soul?" A technologist would complain about the designer in these terms: "How can you work with someone who has the aesthetic curse?" And the manager would have his gripes too. "The buzzards—referring to both designer and technologist—"are making my project a career," referring to the fact that the project was behind schedule.

It was not too many months before the trios were working together in effective team action and making joint presentations to clients and to in-house CRS juries. More important, they were learning to have an appreciation for and to depend upon professionals of other talents and disciplines.

TROIKA TEAM
THE "TEAM" IS A TEAM. THERE IS TRUE COLLAB-ORATION.... GROUP DYNAMICS.

The greatest adjustment for adapting to the troika idea had to be made by the designer. Up to then he had run the show, and was accustomed to having his way. The manager, however, was beginning to have his say, but the technologist was relegated to second-class citizenship. He had the most to gain. And in one sense the designer had the most to lose. As it turned out, without exception, the designers, who had a burning desire to help create architecture, began to appreciate fully the contributions both the manager and the technologist could make in the development of buildings which possessed the aura that is architecture.

54

Match the team to the task

The troika idea began to take hold in the early fifties when CRS had reached the size which allowed us a choice of personnel to match the team to the task. Also we were compelled to rid ourselves of the false pride of thinking that since we were architects we could do everything (another education vestige). So we started going outside the firm for help.

The first rule of organization for team action is to bring together the combination of people who can do the best job for a specific task.

In 1954 when CRS was commissioned to design the Brazos County Courthouse in Bryan, Texas, we deliberated considerably about just whom we should put on that job to produce what we hoped would be one of the best civic buildings in America. We were then producing some of the best little schoolhouses in the nation, according to the competition juries. So why not shoot high? We decided to put our best school team on the task—William Pena on programming, Frank Lawyer on design, Al Martin on structure, Earl Merrill and Brawley King on production. I served as the partner-in-charge, a kind of team captain. Since we had no inhouse mechanical/electrical engineer, we brought in J. W. Hall, Jr. And because we had never done a courthouse before, we asked Professor Gail Vetter of Texas

The Brazos County Courthouse, which in 1956 was a national award winner for "its unique kind of civic architecture," consists of seven different units to separate the seven major functions of county government. Walter Cocking's brilliant input of using nonschool buildings for public education manifested a classroom, but the users did not take to it. The idea is still valid. Is there a better place to study government than in a governmental building?

A & M University to join our team and dig deep into the literature as a "research member." We had to find out something about courthouses and jails in a hurry.

Pena and I visited a considerable number of courthouses and jails. We deliberately stayed away from new ones, however. We thought we could learn more from past mistakes than be influenced by dazzling new buildings without history.

It was a good team. And we just about accomplished our goal. In 1957 the Brazos County Courthouse won the First Honor Award, AIA National Competition, a real team effort. A few years later when Burchard and Bush-Brown brought out "Architecture of America," our team was slapped in the face with a wet towel when the building was referred to as a "courthouse . . . built by Caudill." Certainly Lawyer played a much stronger role than I, in design. But designing the courthouse was a team effort. And we matched the team with the task.

We did not realize it at the time, but we had essentially a task troika which led the twenty- to thirty-man team—Lawyer on design, Merrill on technology, and Caudill on management.

When CRS was given the opportunity to design Houston's concert hall, the Jesse H. Jones Hall for the Performing Arts, our ideas about team action had expanded considerably. For one thing, we had not the slightest hesitancy to go outside of CRS to ask for professional help. If there were people in the firm who could not cut the mustard then we would find someone else who could. Or if CRS had certain talent voids we did not mind buying the talent needed to fill them. We were beginning to be ready for the expanded team.

TASK TEAM LED BY **TASK TROIKA**

The first outsider we picked to help on Jones Hall was George C. Izenour, one of the world's leading authorities on theater planning. Then we brought in Bob Newman, who had the backing of his very large firm, Bolt, Beranek and Newman, to handle the acoustics. On structures we chose Walter P. Moore and his firm. On mechanical/electrical we brought in Bernard Johnson Associates, a large firm in its own right. We assembled a team of teams to do the task at hand.

To lead this team of teams we had a CRS trilateral arrangement, with Charles Lawrence in charge of design, Tom Bullock in charge of management, and James Gatton in charge of technology. We did not call this trio a troika, but it was. This project more than any other led to the troika plan which went into effect eight years later. It takes some time for us to catch onto a good thing.

As with the other example—the courthouse—we had never done a concert hall. Also as with the courthouse, we lined up the most experienced talent we could find. Lawrence brought into action a large group of designers, including Lawyer, who led the courthouse design group; Bullock called upon many programmers, including Pena, to pin down the problems on function. And Gatton was surrounded with an array of technological talent needed to make this multifunction, multiform structure work. Even Scott and I got into the act during the conceptual stages and served as uninvolved critics.

And again as with the courthouse, Jones Hall won one of the highest awards of the American Institute of Architects—a big team effort if there ever was one.

HE WANTED A
GLAMOROUS SHOT
WITH **THE** ARCH-
TECT'S HEAD IN
THE FOREGROUND.

Just prior to the dedication of the Jesse H. Jones Hall for the Performing Arts we were confronted with a group of reporters. One of the reporters wanted his photographer to take a "glamorous shot with *the* architect's head in the foreground showing the new building in the background." He had his photographer ready to go. All he needed was *the* architect. "So where is the architect?" He was a bit rattled when one of us said, "The architect is a team." He was shook up even more when he was told that 61 of us worked on the design, putting in $13\frac{3}{4}$ man-years. We had to work together. We had only fourteen months to get out the plans. But he wanted a shot of only one head. We compromised and said, "We'll give you three —Charles Lawrence who took the lead in design, Tom Bullock who managed the project, and James Gatton who served as the technologist who led our group in putting the pieces together." For the photographer, three were too many. No pictures were taken. More than one reporter called it the Caudill design. Yet I had a minute part.

55
The three disciplines of architectural practice are interrelated

With any architectural firm, the main task is the creation of architecture. Whether the task is detailing a window or programming spatial requirements for an immense building complex, the creation of architecture is the overriding goal. All other nonbuilding tasks such as accounting, recruiting, promoting, are subservient to this main task—creation of form and space which radiate architecture.

About 1962 the School of Architecture, Rice University, saw fit to revamp its curriculum to correspond with these three disciplines within architectural practice—an acknowledgement of the validity of the process theory.

Whatever the task, it is necessary that the task team be matched to it; that people with talent and capabilities best suited to the work at hand be pitted against the problem so that the optimum solution is created with maximum efficiency.

I repeat for emphasis: Matching people to task should be based on the premise that every architectural task, regardless how large or how small, requires three kinds of thinking/action—those that relate to design, those that relate to management, and those that relate to technology. These three are distinguishable, yet inseparable. To perform any architectural task takes these three kinds of thinking/action.

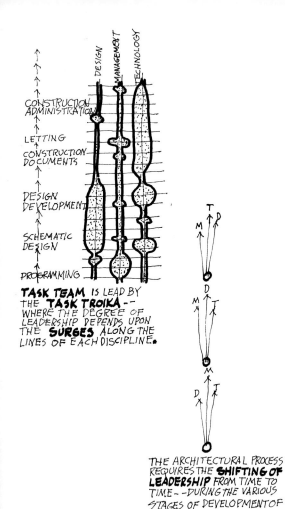

CONSTRUCTION
ADMINISTRATION

LETTING

CONSTRUCTION
DOCUMENTS

DESIGN
DEVELOPMENT

SCHEMATIC
DESIGN

PROGRAMMING

TASK TEAM IS LEAD BY
THE **TASK TROIKA** —
WHERE THE DEGREE OF
LEADERSHIP DEPENDS UPON
THE **SURGES** ALONG THE
LINES OF EACH DISCIPLINE.

THE ARCHITECTURAL PROCESS
REQUIRES THE **SHIFTING OF
LEADERSHIP** FROM TIME TO
TIME — DURING THE VARIOUS
STAGES OF DEVELOPMENT OF
THE PROJECT.

Obviously, there are many other ways to divide and label various facets of architecture practice. But no matter how you slice it, the design aspect, the management aspect, and the technological aspect are the names of the practice game.

Let me try to strengthen the case for the task troika and point out the necessity for the collaboration: Most every task requires design talent. There should be on the task team in leadership position a designer to create the right kind of form and space to make the building work functionally, economically, and aesthetically. A designer is like a surgeon; he operates after others have diagnosed the problem and prepared for the operation. Whether or not the patient lives—living architecture, if you please—depends largely upon his skill and experience. He alone cannot be responsible for the phenomenon of architecture, but whether or not architecture emerges depends considerably upon his sensitivity to human needs. (There are few competent designers and it seems that schools are much more interested in turning out architectural analysts and critics than architectural surgeons.) The troika idea does not in any way diminish the importance of the designer.

Most tasks too need managerial talent. Someone must be held responsible for bringing people and things together at the right time in the right place and with the right amount of money. That's the manager's job—to manage the task. Managing implies direction and control of people and things. The task manager makes judicious use of means to accomplish the end. The manager is a process-oriented specialist, whereas the designer is product-oriented.

And third, most tasks require technological talent. The technologist is both product and process minded, concerned with a practical purpose—putting

Moody Hall, of St. Edward's University, Austin, Texas, designed in 1965, illustrates the importance of composition skills.

THE DANGER OF THE **TASK TROIKA** IS THE TENDENCY TOWARD **DISPERSION** OF EFFORT AND FRACTURE OF GOALS.

THIS NEED NOT HAPPEN IF THE 3 LEADERS PULL TOGETHER IN THE **SAME DIRECTION.**

WITH THE SAME GOAL — **THE CREATION OF ARCHITECTURE** — AS THEIR FIRST OBJECTIVE.

things together. In a very small firm he would be Mr. Inside Man, doing the working drawings, writing the specifications, and serving as the construction administrator. In a large firm the group of technologists would include specialists.

With the coming of industrialized building and building systems making such strong impact upon the scene, the top technologist will eventually be the building system expert. He would be the person on the team responsible for integrated design—the coordination of all of the subsystems. You might say he would be a technological generalist who must know something about all aspects of the technology of building.

In any case, technological talent is necessary to put the pieces together, to build up the major and minor forms, and to span and define spaces in the most efficient and economical manner.

It is imperative in understanding the triad theory of process that one realize that management, design, and technology overlap. How can design be separated from technology or from management? It can't. Consider the space which you presently occupy. It is defined by walls, floor, and ceiling, each of which have certain proportions, certain colors, and textures—formal items which would fall in the category of design. But how can these be considered without knowing, technologically speaking, how the floor and ceiling are held up and how the components are connected? And how can they be considered without a knowledge of prior programming of the spatial requirements which fall under the heading of management, not to mention the management of getting the space designed and built?

Although design, management, and technology are distinguishable, they most certainly are intrinsically interrelated. But for the most part the scope and complexity of architectural tasks are more efficiently dispatched when the team is brought into action with these three main roles played by different people.

56

Three sponsors form the CRS Troika

Central to operating the Troika Plan, there is a committee of three, called the CRS Troika, previously mentioned. It is appointed by the Board of Directors. Each member is called a sponsor. This appointment is made primarily because of his special commitment to one of the three practice disciplines—design, management, and technology. A sponsor is charged with:

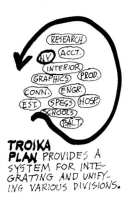

TROIKA PLAN PROVIDES A SYSTEM FOR INTEGRATING AND UNIFYING VARIOUS DIVISIONS.

• Serving as patron of his assigned discipline—be it design, management, or technology.

• Causing activities such as open forums and seminars which will generate new thought in the assumed discipline.

• Using his influence to promote advancement within his discipline.

• Initiating procedures leading to proficiences.

• Encouraging research and advising individuals to delve.

• Using his influence as a high-level CRS member to improve quality.

The CRS Troika was established with the authority to examine, evaluate, and judge any CRS output—products or services. Along with the authority goes the responsibility of initiating group or individual action which will create enthusiasm, even excitement, within each of the disciplines.

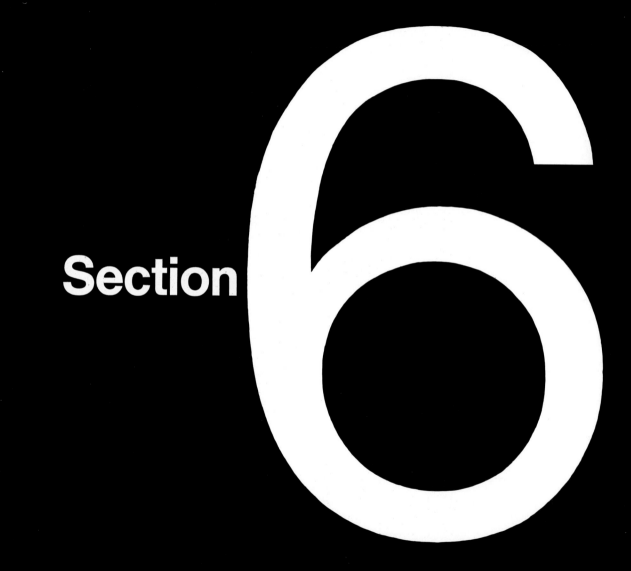

Section 6

Product Evaluation by Jury

Since team action is not a one-man operation, evaluation of team products should not be made by one man alone. No design czar should judge the work of many. The belief in the team concept induces systematic, thorough judgment of team effort. The schools' conventional jury system is brought into the office and raised to a higher level of sophistication by using the function/form/economy yardstick and by forming juries with equal representation in management, design, and technology.

57

Everyone judges buildings

A person walks into a room and he says to himself, "This feels good. How pleasant! Even inspiring! I want to come here more often." Unquestionably there is architecture in that space—for him. The person has experienced and judged the space. It is a simple procedure—a personal experience.

A man walking down the street sees a building and says either to himself or to someone who might be walking with him, "That's certainly a good building," or "What a terrible building." Or he might think nothing or say nothing because the building evokes no response—either of delight or distaste.

When I taught in short hitches at Washington University, Cornell, Princeton, and other schools, I was listed as a "visiting critic." My job was to guide the students by giving them criticism. With or without evaluative criteria, I acted as judge.

One miffed student asked, "What right have you to judge?" He had a point. I would only say, "At this time, I am the only critic you have. If I can't help you, you must help yourself."

When I was at my best as a teacher, I taught my students the art of self-criticism. I let them help themselves and make their own mistakes. As their critic I tried not to judge their work so much as their professional development. They then would be the judge of their own work. But no matter how analytical they were, value judgment was an important factor in the evaluation.

WE LIKE THIS SPACE!

Now if a half-dozen professionals come together to judge a building, as in a typical AIA Honor Awards Jury, even more thought would be given to the final evaluation. Certainly some kind of procedure and balloting method would be necessary. However, having served on a considerable number of these juries, I must confess that the majority of them are conducted without evaluative criteria. A common procedure is for each juror to take an hour or so and go through all entries by himself and list his top ten, after which the jurors get together and compare their lists, and start their fight —with no ground rules.

Interestingly enough, if there is to be only one winner, there is not too much argument. The runners-up cause the most fuss since the jury must deal in the nuances of grays. Here is the area in which evaluative criteria are greatly needed. But even with evaluative criteria, there still must be value judgment.

58

Is value judgment sound?

EXPERIENCE IS A DYNAMIC SYNTHESIS OF **FACTS** AND **VALUES.**

Precision is desired in judging. More precision must be introduced during the design development stage so that the product becomes better. As it stands, most designers judge intuitively. Value judgment by groups is used every day. Professional competitions and school juries go on all the time; so team judging is not new although most juries practice it haphazardly, without any degree of precision.

How can precision be obtained where value judgment is used? Value judgment is susceptible to human error. It is not a fact. But a person never experiences a pure fact. When a team, rather than an individual, judges something, the chances of human error are diminished somewhat because the judgment is based on combined talents and experiences.

Despite the drawbacks, the jury team for making evaluation is still the best way we have to judge. The more sensitive the jurors and the more sophisticated the evaluative criteria, the more valid the judgment. In any case, value judgment is part of the judging process. Value judgment has a place in the design process, and it has a place in judging the product. Value and

How old is this school? The "open plan" gives a clue. The low ceiling and plate glass windows might suggest a date of its conception. Actually this College Station, Texas, High School—the granddaddy of open planning—was designed by the CRS team over seventeen years ago. As a pacesetter it has more of a time quality than timeless quality.

fact go together. Of course there must be an awareness and use of established facts, accurately accumulated and organized to be used as bases for judgment. With such bases a team of jurors can evaluate both process and product most effectively. The jury system is valid when agreed-upon evaluative criteria form the basis for judgment.

Obviously the more qualified the people on the judging team, the better the judgment—if they know how to work together. There is safety in numbers —an argument for team evaluation. All dodos on the judging team will not add up to a highly qualified one-man jury.

There is a lot of argument against the jury system. One is that no two juries judge alike. One jury will give an entry an award; another jury would say thumbs down. Quite true. This can be explained on two counts—the makeup of the jury and the criteria used.

In many cases one man has been known to completely dominate the jury. I have served on juries with Eero Saarinen, Louis Kahn, Jose Sert, and other distinguished architects who, through knowledge, skill, and charismatic characteristics swayed the jury single-handed. When this happens it is still a one-man jury—a design czar—with all the disadvantages.

If the jury is composed entirely of architects, the judgment might be quite different than if the team were of an interdisciplinary makeup.

And obviously, the criteria used change the situation tremendously. For example, if function were considered above everything else with little value placed on form and economy, the winning design in a competition would be quite different than if the criteria gave equal weight to function, form, and economy. For these reasons, it is important to have preagreement on criteria before judgment is made. By doing so, there can be precision.

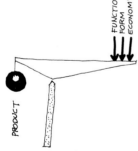

IN ACCORDANCE WITH THE **TRIAD THEORY** RELATING TO BOTH **PRODUCT** AND **PROCESS**, THE PRODUCT SHOULD BE MEASURED IN TERMS OF THE THREE FORCES WHICH SHAPE BUILDINGS AND THEIR COMPONENTS AND SPACES.

59

In the sixties, CRS initiated a jury system

From its very beginning the CRS team felt the need for a systematic approach for judging its output. And as the team began to evolve, this need became more and more acute. It was not until 1960, however, that we actually put into effect a system of judging.

Three of us took the lead in its development—Charles Lawrence, Frank Lawyer, and myself—all designers. At the time the climate was so against any kind of evaluation and designers were so supersensitive about having their work criticized that CRS could never have gotten the program on the road if designers themselves had not originated the idea. The "design is everything" contention prevailed at the time.

As it was, we had a mild rebellion on our hands, a pattern that seems to have always been associated with CRS, because Tom Bullock and Herb Paseur suggested we call the "jury" a Quality Control Board! The designers howled! They wanted no part of being "controlled." It was finally called the Design Board, with the purpose of reviewing, evaluating, and establishing quality profiles for various projects. Prior to the first jury we developed, during a series of seminars, a yardstick to measure product.

The evaluative criteria included these eight intrinsic qualities:

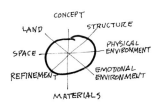

(1) The building must have a *concept*. A good building has a job to do. It must respond to its intended function. A great building expresses a clear-cut concept giving harmonious union of function and form.

(2) The building must have decisive *structural order*. Most good buildings have structural consciousness. Some "show their bones" and do it with

meaningful and pleasant rhythm. Others express strength in their skins. In both cases, there must be structural significance.

(3) The building must honor and respect the *physical environment*. Obviously a building must do a good job of keeping out the heat, cold, rain, sun, wind, and snow. But it also must keep out extraneous sounds, excessive humidity, dust, odors, and smog, and provide its occupants with proper hearing conditions, the right lighting, and correct thermal comforts. The physical environment should provide for physical comfort.

(4) The spaces must provide the desired *emotional environment*. Emotion is in all great architecture. A great building is more than a dead, structural shell. It possesses a spirit, giving man a feeling of importance. The emotional environment should provide for emotional comfort.

(5) Full advantage is taken of advanced *technology*. A well-designed building usually takes advantage of the day's technology. Great buildings are pioneers of new materials and techniques.

(6) There is the necessity of skillful *refinement*. A great building, like great music, must have behind it the skill of great technicians—the design developers. The refinement of a building gives meaning to all parts, continuity of details, unity of form, texture, and color; and brings together a union of opposites—darks and lights, lines and planes, solids and voids.

(7) The building must have meaningful, memorable *space*. The experience of inspiring space can be more satisfactory than that of a great painting, a classical musical composition. Space can be awesome or intimate, cheerful or depressing, confining or nonconfining, stimulating or sedative. The art of defining space is most important. How well space is subdivided determines the success of a building.

(8) The building is a part of the *land* on which it rests. There must be a successful marriage of building and land. A good building must look and

act in such a way that its components are integrated as parts of a total composition, including terrain, trees, and sky.

It was not easy getting complete agreement on their eight qualities for judging a building. Every designer, manager, and technologist has his own way of categorizing and expressing specific, intrinsic qualities of a good building depending upon his specialty. During CRS seminars, we agreed early that "great buildings must serve and better man." Thereafter agreement eluded us. For months we tangled on specifics. The approved eight intrinsic qualities just barely made it.

Using these eight as criteria, we initiated a program for evaluating building projects which came through the office. Evaluations were made by the Design Board which consisted primarily of designers—a mistake. We should have had managers and technologists judging the work as well. Ten years later we finally broke the design barrier—the Beaux Arts tradition that "design is everything."

60
The product theory gives equal emphasis to function, form, and economy

Late in 1969, the two triad theories—theory of product and theory of process—were taking hold and being translated into various methods of practice, but somewhat haphazardly. There was a need to bring the two together.

About the same time we began to realize that the CRS output was more than building designs. People were judging the performance of the CRS

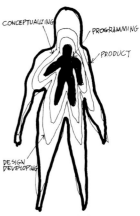

CONCEPTUALIZING
PROGRAMMING
PRODUCT
DESIGN DEVELOPING

A DESIGN PRODUCT **GROWS LIKE A BABY** AND WITH THE OMNI-DIRECTIONAL APPROACH EVALUATIONS CAN BE MEASURED AT EACH STAGE OF DEVELOPMENT.

team on feasibility studies, planning reports, building systems studies and articles—not just buildings. We needed to develop further our method of product evaluation to include total CRS output.

The CRS Executive Committee—Bullock, Scott, Paseur, and I—became quite concerned about the quality of total CRS output. We were embarrassed by some of the ordinary reports and poor graphics produced by the firm. And we were particularly alarmed at the designers' lack of cost consciousness. There were too many proposals our clients could not afford, too little attention to the cost leg of the tripod.

Paseur, as the managing director, assigned Bullock and me to devise some plan to stimulate more interest and cause more precision in the design process to assure a better product in every kind of CRS output. From our efforts came the Troika Plan. We asked Charles Lawrence to be the design sponsor of the Troika and help us find better ways to evaluate the output —both services and products. Bullock became the sponsor of management and I the sponsor of technology.

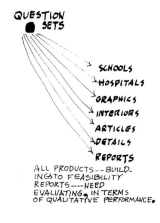

QUESTION SETS

→ SCHOOLS
→ HOSPITALS
→ GRAPHICS
→ INTERIORS
→ ARTICLES
→ DETAILS
→ REPORTS

ALL PRODUCTS -- BUILD-
ING TO FEASIBILITY
REPORTS -- NEED
EVALUATING, IN TERMS
OF QUALITATIVE PERFORMANCE.

We decided upon three categories that would be applicable to any of the CRS output: a *function* category, a *form* category, and an *economy* category. We then agreed that individual question sets relating to each element of the triad—function, form, and economy—would be needed for a single building, for campus plans, for building subsystems, for architectural graphic design, for interior design, for feasibility studies, for university planning, for programming, one each for building types such as elementary schools, middle schools, high schools, community college buildings, and university buildings—even a question set as a yardstick for judging a speech or an article.

We decided that the question sets must be revised and dated at regular intervals. Some questions must be discarded, others added. Keeping question sets up to date is absolutely essential.

More important, each set must have the approval of everyone concerned, and each question must be tied directly to the philosophy and goals of the firm—for these question sets serve as excellent devices for measuring the performance of the total firm.

The question set for a single building is included here. It reflects a deliberate attempt to give equal emphasis to each of the three elements of the product triad. We felt at the time that both function and economy were being neglected by designers in their efforts to create beautiful form. We reasoned that since the question set would be used as an evaluative criterion during jury and as a guide during the design process, the two neglected elements would be brought back into full play and we would get more integrated buildings—integrated as to function, form, and economy.

The single-building question set follows:

FUNCTION

(1) Is there a *concept* (underlying idea), and are the spaces grouped, sized, and shaped to reinforce this concept?

(2) Do the spaces have affinities which allow people and things to *flow* with efficiency?

(3) Have the shelteral considerations and environment *controls* been recognized?

(4) Does the building work in the *generic* sense as a school helps to teach and a hospital helps to cure?

(5) Is the plant—buildings and grounds—*imaginatively* conceived?

(6) Have the major operational problems (security, maintenance, routine operation) been considered for the *future* as well as the present?

FORM

(7) Is there *propriety* in the forms and spaces reflecting the concept?

(8) Do forms and spaces possess the *spirit* of the times without being faddish?

(9) Do the forms—major and minor together with their connections—take advantage of up-to-date *technology?*

(10) Does the *composition* of form and space contain both variety and unity projecting an aura of architecture?

(11) Are all forms *meaningful*—from mass to details?

(12) Is there a systematized *integration* of structure, mechanical and electrical?

ECONOMY

(13) Are the *forms* "lean and clean," without sham, yet nothing wanted?

(14) Do the *spaces* permit efficient operation capitalizing on the idea of maximum effect with minimum means?

(15) Has *industrialized* building method been given serious consideration by saving time and labor on the site?

(16) Is there a realistic solution to the *budget* problem?

(17) Can this building be *changed* economically, either through conversion or expansion, to meet future requirements?

142

(18) Can this building through its elimination of waste, dignity through restraint, and *simplicity* of construction, be classified as "most for the money?"

The use of a question set such as this allows us to make evaluation on a wide range. We were then and still are interested in systematic evaluation of all CRS products regardless of scale. I have used the expression "doorknobs to cities" many times in this book. Perhaps I am belaboring the point, but it is an important one. Every architectural product, be it a doorknob or a city, must be considered in context. Everything relates to something else. The doorknob relates to the door, which relates to the house, which relates to the neighborhood, which relates to the city, which relates to the region.

Because of this wide range of architectural products—cities to buildings to windows—there must be a wide range of talent. We need doorknob people, and we need big-city people working together as a team to make the environment a decent place to live. And we need methods to evaluate the products which these people produce. The question sets help to provide the method.

THE **MATHEMATICS** OF A WHOLE NOTE

IS SIMILAR TO THE MATHEMATICS OF A **CITY**. THE DOOR IS TO THE HOUSE WHAT THE HOUSE IS TO THE NEIGHBORHOOD WHAT THE NEIGHBORHOOD IS TO THE CITY... THE CONCEPT OF **ORGANIC UNITY.**

61

CRS Troika took over the juries

I have already mentioned the advantage of a marriage of the two triad theories. Consummation took place when the question sets were organized around the product theory and when the CRS Troika took over the jury system, created the Quality Panel, and insisted on equal representation from management, design, and technology.

Jack DeBartolo, one of our design leaders, is shown here answering questions during a 1970 CRS six-man jury. Richard Anderson, serving as the technologist of the task troika, is helping defend the proposal. The Task Troika has thirty minutes for presentation, and then there is another thirty-minute period for questions and answers before the jury makes the evaluation through use of question sets.

When the Troika Plan came in, the CRS Design Board went out. The Quality Panel took its place. These factors distinguish the Design Board from the Quality Panel:

• The Design Board put emphasis on design only, while the Quality Panel emphasized management and technology as well.

• The Design Board responsibilities were generally limited to buildings, while the Quality Panel's activities covered a broader scope and were concerned with the total CRS output, not buildings alone.

• The CRS Troika, consisting of people at the board of directors' level, ran juries selected from the Quality Panel and had authority to act if the quality was judged low, while the Design Board was primarily an advisory group.

• The Design Board was primarily composed of designers, while the Quality Panel had equal representation for design, management, and technology.

144

Appointed by the CRS Troika, the Quality Panel consisted of seven specialists, who had management emphasis, seven design-type specialists, and seven technology-type specialists. The three sponsors were included in the membership.

The essence of the CRS Troika is assurance that no discipline—management, design, or technology—is overlooked or undervalued.

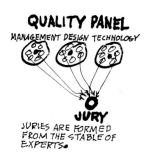

QUALITY PANEL
MANAGEMENT DESIGN TECHNOLOGY
JURY
JURIES ARE FORMED FROM THE STABLE OF EXPERTS.

62

We quantified quality

Like it or not, everyone gives grades. Everyone gets them. School children get them. I take them home every month in the form of money; my salary is my grade. The amount is determined by people who judge the quality of my performance. There is nothing new about assigning numbers to quality of performance.

SYSTEMATIC JUDGING BY TEAM HAS ADVANTAGE OVER JUDGMENT BY THE INDIVIDUAL.

We decided to grade projects which come through the juries. In doing so, we could compare one project with another and the work of one task team with that of another task team. Such a grade, we agreed, must relate to the triad theory of product and must reflect both the magnitude and balance of function, form, and economy, at every stage of development all the way to the finished product.

On the basis of the triad theory, a logical approach to solving problems relating to architecture would be simultaneous consideration of function, form, and economy. An objective is to keep these elements of the product

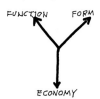

CONSIDER SIMULTANEOUSLY THE FORCES:

FUNCTION   FORM

ECONOMY

ONE OBJECTIVE IS TO EQUILIBRATE THE FORCES.

People judge buildings. This one, the library of Southern Colorado State College, designed in 1963, is immediately judged by everyone who sees and experiences its interior space. Most people have strong feelings about it. They either love it or hate it. Professional juries have given it a high rating. Charles Lawrence, Jim Hughes, and Herb Paseur served as the Task Troika for the project. Our associates were Rogers/Nagel.

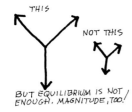

THIS
NOT THIS
BUT EQUILIBRIUM IS NOT ENOUGH. MAGNITUDE, TOO!

(forces during process) of the triad in equilibrium. When an equilibrium is achieved, there is achieved the desired union of the elements.

Achievement of this equilibrium is not enough. The approach must also concern the quest for strength, working toward making each element of the triad the greatest possible magnitude.

146

Let us assume we record strength by making use of the question set like this. Zero is zero. Ten is perfect. Five is just so-so.

Now let's assume the impossible—that the jury decided a project rates 10 on each of the three elements of the triad. By triangulating the three forces of the greatest magnitude, each valued at 10, we would have a symbol which might be designated as the "triangle of perfection."

This 10–10–10 triangle has an area of 129.89 (call it 130). If the jury had decided the project rated (its value judgment) a 5 on all three counts, the project as big as a building or as small as a doorknob, would have that needed balance, but because of the low magnitudes of the forces, the area of the triangle would be much less—to be exact 32.47 (call it 32).

Now let's get a bit closer to what may happen when a jury judges a project. Say it is a small elementary school. After presentation and heated debates, a vote was taken. The average of the scores went something like this: function 8, form 3, and economy 2. Triangulation of this 8–3–2 triangle would produce what might be called the "triangle of reality" which has an area of 19.91 (call it 20).

Now let us compare the three triangles. The 5–5–5 has a greater area than the 8–3–2 despite the fact that the function leg of the latter was very high. Here is a case where "balance" won out. Neither approached the area of the "triangle of perfection" which has balance and great magnitude. Since the areas of these triangles, therefore, express both balance and magnitude, we now have a coefficient which will give us a numerical value of the quality of the project or product judged. This coefficient is designated as the quality quotient.

To save time, the CRS team made use of the computer and developed a set of tables which at a glance would give us the quality quotient.

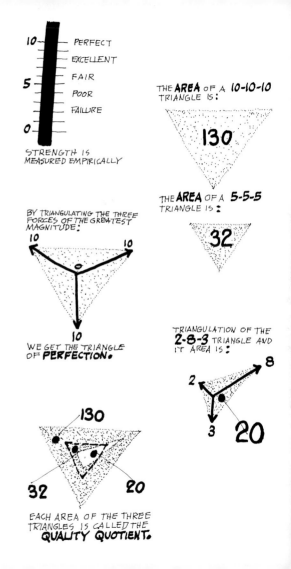

10 — PERFECT
EXCELLENT
5 — FAIR
POOR
0 — FAILURE

STRENGTH IS MEASURED EMPIRICALLY

THE **AREA** OF A **10-10-10** TRIANGLE IS:
130

THE **AREA** OF A **5-5-5** TRIANGLE IS:
32

BY TRIANGULATING THE THREE FORCES OF THE GREATEST MAGNITUDE:
10   10
10
WE GET THE TRIANGLE OF **PERFECTION.**

TRIANGULATION OF THE **2-8-3** TRIANGLE AND IT AREA IS:
2   8
3   **20**

130
32   **20**

EACH AREA OF THE THREE TRIANGLES IS CALLED THE **QUALITY QUOTIENT.**

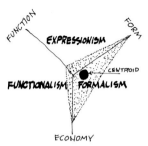

THE LOCATION OF THE **CENTROID**
OF THE TRIANGLE INDICATES THE
TENDENCY TO FUNCTIONALISM,
FORMALISM, OR EXPRESSIONISM.

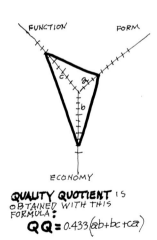

QUALITY QUOTIENT IS
OBTAINED WITH THIS
FORMULA:

$$QQ = 0.433 (ab + bc + ca)$$

63

The quality quotient compares one product with another

Let us look back to the 8–3–2 situation with its quality quotient of 20. Frankly that is a very low score. Compare that to the score of 69 which a CRS jury gave to the high school designed for San Angelo, Texas in 1955, or to the dome school designed for New York City in 1962, which had a score of 55, or to the 60 score of Larsen Hall, Harvard University, designed in 1963. Note that there is a tendency to formalism (location of centroid) in Larsen Hall and a slight tendency to functionalism in the New York dome school. One of the best scores given to a finished building designed by CRS was the 85 quality quotient given to Jones Hall for the Performing Arts, designed in 1963. The CRS Houston office during a jury in April 1970 received a score of 92.

So that we would have something to compare with our own work, we had to judge other buildings. The quality quotient for Wright's Guggenheim Museum turned out to be 87.

The CBS building designed by the Saarinen group rated a 96 by a CRS jury. And even better, both the Seagram building (Mies with Johnson's help) and the Tennessee Gas Building (San Francisco office of SOM) in Houston were rated 100 each by a CRS jury.

On the basis of these comparable scores, we informally came to an agreement which gave us a quick measuring yardstick:

(1) If the quality quotient falls below 32, there is not much chance that architecture will emerge. A quality quotient of 32, as you recall, is the 5-5-5 triangle. It is also close to a 2-7-7- triangle, a 3-4-9 triangle, and a

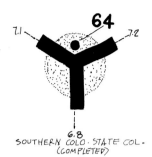
7.1   **64**   7.2

6.8
SOUTHERN COLO. STATE COL.
(COMPLETED)

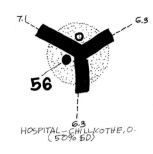
7.1   6.3

56

6.3
HOSPITAL - CHILLICOTHE, O.
(50% BD.)

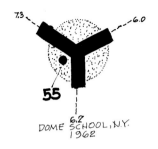
5.9   8.0

60

6.6
LARSEN HALL, HARVARD U.
1963

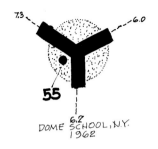
7.3   6.0

55

6.2
DOME SCHOOL, N.Y.
1962

8.2   8.3

92

8.8
DEL. TECH. COMMUNITY COL.
PHASE I (SD)

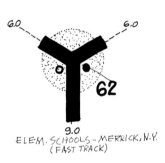
6.0   6.0

62

9.0
ELEM. SCHOOLS - MERRICK, N.Y.
(FAST TRACK)

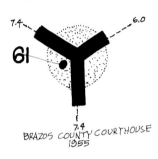
7.4   6.0

61

7.4
BRAZOS COUNTY COURTHOUSE
1955

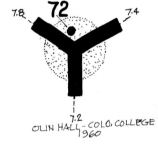
7.8   **72**   7.4

7.2
OLIN HALL - COLO. COLLEGE
1960

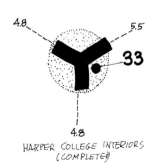
4.8   5.5

33

4.8
HARPER COLLEGE INTERIORS
(COMPLETED)

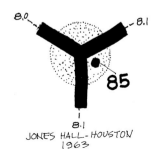
7.0   6.6

67

7.9
CIVIC CENTER - AMARILLO, TEX.
(COMPLETED)

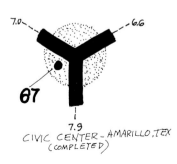
8.0   8.1

85

8.1
JONES HALL - HOUSTON
1963

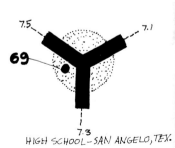
7.5   7.1

69

7.3
HIGH SCHOOL - SAN ANGELO, TEX.

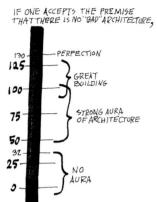

130
125 — PERFECTION
100 } GREAT BUILDING
75 } STRONG AURA OF ARCHITECTURE
50
32
25 } NO AURA
0

bit more than a 4-4-6 triangle. As 32 on the thermometer is the point of freezing, the quality quotient of 32 marks the point of the beginning of the architectural phenomenon—the appearance of the aura—the point at which mere structure emerges into architecture. While such numerical definition may be arbitrary, it nonetheless has helped us to make quick comparative use of the quality quotients.

(2) If the quality quotient is in the 90 range (it will never reach 130, the point of perfection) the product, if a building, may lie in the realm of "great architecture," as historians would describe it. In our terms, such a building would unquestionably possess a very strong architectural aura, experienced by almost everybody who viewed the building and felt its spaces. A building having a 90 to 100 design quotient would be a masterpiece in its fusion of function, form, and economy. In order to see what it takes to do this, let me give you a few triangulation scores. An 8-8-9 triangle will barely yield a 90 quality quotient. A 9-9-9 triangle reached over the 100 mark (105). But a 9-9-7 hits 90 on the button. So if you wish to design a 90 plus, using our yardstick, two of the elements of the triad must be very strong.

Of course all juries will tend to award different scores to the same product. The same jury judging the same building at a different time might well give the product a few points higher or lower depending upon its collective mood. The Olin Hall of Science received 72 as its quality quotient, judged after the dedication. Three years later another jury visited the building and after talking with satisfied users judged the building 84. Well-organized verbal and graphic presentations seem to sway juries. Value judgment is like that. We have not yet reached the state of sophistication at which we can discard value judgment for something better. All we can do is to try to bring method into play when we make value judgments on quality performance. This we have done. Despite the weakness of this method of evaluation, the results are, surprisingly, accurate enough to give us bases for making comparisons.

64

Grading need not be repugnant

Architectural juries have always had to deal in numbers, if only to select the first, second, and third prizes, and a few "honorable mentions." Architectural professors have always had to assign numbers to their students' work. So assigning numbers is nothing new. Nevertheless, most architects and some engineers hate to have their work graded. Any one of them would be horrified if someone were to say to him, "George, on your last project you made a near bottom score." That is just what happened in CRS to one of the key designers who, at that time, was leading a team to design an educational plant. In fact "George" flunked. The jury from the Design Board saw fit to grade the project so low it did not fall "within the realm of architecture." It was below 32.

In this particular case "George" was running more of a one-man gang than a team. The members served more as pencil caddies than full participating team members. He rightly got the blame. He had bullied the whole "team" into doing what he wanted to do. He considered the other members' opinions valueless regardless of their special talents or experiences. The product reflected this narrow approach. This happened before CRS initiated the Troika Plan.

With the project team, assigning the number is much more palatable. In fact, each member of the Troika wants to know the comparative score; if the product being evaluated shows a weakness in one Troika member's specialty, then he can remedy the situation. It is easy for a true team, in contrast to the one-man gang, to accept numerical evaluations.

Section 7

Education
for Team

How can architects best be educated to play on inter-disciplinary teams? How can nonarchitects best be educated to play on teams whose prime purpose is to produce buildings and spaces which possess the architectural quality? How can architects and nonarchitects work together? Even more basic is the question: Can team action be taught? How? And when? In the schools or in the offices? Education for team is a difficult enough problem, but included in the overall problem are the many paradoxes of architecture education. The intent of this section is neither to present a survey of what is going on in education, nor to make a comparative analysis of various curricula. Curricula come and go. Yet there are some basic elements of the education of architects which have always been with us and most likely always will be.

65
Education of architects is in a state of flux

For years architecture education has gone merrily along, relatively un-changed and unhurt. The hardened armor of the Beaux Arts systems (where the emphasis was placed primarily on design development and impressive renderings) easily warded off timid attempts at change, except for a few dents dealt by Wright with his own school in the thirties, by Gropius of Harvard, by Mies of Illinois Tech, and by less well known but just as de-termined educators scattered throughout the United States. By the time I was in school, the shiny armor had measurable dents and was beginning to dull. I, for one, was completely against the establishment.

To me it made no sense at all for students in an Oklahoma college to be directed from New York. More specifically, we were handed a piece of paper from the Beaux Arts headquarters in New York, which said in essence: "Son, we want you to design a monastery for Tibet. In nine hours turn in a conceptual sketch. We are going to keep that sketch on hand for five weeks, at the end of which time you will have completed design de-velopment drawings for the monastery of certain scales, on a certain size sheet of 'double elephant Strathmore' which of course will be 'stretched' on your drawing board. No color please, Son. And you must render your drawings in Chinese ink which you will grind yourself. A warning, Son, you'd better not change from that original sketch or we will get you. Or rather, we will mark a big red 'X' over your drawing. So, be good and follow instructions." (I did, but I didn't like it.)

Most of us in practice today at the "senior vice president" level were indoctrinated in the Beaux Arts system. Our buzz words were *"poché* the

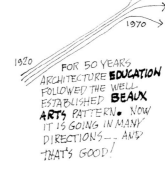

FOR 50 YEARS ARCHITECTURE **EDUCATION** FOLLOWED THE WELL ESTABLISHED **BEAUX ARTS** PATTERN. NOW IT IS GOING IN MANY DIRECTIONS... AND THAT'S GOOD!

John Rowlett entered the profession in 1938, better pre-pared than most graduates. He was trained for a specialty —educational architecture—since he had degrees in both education and architecture.

parti," "en tourage," "charette week," "esquisse" (that is the nine-hour sketch), and "esquisse esquisse." (That is a twenty-four-hour sketch problem.)

During my eight years at Rice University as Director of the School of Architecture I had hanging on my office wall one of the many ink wash renderings I made while at Oklahoma State (then Oklahoma A&M) with a current, contrasting conceptual sketch of a CRS project. When a student or a grievance committee came in to complain about the program or their professors, I would point to the old ink wash drawing and say, "This is the way I was taught." Then pointing to the CRS sketch, I would add, "This is the way I practice." Then I would give them the clincher. "My profs didn't know what the hell they were doing either."

But they did. They taught us how to take a rough conceptual sketch and develop it. And they taught us to draw. Despite my objections, there were a lot of good things about the Beaux Arts system, including ridding the inferiority complexes of students from midwest cow colleges when they won higher honors on a competitive basis than those students from more prestigious eastern schools. The Beaux Arts system taught the students to compete. The system taught us the tracing paper study technique: One could tell the degree of design skill by the amount of yellow tracing paper studies, to be uninhibited about putting ideas down on paper—to think with our hands.

In 1939, fresh out of MIT, I went to Texas A&M to teach, primarily because of professors Jack Finney and Sam Zisman, who would not touch the Beaux Arts system with a ten-foot pencil. It is my guess this school was one of the first to make a clear break from Beaux Arts, and perhaps the first to stress programming at the undergraduate level. What we lost in teaching our students design skills, however, may not have been worth

156

the switch of emphasis. But I was satisfied. I loved tearing down the establishment—and trying to build back a better one. We did.

Just where architecture education is today is a difficult question to answer. Beaux Arts is about "washed out." At least no more grinding of ink and making the tedious ink washes (I recall the time I took six weeks to render a Corinthian capitol).

Educators are taking their charges, or more accurately their charges are taking them, in many directions, at once ranging from an extremely social-conscience emphasis to highly computerized design methods. Curricula are becoming broader if you look at them in one way and watered down if you look at them from another point of view. Students are demanding and getting more choices of options. The "cafeteria curriculum" is becoming real.

Both students and teachers are more interested in *process,* particularly through programming, design methodology, and system building, than in *product*—the main concern of the Beaux Arts system.

PROCESS > PRODUCT

Students now have a deeper desire to help build a better world through architecture practice; so their concern is primarily the users' welfare. One way of looking at it is that there is a return to functionalism, but it is a new kind. It is social functionalism.

Students today are less inclined to worship the prima donnas than my generation did. I have a friend, however, who still reads a chapter of Frank Lloyd Wright every night before he goes to bed. The heroes of the new generation are nonarchitects—the social reformers, the communication czars, and the space psychologists. Unquestionably, this new attitude will be reflected in the buildings when the students of this day become "senior partners" (if there is such a thing by then).

157

Students also have greater opportunity and willingness to work on teams. They realize, probably more so than do most of the professors, that "together we can do a better job than we can separately." They also have a comprehension of the giant tasks ahead of them in changing the physical environment and know that to do the things that must be done, giant teams are necessary. They know that architects of the future will have to be more sensitive to human needs and values and they welcome the behavioral scientists as members of these teams. They know, too, that to have the right kind of physical environment will require using the most advanced technology; so they are willing to have the technologists on their teams, particularly the building system experts. (A few want to be technologists, but not many.)

Unquestionably, new buildings and their spaces are in for a change. Education will see to that.

In December 1969, CRS moved into the first building specifically designed for the CRS team. Our intent was to have a "home" which would not get in the way of team action. We committed CRS to "open planning"—which we could redesign and rearrange in a matter of hours. We wanted no typical corporation setups like thicker carpets and larger ash trays for the brass. We wanted gang toilets—no "officers' country." So far it works fine. One of the nicest compliments paid to us was from three architects outside of the firm who said, "Your new building is a perfect statement for a uniquely dynamic firm and further testimony for the team approach." Our "place," which is over a block long and a little less than half a block wide, is essentially loft space that can be changed at a moment's notice. This kind of space for architecture by team would make a good building for a school of architecture which has team teaching and an integrated curriculum.

66

The seven paradoxes of education do not change

There are certain changes we can always count on—the number of students to be taught; the curricula designed to teach them; and the makeup of the faculty. What does not change are certain paradoxes of architecture education.

Permit me to list seven paradoxes that have been bugging educators for as long as I can remember.

(1) Should the student architect be taught to rely solely on the broad bases of intellectual, interdisciplinary rationale at the risk of knowing "little about a lot of things?" Or should he be taught marketable skills which allow him to make a living in a competitive profession, risking a "trade school" education which later may stifle professional growth?

(2) Should the student have a master-teacher to offer strong guidance and deep understanding of a particular philosophy at the risk of narrowness and exclusion of other philosophies? Or should he be exposed to many strong teachers, and many philosophies so that he can formulate his own but at the risk of overexposure and confusion to him?

(3) Should competition be stressed to give readiness to the student who must enter a highly competitive world, but at the risk of his becoming a thwarted, overcompetitive individual? Or should the student be taught to compete only with himself to maximize intellectual and professional growth free of the energy-consuming jealousies which go along with fierce class competition, but at the risk of his becoming a "hothouse plant" which withers when the going gets hot?

THE
PARADOXES
OF
EDUCATION

THINK	DO
MASTER TEACHER	TEACHING TEAM
COMPETITION	NO COMPETITION
INDIV. PROBLEM	GROUP PROBLEM
GENERALIST	SPECIALIST
START NOW	START LATER
INTEGRATED CURRICULUM	UNLIMITED CHOICE

(4) Should the student be given individual problems to meet his own individual situation for material growth and development, but at the risk of self-indulgence and self-isolation? Or should the student be given collaborative problems which foster human relationships, leading toward mastery of the art of collaboration, but at the risk of sacrificing the individual's self-actuation and the risk of his using the team as a crutch?

(5) Should students be given general education which covers the broad aspects of architecture to prepare them to deal with the broad scope by developing an awareness of the interrelationship of various elements of the physical environment, but at the risk of their having no depth in any of the aspects of the environment? Or should those students specialize to achieve the depth needed to contribute to improving the environment at the risk of becoming too specialized and approaching the problems with too limited points of view?

(6) Should education of architects begin during the freshman year with all its advantages of motivation which goes with early decision of choosing a profession, but at the risk of overspecialization? Or should the student first obtain a thorough liberal arts background with an undergraduate degree before entering a professional school so that he will have the intellectual and cultural base on which to build his professional training, but carrying the penalty of forcing the student to wait four years to do the thing he wanted to do in the first place—study architecture?

(7) Should the curriculum offer an unlimited variety of options so that the student can take almost any courses he wants to fulfill his individual needs, but at the risk of pursuing his education in so many different directions that his education is disconnected and has "too many loose ends" at the time of graduation? Or should there be an integrated curriculum which unifies the various subjects into one general course eliminating the weak-

nesses of piecemeal programs, but at the risk of imposing limits on individual courses the student may take?

These paradoxes of architecture education will always create problems for educators. On the other hand, there are reasonable solutions to the problems. There are better ways, even best ways.

When the problem of education for team is superimposed over the ever-changing and confusing picture of what is now architecture education, to pin down what is best for a specific situation is even more difficult. The only thing certain is that there is no stock plan education. Schools should be different. By necessity and by choice every university must examine its own resources—financial, physical, and human—and then design its curriculum accordingly so as to equate resources with goals. Educators have to balance the books—do what resources will allow. So there will be no pat education for team.

Delving deeper into the paradoxes, however, will help us understand architecture education in general and that which is required to help the students appreciate and perhaps develop skills for team action.

67

Paradox one: The problem of think and do is a dilemma for every teacher

In September, 1961, Bill Lacy, Coryl Jones, and I left CRS (my departure was on a one-half time basis) to try to put the Department of Architecture, Rice University, back on its feet. The department had lost its accreditation.

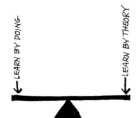

↑ LEARN BY DOING ↑ LEARN BY THEORY

THERE MUST BE A **BALANCE** BETWEEN PRACTICE AND THEORY. ALL THEORY AND NO PRACTICE WON'T DO. ALL PRACTICE WITHOUT THEORETICAL REASONING IS WORSE.

Hopefully teams will create new kinds of spaces and forms which truly cater to physical, intellectual, emotional, and social needs of most people. We are a long way from doing this at a high, sophisticated level, but we are on our way. Architecture by team holds great promise. So does education by team.

Bill was a CRS designer with a strong academic bent and Coryl was my secretary. We were a smooth-working team, by our own admission.

The coming of the Caudill/Lacy combination created the usual fears among some faculty members. "Are these cornfed cowpokes (Bill and I were both Oklahoma State graduates) going to try to convert Rice into a trade school?" To make matters worse, I was tainted with commercialism, being a practitioner and having obtained my advanced degree from MIT, that "trade school" down the Charles River from Harvard.

Rice's Department of Architecture had been in the business nearly fifty years. It had been a monument of stability until the last years of the fifties. There had only been two other chairmen before me. And it was Ivy League with a southern accent. In fact, most of the faculty had gone to Princeton.

There were apparently good reasons for fearing that Caudill and his little friend (later Dean of the College of Architecture, University of Tennessee) would lower the intellectual prestige of the Department. Rumors radiated from some source that I was anti-intellectual. It got around too that our intent was to get things done at any cost, even at the sacrifice of catering to the *thinkers,* that I was only interested in producing *doers.*

There was a bit of truth in those rumors. I remember telling some of the students, "Give me a not-so-smart but highly motivated student any day over a smart but lazy student; I have a better chance of making an architect out of him." I still believe it. But how nice to have highly intelligent, greatly motivated students. And we had quite a few such students go through Rice and become top-flight professionals.

I had not been at Rice three months when I was brave enough to confront the Rice Architectural Alumni Association. (I fondly called it my PTA.) I recall telling the horrified, mortified, alumni group this: "Our problem is neither poor faculty, inadequate finances, nor wrong curriculum, as you might think. Our problem is that we are not attracting good enough students." I went over like the proverbial lead balloon. Rice had always glowed in its reputation of getting the brain power. We were still getting the brains—highly intellectual students who could *think.* But for some reason the majority of them did not choose to *work.* We were failing to attract the doers. It was the *do* that was our problem. Because to make an architect out of a youngster, he has to *think* and *do.*

So we went recruiting. If Jess Neely, then the Rice football coach, could recruit, so could we. We recruited both at the graduate level and at the undergraduate level where our problem was. To stimulate the *do,* I found and persuaded some "mechanical rabbits" to come to Rice specifically to make our kids run. And run they did.

MECHANICAL RABBIT NEEDED AS **PACE** SETTER.

One of these rabbits (lions in my opinion) was Bud Luther, who had spent four years at Texas A&M. Since he had worked two summers for CRS, I knew Bud was a highly talented doer. And what a great job he did for his classmates and, I must add, for himself. He was a real pacesetter.

He later went on to Harvard for his advanced degree, won and took advantage of a coveted traveling scholarship culminating formal education in both thinking and doing which gave him a professional readiness that is hard to beat. He developed fast as an understudy under my design partner Charles Lawrence.

Bud Luther was able to handle the paradox of think-and-do quite well. He gave added validity to John Dewey's expression "Learn by doing."

Because this is such an important point—resolution of the paradox of thinking and doing—I will dwell on it a little longer.

After four years at Rice I began to understand and appreciate the pure intellectual approach. Neither the professors nor the bright students wanted to blindly go about doing things just to be doing. They did not wish to be caught in the trap of the Navy gob who had as a precautionary policy—"If it does not move, paint it. If it does, salute it."

These intellectuals demand reasons. And they sought perfection, which probably was their biggest hang-up. They wished to do nothing unless it was perfect.

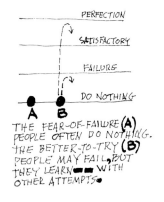

THE FEAR-OF-FAILURE (A) PEOPLE OFTEN DO NOTHING. THE BETTER-TO-TRY (B) PEOPLE MAY FAIL, BUT THEY LEARN ▬ ▬ WITH OTHER ATTEMPTS.

Evidence of this was that some of my most intellectual professors found it difficult to write articles, books, and make public lectures because they demanded of themselves absolute—and unfortunately unattainable—perfection. They did not give themselves the privilege of making mistakes.

Here is Bud Luther in action. Luther, at the time a relatively young man fresh out of college, was given the opportunity, as a rookie on the team, to explain to a tough multiheaded corporation client a certain phase of the work which he had helped to develop. So often students of architecture are under the impression that the three years between graduation and registration are "professional slavery." Nonsense. It is important that every member of the team has his chance for fast professional development. Team leaders see that the rookies have the opportunity to grow, because when they grow the team becomes stronger.

And, unfortunately, they did not want to give their own students the opportunities which mistakes offer to learning. An obsession with perfection inevitably leads to a terrible fear of failure which hinders growth and development of the individual.

Doing without thinking is bad, but just as bad is trying to think everything through and doing nothing. In CRS we have a maxim: It is only a mistake if it gets out of the office.

There are cases where it is good to do it wrong.

My sister Lil, four years older than I, used to protect her little brother, and bolster my spirits after I had goofed up on some high school situation, by saying, "Bill, you must remember that failures are the stepping stones to success." (I've certainly had enough of them to be a great success.)

Four years at Rice among the thinkers, by the way, helped teach me to think, and gave me an insight to some of the problems our students had.

For one thing, Rice was an environment in which a large percentage of the professors, mostly outside the School of Architecture (we were elevated from "department" to "school" my fifth year at Rice) but not entirely, felt strongly that education had nothing to do with making a living.

Our kids in the School, which in essence was a professional school, naturally received a lot of flak about the evils of professionalism. The term professional was dirty. When Lacy and I came on the scene, we were shocked at the anti-profession attitude. We learned that a large number of faculty and students honestly believed that practicing architects were either incompetent or downright crooks. As we became more familiar with the situation, we understood why. There was a credibility gap between thinking and doing.

The preceptorship plan allowed a student to spend a year between his four and fifth year under the guidance of a distinguished architect in an outstanding office. This plan was put into effect shortly after we arrived and was designed primarily to dispel this notion. It worked. When the preceptee became intimately acquainted with his preceptor—his work and his thinking—the student began to appreciate the architect and to value the *doing* aspect of architecture. And he came back to Rice motivated to develop professional, marketable skills.

I've often told my brightest students at Rice, "You have a disadvantage over most students. When you become architects, if you do not have the design skills to create beautiful functional buildings which radiate the aura of architecture, you will be frustrated to a point of extreme unhappiness. Some other students, who perhaps will produce buildings of lesser quality than yours, will be happy as larks, believing that their buildings are really good. They won't know the difference. Unfortunately, you will. And it is going to bug the hell out of you. You will find you now have the philosophy (you can talk architecture) but do not have the skills to create architecture. Don't put off *doing*. Make your mistakes now. Skills come by doing, by profiting from your mistakes. Put something down on that cheap yellow tracing paper. If it does not turn out right, nothing is lost, and the next sketch may be better. Think with your hands as well as your head."

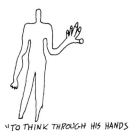
"TO THINK THROUGH HIS HANDS"

In my experience as a teacher in various schools from cow colleges to Ivy League schools, I find that students are about the same. About one-third really have what it takes to be an architect—the ability and the desire. There is also the middle third with ample ability, but lack of desire. What a challenge they present. Then there is the lower third, unqualified for architecture, but highly qualified in other fields. Too many students are pushed into architecture by poor guidance or parental persuasion.

The top third, highly motivated, highly intelligent, talented students who can think with their hands as well as their heads make teaching one of the most gratifying professions there is. That is why I like to teach at Rice. We have more than our share of the top third. (I must confess, however, during my administration at Rice, particularly the last half, the input was better than the output. We could have done more with the middle third and we could have given better advice to the lower third.) A think-do student with just a little luck unquestionably makes a highly competent professional.

THE ONE GREAT TEACHER IS IDEA CONTRADICTORY TO TO THE:

TEACHING TEAM CONCEPT, BUT BOTH ARE NEEDED AT TIMES.

68

Paradox two: Which is the better—master teaching or team teaching?

The second paradox of architecture education is how best to deal with master-teaching/team-teaching problems. Let me repeat the predicament. Should the student have a master-teacher, the great man or prima donna, if you please, who will give him strong guidance and deep understanding of his (the great man's) philosophy, or should the student be exposed to a team of teachers with many different philosophies? There are good arguments for both sides.

Structural system designers, lighting system designers, heating and ventilating system designers are architects in the sense that they help to cause architecture to happen. The common practice of labeling working drawings with such titles as "structural," "mechanical," "lighting," and "architectural," implies that "architectural" is a leftover. This is ridiculous. All systems relate to architecture. That's why the architectural team must be interdisciplinary. It is another good argument for team teaching.

169

Socrates taught Plato. Haydn taught Beethoven. And we all know Sullivan taught Wright. There is much validity to the premise that one strong man should do the teaching—the age old master-apprentice idea.

In 1947, I took my fifth-year design class from Texas A&M on a field trip to the West Coast. We spent a day with Frank Lloyd Wright, a day with Richard Neutra, a day with Ernie Kump, and one with John Lyon Reid, who was one of my teachers at MIT. Frankly, I wanted my students to be exposed to some really great teachers. (And I wanted to be, too.)

At Taliesin West, I was either reticent, or just plain scared of Frank Lloyd Wright. I had heard he hated professors. So I kept as quiet as I could and tried to camouflage myself to appear as a student. It was not hard, since some were as old as I. (No reflections on Willie Pena, but he was in the class.)

Our evening at the Neutra home was something else. I bolstered my courage to speak out against the master-teacher method of teaching. Why shouldn't I have been against it? Being a young instructor I was no master.

Mr. Neutra, being a very kind man as well as a great architect-teacher, permitted my indulgence. He let me talk. Mr. Wright would not have allowed me to expound even if I wanted to, nor would my students have wanted me to when the "master" was around. And I wouldn't have blamed them. But Mr. Neutra let me talk. I should have been listening. I blurted out, "Mr. Neutra, I think the master/apprentice method of teaching has had its day." Mr. Neutra, with all my entourage around his feet, elegantly but in no uncertain terms fired back that I was all wrong. He said that the sensitive student needed and wanted a strong person to guide and teach him the reasons behind architecture and to help him develop the skills and techniques to create architecture. He abhorred the "current fad" of the schools throwing the students in a complete state of confusion by foisting upon them teachers who, regardless of their competencies, had completely different philosophies. I could understand what he was talking about too.

He had a point. But so did I, and said something like this:

"Mr. Neutra, you are right—in your case. You are a great architect-teacher. But there is not a Neutra at A&M. We deliberately hire professors with different philosophies. We want them to be incompatible in terms of architectural beliefs and methods. Hopefully, they will have social compatibility, but this doesn't always happen. We'll take that chance. We want our students to be exposed to many kinds of thinking; to be familiar with the works of many architects" (I ran some unscheduled seminars each Monday night at the "Y" to increase this exposure); "to try out different ways to do things, so that each student may develop his own philosophy." And then I added, "You would not want to see little carbon copies of Caudill coming out of A&M, would you?" He could not argue with that point.

Mr. Neutra did rebut, magnificently. I had to eat a few words. The debate bounced back and forth until Mrs. Neutra told the "master" it was his bedtime, since he arose at 4:00 A.M. So he excused himself and we thanked him for a wonderful evening.

My students thoroughly enjoyed this verbal ping-pong. As for me, I felt pretty bad about it. I went back to the hotel feeling I had been rather rude to argue with such a great man—and in his own home. I was a bit ashamed.

Before 7:00 A.M. the next morning the phone rang. Much to my surprise, it was Richard Neutra. He said that since he had risen at 4:00 A.M. he had had time to reflect on our discussions. He wanted to apologize for what might have been an embarrassment for me before my students. "That's the last thing I would want to do. As you know, Professor Caudill, I hold you in high esteem because of Bob Simpson" (a former student of mine who was Neutra's lead man). "If I offended you, please forgive me." I was taken aback by the humility and sensitivity of this famous architect. I could only say, "Mr. Neutra, how can I be offended by a great man?"

I recall while at Texas A&M, a fine teacher, Bill Allen, fresh out of Harvard, joined our faculty, He believed that "there was only one way to go—the Corbu way." According to Bill, Le Corbusier wrote the Bible; Gropius preached and practiced it. Bill taught the fourth year at A&M. I taught the fifth. I could not understand what he was trying to do and he could not understand what I was trying to do—at least for his first year. When his students entered my class, I spent two or three weeks trying to undo what he did. They had *cubitis,* if you please—trying to work within the confines of a cube. They thought the Savoye House was the greatest thing since sliced bread. I thought it was a fake. (They were right; I was wrong.) Their buzz phrases were, "let's complete the cube," "let the building float," "physical manifestation of the conceptional idea," "divorced from nature," and "machine for living." (I've used them many times since.) At the time, Bill and I had such philosophical differences that I was forced to join Frank Lloyd Wright's side and read Le Corbusier on the sly.

The master-teacher method unquestionably has its place in education of the architect. We need great teachers—teachers like Jean Labatut, Walter Gropius, Mies van der Rohe, and Lawrence Anderson to name a few. There is no argument about that.

The concept of team teaching is based on the premise that all teachers are not equal, either in talent or in experience. A teaching team, therefore, consists of a group of "unalikes" who work together in a complementary arrangement. To be effective, each must recognize his own weaknesses and acknowledge the corresponding strengths of the others. And that is tough for a typical college professor. He has been taught that he should know everything about everything—from determining the amount of steel in a reinforced concrete beam to knowing how much burnt sienna to put in the paint bucket to get the right buff hue for the ceiling of the master bedroom toilet.

After six years of administering team teaching at Rice University I became convinced that my students knew more about teaching by team than did my professors. If a student had a problem concerning color, he would say to himself, "I'll discuss this with Professor Todd, who knows more about color than anyone else." Or if he was confronted with a situation that called for figuring the wind stresses on a high-rise building, he would say, "Only Dr. Krahl can help me on this problem." In other words the students were smart enough to recognize the strengths and weaknesses of the professors and went to the teachers who could do them the most good. The professors themselves were not as aware of their own weaknesses and strengths and were reluctant to send their students to other professors for help.

The problem of getting the professors together in team action is particularly exaggerated in an integrated subject matter curriculum as we had at Rice. I suspect that is why there are so many cafeteria-type curricula where the student has many choices of subject—a little from this prof, and so on. (And it doesn't seem to make too much difference if the professors barely speak to each other.)

Team teaching can be effective. The University of Houston School of Education contracted with CRS to conduct a ten-day course on school planning. It was a team effort involving nine CRS architects and engineers; teachers who specialized in different aspects of schoolhouse planning.

Oddly enough, in my experience the best example of team teaching occurred in the Houston office of CRS. Rice's School of Architecture had made an arrangement with CRS to give the returning preceptees (the fifth-year students who had spent a year working directly under distinguished architects throughout the country and abroad) a two-week block-of-time course called "Path of Design," the purpose of which was to expose the students to the latest procedures of management and design. Why at CRS? Frankly we had more qualified "teachers" since the CRS team was on the leading edge of office practice. And where else would there be a better place to teach office practice than in an office? So we did. And with a team of fourteen "professors."

We need teaching teams—the interdisciplinary teams which we have been trying to produce these past years, at Rice University, to teach management, design, and technology as one single course called architecture.

There must be both—great teachers and teaching teams.

The paradox can be resolved.

Both the master-teacher and the teaching team can help the student realize the necessity of architecture by team and point out some ways in which the student may develop the art of collaboration and still retain strong individuality.

174

69

Paradox three: To compete or not to compete?

The third paradox of education of architects—to compete or not to compete—is still a hot issue. The current crop of students seems to be against competition of any kind. As of this writing, Rice students have voted to discontinue the William Ward Watkin Traveling Scholarship Competition—one of the oldest traditions at the School. They are asking the Architectural Alumni Association to raise the money and give it to the sophomore class for its annual field trip. This is disconcerting to the alumni, particularly to those old-time winners of the competitions, and to me too. I was discussing this with Tom Bullock and Charles Lawrence. We agreed that this fits into the national picture and that most students are resisting any kind of competition. Rice students, too, are bucking the grade system. They want "pass or fail." Tom said, "The way things are going now, the student will want 'pass or fail' for the class as a whole." I doubt if things will go that far, although I have used the expression "the team failed" many times.

Too much stress on competition can be blamed for the prevailing student attitude. They are too often caught in the pinch of competitions for scholarships. If you are a high school student, you had better be in the upper ten percent of your class to get into Rice. And if you are a senior at Rice, you had better be among the top three students in grades to get into Harvard. And so it goes.

I have publicly stated many times that some CRS competitors have taught us more than some of our partners. We shall always be grateful to Lawrence Perkins, John Reid, John McLeod, and many others. They taught us so much, and made us work so much harder.

When John Reid of San Francisco took the best Texas school client we ever had away from us, I did not hear one derogatory word from any CRS partners. We owed Reid a debt we can never repay. He and others like him did something the schools could not do—make professionals out of us, through competition.

Competition does have its advantages. Although it may deter a few students, it offers motivation to most of the others. Some students can compete only with themselves and unquestionably that's the most noble way of all. Comparative grading is rough to a relatively weak person who should not be competing with a strong person. In another league that relatively weak person might well be strong. So, obviously, if there is competition, there should be limits. It is questionable whether the limits should be as broad as "pass or fail." If grades are a sore point for students, the paycheck of the embryonic architect will be doubly so. In essence, salaries are grades.

So are jury reports. And so are results of competitions.

I contend, therefore, that if educators are fair to the students, they will stress some competition to provide the readiness necessary if they are to enter a highly competitive world. Admittedly, the world will change, but very, very slowly in this respect. On the other hand, there must be in any program relating to education for architecture, the chance for the individual to grow and develop, free of energy-consuming jealousies that go with fierce class competition.

This paradox, therefore, is resolved by a commitment to both competition and non-competition. This is absolutely necessary in following the practice of architecture by team.

Every position on the team should be open to competition. The team cannot get better unless its individual specialists get better. If they don't, they should be replaced. That is why there is a bench. And the team itself must have a highly competitive attitude. There must be the desire to win, or, to put it more bluntly, to beat someone. When you are standing in line to be interviewed for a job you'd give your right arm to get, you feel competitive—you want to beat everyone else.

Getting on the team is competition of the highest order. When the team is in action, either against another team or by itself, there is still competition of the highest order. Once on a team and occupying a position which depends upon other positions for successful operation, there can be no competition among team members. It has to be "brotherly love"—helping the other guy, in the truest sense. There must be togetherness—"together we can do a better job than we can separately."

Educators must be cognizant that there must be both competitive and noncompetitive education. Hopefully they will have the judgment to know when competition stimulates and when it deters learning.

70

Paradox four: Should there be individual projects or group projects?

Visiting critics love to do group problems. At the end of their two to five weeks stint, they have something big to show for their endeavors. I know. I like to do them.

The trouble with the group project is that to produce the best results, every member of the group should "do his thing," that which he can do best. And in team effort, this makes good sense—let the specialists specialize. But should the student specialize at this stage of development?

While serving as a visiting critic at Cornell, I pulled a double cross in this respect. The time was so short and the project so large that we decided to split the class into four teams. I met with each group separately to help them get organized. I pointed out how important it was to survey and evaluate the talent available. To know what we have in the way of human resources is the key to group action. After each group evaluated the talent, that's when I threw in the double cross. It went something like this: "Jones, I hear you are the best delineator in the group; so you will be in charge of the programming part of the project." "Smith, I understand you have great managerial talent, but can't draw for sour apples, so your job is to be in charge of the visual presentation. We expect you to do at least one presentation sketch with your lily white hands." "Thompson, they tell me you are tremendous at conceptual design. Great! The world needs conceptual designers, but you are not quite ready for the world. I understand you and structures don't get along so well. So doesn't it make sense for you to serve as the structural specialist on the team and do a catch-up?" "And Brown, you are assigned to be the conceptual designer. Your long suit, I know, is structure, but what an opportunity you will have to develop skills sadly lacking in design!"

The results left much to be desired in terms of functional, economical, and aesthetic solutions, but in terms of learning, the project was quite successful. To do this at the undergraduate level has much merit. At the graduate level, it is questionable.

178

When schools were smaller, some of them had group problems which involved the entire school. We had one at Texas A&M in 1940. For one class it lasted two years. The problem was a Negro slum clearance project for Bryan, Texas, the little city next to College Station where the university is located. The "now generation" did not invent social consciousness. Our students had it then. And so did the young professors.

The way this super-collaborative problem went was something like this.

The freshman class's task was to go into the ghettos, and with carefully worked out questionnaires, determine some of the sociological problems which had architectural implications. My sophomore class was to be responsible for designing educational facilities for the housing project.

I recall very vividly one specific project—a nursery for the children of working mothers. The project was done on an individual basis—a case of individual projects within the context of a group project. One of my students wanted to develop a two-story scheme. While a two-story nursery was not very practical, I could see the great opportunity of his learning about stairs and the problems connected with two-level planning and detailing, so I told him to go ahead. Come jury time, my boy was given a failing grade. On the jury was that great guy (and, fortunately for me, very forgiving person) Mr. Ernest Langford, the head of the Department of Architecture. Seeing the terrible injustice that the six-man jury did to my student, I completely lost my temper and fired the jury in go-to-hell terms, saying "I'll judge the problems myself." And I did. My boy with the two-story nursery received an "A" from me and I ignored the "F" by the jury. Mr. Langford was magnanimous. He allowed me to teach classes the following day.

This incident caused me to formulate my own policies about grades and juries. They should be separated. This I carried to Rice. I contend that grades must reflect effort and individual development, while jury judgments reflect the product only and perhaps the presentation of that product, both verbally and graphically.

My sophomore class later designed an elementary school for the housing project in this super-collaborative project. The junior class, as I recall, designed a shopping center and a church as its contribution.

The senior class was the one that took most responsibility, and the longest time. They were still working on their portion during their fifth year. The seniors' assignment was to design and do the working drawings for the houses themselves. And they did a fine, creative job under Professors Tommy Thomson, Jack Finney, Hal Moseley, and Sam Zisman, who later obtained governmental grants to carry through the housing. The fifth-year class were the planners.

This all-school effort was an exciting project. The lower classes were particularly pleased to work as a team of classes which included the upperclassmen. Within the big problem were a considerable number of individual problems. So there were many benefits.

There were a lot of bad things too. The seniors became bored working at one project for so long. The freshmen, playing the role of sociologists, missed out in learning architectural skills. A few students took unfair advantage of group action by letting someone else do their work. I suspect three or four students completely wasted a year.

There is no "yes" or "no" answer to the question of individual projects versus group projects. I am convinced that the student should have both kinds of experiences, but certainly he should do many projects on his own and carry the full responsibility.

We had a bright fifth-year student at Rice, Hank Winkelman, who was completely dedicated to learning hospital design. We allowed him to go his own way to achieve this goal on his own initiative. He worked up an arrangement with the Texas University Medical School in Galveston, actually living with one of the doctors to collaborate on a specific project—a real one. He would call on the Rice faculty only for guidance and criticism. Hank did quite well. He was motivated; he had the talent; and he had enough practical experience to be left on his own. Other students in his class apparently had not reached the point of maturity for this kind of freedom, and they goofed up. For them, it was a bad experience and in a case or two, a real setback of their growth and development. So it is difficult to tell just how much a student can do on his own and how much strong guidance and hand-holding he needs before reaching maturity. Only the best teachers know when a student is ready to handle individual projects with minimum guidance.

One of the greatest advantages of using individual problems in the customary, nonisolated manner where each member of the class is given the same problem, is that at the end of the project, during an open jury, the student will see that there are many ways of solving architectural problems. He has the opportunity to compare his solutions with others. I am completely convinced that students sometimes learn as much from each other as they do from their professors. Maybe this is the best argument for group projects. It is also a good argument for competition.

Allow me to say it again: There is no "yes" or "no" answer. Which is best? Group projects? Individual projects? Both are needed in any architecture curriculum. Concerning education for team, this is particularly true. To be an effective member of a team, one must first be a highly competent individual performer, and second, be a person who has developed the art of collaboration.

71

Paradox five: Should a student be a generalist or a specialist?

A sophomore student at Rice came to me one day, quite disturbed because he could not take all of the sociology courses he wanted. He emphatically pointed out that architecture was irrelevant without a thorough understanding of the behavior of people. I could not argue about that. He went on to say that the architect must be a broad person. And I could not argue about that except to add, "He should not only be knowledgeable in the humanities/arts, but also in science/engineering" (which, as it turned out, did not interest our student in the least). Being a persistent, persuasive, articulate fellow, he kept insisting that we should water down the curriculum so he could get a minor (whatever that is) in sociology.

SOCIOLOGY TO AN
ADVANCED ARCHITECTURE
STUDENT WILL BE MORE
MEANINGFUL THAN TO
A SOPHOMORE.

Finally in order to get rid of him, I had to say, "John, if you want to be a sociologist, why don't you transfer to the Department of Sociology?" He replied, "But I want to be an architect!" Then I hit him like a hard-nose practitioner would. "John, our firm is committed to the team concept. Every man on a task team is a specialist. Now if the task requires a person on the team who is talented and experienced in sociology, for sure we are not going to fill that position with a so-so architect who is an amateur sociologist or a so-so sociologist who is an amateur architect. We are going to find us the best damn professional sociologist that our money can buy—then teach him to play on our team." I added, "Of course, John, a specialist must be a good generalist, but when someone has to operate on my heart, I'll want a great heart man to do it, not a general practitioner. And I'll want the best my money can buy." The profession of architecture is like that. All of us have to know about a lot of things, including sociology, but to contribute to making this world a better place, each of us must know a tremendous amount about at least one thing.

We had a very bright student at Rice who, after his third year, discovered he had neither the talent nor the desire to be a designer. At the time, we had dreamed of developing a completely individualized curriculum for Rice; so my faculty and I decided to let this young man specialize. We all knew he would never make a good designer, but we felt that he had the intellectual and analytical capacity to make a top-flight technologist, which the profession sadly lacks. So we designed a special course just for him with a specification writing emphasis. We even had him taking courses outside of Rice and attending professional seminar/clinics and conventions. He was graduated with an undergraduate specialty.

How did it all end? Two things happened: Five years after graduation, he held down, in a most competent manner, an important job in a fine architectural firm. He grew to be a professional in the technological and altruistic sense—an expert in specification writing. The second thing that happened was this: He failed the design part of the architectural registration examination three or four times. Here's where we goofed up. We did not give him enough design at Rice to be registered as an architect.

I think he finally passed it. If so, he developed the design skills on his own. I have not decided whether this is a success story or not. Perhaps the only thing that was wrong is the registration laws. Whether the man was registered or not, Rice helped to turn out a highly competent specialist greatly needed in the profession. There are advantages of specialization in the school, but at the undergradute level it is a bit risky.

Let me now give an opposite picture of the specialist-generalist problem. CRS is a team of specialists. Every one of us is trained to do at least one thing with the highest degree of competency, hopefully better than anyone else in the United States. I'll put Frank Lawyer against anyone on design. I'll put Willie Pena against anyone on programming. If there are any better, he taught them. I'll put Phil Williams against anyone on the educational/analytical aspect of campus planning. And I'll put myself against anyone in the world on bragging about my teammates.

Most of the specialists we have, received their training, or the greatest growth or professional development, in CRS. Bob Mattox, one of the nation's experts on the use of computers in architecture practice, never took a course in computers while at Rice University. After working in the CRS production section, he asked to be transferred to programming under Pena and that was where he became interested in the use of the computer as a programming tool.

James Thomas never took a course at Rice in interior design. He did, however, work for an interior designer before coming to CRS to organize and build our Interior Design Section.

Andy Belschner, who started the CRS architectural graphics section, never took a course in architectural graphics at Rice.

Bob Williams, in charge of computerized construction specifications, was never given a specification emphasis like the other Rice student I mentioned.

Wallie Scott, number one promoter in CRS, never took a how-to-get-a-job course at A&M. His great talent at the interviews was developed strictly through his experience in CRS and from guidance given to him by his partners. Now he is teaching others.

William Pena, too, developed his specialty of programming after graduation.

Herb Paseur, who handles the managerial and financial operations of CRS Design Associates, never took a business course while he was at Oklahoma State.

Herb Paseur, one-time chief designer of our Oklahoma City office, never took a business course as a student at Oklahoma State University. Being a person of great adaptability with qualities of leadership, Paseur, through CRS planned experiences and intense study, has developed into a highly competent, responsible corporation administrator.

What all of these specialists who developed their specialty after graduation have is this: Each received excellent general training at good architecture schools.

Here is a point that should be emphasized. The study of architecture in the traditional manner gives the student a liberal arts background unequal to any other major. The course that a student of architecture must take runs the gamut from science to art.

I recall overhearing two professors in the Rice Faculty Club, an English teacher and a history teacher, talking about a new man who was going to join the English department. The conversation went something like this: History prof: "I hear you are getting a new man." English prof: "Quite right. Strictly first class. He's Fifteenth Century." History prof: "Fifteenth Century? I thought you were Fifteenth Century." English prof: "Right but I am Fifteenth Century English literature. He is Fifteenth Century Spanish literature." That's when I decided architects were not such narrow-minded specialists after all.

The paradox of generalists versus specialists at the student level can be resolved, provided each individual is considered separately. It is my empirical judgment that most students should delay specialization within the general field of architecture until the graduate years. But most certainly the graduate work should emphasize a specialty.

An example of graduate studies leading to successful professional specialization is the case of Jim Falick, of our team. After completing his undergraduate course at Columbia University, he entered the Hospital Design Program. After getting his master's degree, he hit the field running, saving many years over developing this specialty during the normal course of office practice. At the time, Columbia was one of the very few schools offering this kind of specialization. Dean Charles Colbert was highly criticized at the time for introducing "such a narrow course," but as it turned out, many schools now are following the pattern. Specialization at the graduate level is becoming the rule.

As the schools begin to develop their programs in this direction, one would think offices will have fewer in-training programs such as CRS has had throughout the years. It is my guess, however, that things will move so fast during the next few years that the schools will find it hard to keep up and big firms will have to develop specialties.

WITHOUT **MIXING** GENERAL
EDUCATION WITH SPECIAL-
IZED EDUCATION THERE IS
THE DANGER OF THE
PROFESSIONAL SCHOOL BE-
COMING A **TRADE SCHOOL.**

72

Paradox six: When should the education of an architect begin?

If I had a small son with musical talent who wanted to play viola in a great symphony orchestra when he grew up, this is what I would *not* tell him: "Son, first, get a good education. Do well in elementary school. Do well in junior high school. And do particularly well in high school so you can get into a good university. While at the university, take all the courses you want, but be sure and get your academic courses behind you—literature, mathematics, science, and art. So when you begin to pursue seriously your graduate years on your music major, you'll have all that stuff behind you. Then you can concentrate uninterruptedly on becoming the world's greatest viola player."

Everyone knows if you want to become a top-notch violist, you must start as soon as possible, even before entering the first grade.

The 1970 photo (right) of the Cypress College in which Frank Lawyer took the design lead clearly shows that there must be someone on the architecture team who possesses highly developed artistic skills and who has the sensitivity to human physical needs and an awareness of human values. Lawyer started developing these skills before he even entered college. He was a good artist and sculptor by the time he entered his junior year. Designers must start early. They cannot wait until their graduate year. Cypress College, located in North Orange County, California, was jointly designed by William E. Blurock and the CRS team.

I feel the same way about a person learning to be a great architectural designer. Why penalize him by putting him in the academic waiting room for four years until he receives his bachelor's degree? Educational research has shown that motivation grows out of specialization. That's the best argument that I know for specialization and generalization to go hand in hand at every level of the university. The trade school concept at the graduate level may be right for law and medicine, but it is not right for architecture. The master's and Ph.D. candidate in architecture should be able to cross into other disciplines. Accordingly, the rash of 2-4 plans going around the universities, in which a student must go through two years of college before starting architecture, is a detention for designers. As far as I am concerned, architecture education can start in kindergarten if we are going to have highly talented designers on the total architectural team.

In trying to resolve the paradox of start-early and start-late, we fall into the trap of thinking an architect is an architect. This all-alike premise has absolutely no validity. Architects are not alike. Designers are quite a different breed from technologists who are quite a different breed from managers. Every so often, someone comes along with outstanding talent in all three areas, but they generally end up wanting to go only in one direction. It is just as foolish to say that education for all architects should take the same amount of time no matter what the state registration requires.

And it is as foolish for me to say that it is wrong to start architecture after four years in college.

But I did not quite say that. I was referring only to the designer type. I feel very strongly about this contention and I maintain that the earlier the start and the more experience a designer has—in school or out of school—the better chance he has to become first class.

THE STUDENT, WHO IS WORKING ON HIS **MAJOR** AT THE SAME TIME HE IS WORKING OFF HIS **GENERAL** EDUCATION REQUIREMENTS, IS APT TO BE **MOTIVATED.**

To be a technologist or a manager is something else. The length of formal education may be shortened and might well start later in the school of architecture, after the students have had courses in science/engineering or business/management. I would say the 2 + 4 plan or the 4 + 3 plan is quite feasible. I am one of those people who believes that if an illuminating engineer has adequate education and experience to be on an architectural team, then he should be called an architect. By the same token, I believe a sociologist, if his specialty is working on architectural teams and if he contributes to the creation of architecture, should be called an architect. I am only saying that if a person contributes to the creation of architecture, then he is an architect. Obviously, registration examinations will have to change.

Another point: At Rice, we have a 4 + 1 plan at present, but nothing is sacred. At the end of four years, the student receives his Bachelor of Arts degree. With this degree, if the faculty feels that the student has performed satisfactorily during his first four years, then he is admitted to the fifth-year class to pursue his professional degree, the Bachelor of Architecture, requiring one more year.

Because of the successes of the preceptorship plan, there are many on the faculty who wish to go to a 4 + 2 plan (one year as a preceptee and one last year at Rice polishing up) culminating the program with a Master of Architecture and eliminating the fifth-year degree which Rice has had for nearly sixty years. This makes sense to me. A Masters in Architecture today is equivalent to a Bachelor of Architecture when I was in school.

What about the student with a nonarchitecture degree who wants to study architecture? The profession needs such a person and we should not penalize him for late decision.

The 4 + 3 students generally do quite well in the management and technology disciplines. So, when we put the design yardstick on them to measure their performance in design at the end of the third year, with but few exceptions, they fall short by comparison with the regular students. But it is not right to evaluate students only in terms of their desgin capabilities. The profession needs their special talents. The registration boards need to take note of this.

The latecomers come from nearly every field—sociology, music, engineering, and even law. Rice has been so design-oriented that it has been difficult for them. And the profession isn't much better. Take the case of David Colby.

The first I had heard of David was a call I received from Nathaniel Owings of San Francisco, then a letter from John Burchard of MIT. Both were hoping, since Rice was so small, that the School of Architecture could be flexible enough to take on a young man in his thirties who had a degree in economics from Stanford and a master's in business from Harvard, but who wanted desperately to be an architect. After talking it over with the faculty, I said to send Colby down and we would see what we could do.

What we did was a little of everything—from letting him participate in every jury and seminar to giving him a blanket invitation to audit every class, including history or architecture. In order to grasp a feeling for the problems of design, he rode sidesaddle with the freshmen. At the same time, he sat in on some basic structure courses. The purpose of this individualized curriculum was simple, for orientation to architecture in the shortest amount of time, hopefully a year, so that he could go to work in a large office. Nat Owings said, "Send him back after a year and we will put him in charge of our computer department." It sounded like a good idea to me.

We went outside of Rice to expose David to architectural practice. He spent two months in CRS studying our business methods of operation. I remember Tom Bullock saying to him something like "David, the profession needs men like you—highly trained managerial types who consider efficiency first. Don't get the aesthetic curse. If you do, you are lost."

After David spent his year at Rice, he was qualified to go into an office and do what he was trained to do—help manage things. Through Paul Kennon's help, he went to work for Saarinen Associates in New Haven. He did quite well, working himself up to office manager. I was proud of him and of Rice for being so broad-minded about training a nondesigner for the profession. This was a big step in the right direction—developing a new type of person for the architectural team.

It was not much over a year when I received a long letter from David ending with the sentence: "I guess I have caught the aesthetic curse." What happened was that he found that if one does not have that architectural degree and works in an architectural office, he becomes a second-class citizen.

This is no reflection on the Saarinen firm alone. It has happened in our firm. My partner, Bill Perry, an accountant who came to us with a master's degree in business and had college teaching experience, had a devil of a time being accepted as a full contributing member of the CRS team. We understood fully what David was going through. I tried to persuade him to stay by saying that in the future, the nonarchitect in the traditional sense will not only be accepted, but may lead the architectural teams. A good prophecy. At this writing, there are many nonarchitects running schools of architecture, because most architects of my generation are poor managers.

David, however, wanted to come back to Rice and do all the necessary things to make him acceptable in the architectural world, including the registration boards. I was terribly disappointed that he caught the "aesthetic curse" and had to come back because he could not beat the system.

All of us at Rice and CRS were very impressed with his nerve in coming back—a man in his thirties with the responsibilities of a family, competing with the young kids. When at the graduation honor award assembly he received an award for being one of the outstanding architecture graduates, his wife and children must have been even more proud of him than we were.

Sometime in the near future, this profession has to change so that the David Colbys can thrive and contribute. The profession needs highly trained management people like David to help make organization decisions and operational judgments. Sociologists who are real professionals, not amateur architects, educators who can skillfully zero in on the problem of facilities, health facility consultants who devote their entire lives to making hospitals places of joy instead of fear, and engineers who have just as much desire to create architecture as designers. These are needed for future architectural teams.

They will need an acceptance of the team approach—that "together we can do a better job than we can separately," that there must be a basic organizational framework within which the individual can contribute his best talents—whether such talents are in management, technology, or design—in a way relevant to the individual, the task, and the overall performance of the team.

The paradox of *start now* or *wait until* will continue to bug educators as long as they cannot decide what is an architect. Once they decide that architects are many kinds of people emphasizing many areas, then there will be no rigidly set ways to educate an architect—including when to start. The educators will recongize that for the designer-type architect, the earlier the start the better, and for the manager-type architect, it makes little difference when he enters the architecture school, provided he has thorough training in his discipline. He could start the day after receiving a Ph.D. in management, if he wished. If so, he certainly should not be made to go through the regular five-year sequence or even three-year design course. The time at both ends—start to finish—must be adjusted to the individual situation.

73

Paradox seven: Should the curriculum be integrated but limited or unlimited?

When I arrived at Rice, I inherited an integrated subject matter curriculum. All the separate courses had been thrown into one course called Architecture. It made a great deal of sense to me, having had difficulties myself after graduation of tying together all of the loose ends—the specification writing course was not on speaking terms with the course in concrete, nor was the history course in tune with design.

The program at Rice, however, was basically a design course. The faculty, in order to have a more balanced curriculum, initiated a plan which would hopefully give added strength to management and technology, at the same time retaining strength in design. We appointed a coordinator for each one of these three disciplines of practice. They were the watchdogs to see that in every student project, serious consideration would be given to each of the three disciplines.

It was hard for us to give up the expression "Design Professor." But if the single course was Architecture, not just design, then the professor at each grade level who had charge of integrating all subjects needed a more encompassing title, appropriately called "Professor of Architecture."

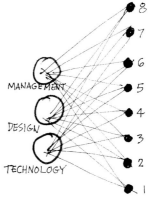

THERE IS A PROFESSOR OF ARCHITECTURE TO DIRECT THE **INTEGRATION** OF THE 3 DISCIPLINES OF PRACTICE.

The trouble with the integrated subject matter curriculum is that the Professor of Architecture must be a super-teacher—knowing a lot about a lot of things, since Architecture covers such a broad area. There are very few super-teachers who can run the gamut. So to solve this problem, there must be available to the students a stable of specialists—such as structural engineers, mechanical engineers, illuminating engineers, acousticians, cost estimators, and the like. The Professor of Architecture at each grade level might well relegate his position to that of a booker. In a few cases, this was true. And to call in the consultants one by one without collaboration simply created confusion, negating the benefits of integration. Then there were some cases where professors who, after scheduling the consultants, would "go fishing." So the integrated curriculum is not free of flaws. Synonymous with the integrated curriculum is team teaching—unpopular with most architectural educators.

In favor of the integrated, team teaching system are these: When the Professors of Architecture are highly qualified, creative teachers, sensitive to the needs and preferences of students, the project method (integrating various subject matter areas and using teaching teams) offers an excellent way to educate professionals. There is no reason why the integrated curriculum cannot be very effective provided it is accompanied by the use of teaching teams—consultants who work together, not just on beck and call. With team teaching, the integrated curriculum has great possibilities. With the consultants performing as a smoothly running teaching team and with the strong leadership of the professor of architecture, a high degree of subject matter integration can be achieved, without the dangling loose ends of a fragmented curriculum.

But students today want more choice. Because of their desire to learn about everything, particularly subjects relating to the humanities, if they had their say they would roam all over the campus taking any course they wished to take. Some schools let them. And rightly so, if education has nothing to do with making a living as some professors think.

Teachers, too, prefer to teach their own little courses without interference of other teachers. The typical professor could care less about team teaching.

There are many advantages to the "cafeteria curriculum." If motivation stems from choice, it is a good idea to let the student choose what he wants to take. If every student needs his own individualized curriculum, then it is a good thing to offer an abundant number of courses to cover the wide range of variances. From an administrator's point of view, it is much easier to manage the unrelated course setup than to run an integrated curriculum. And where crossing departmental or school lines are required, it is a simple matter of referring to the university's catalog. All in all, it sounds like a good plan from the student's point of view, from the faculty standpoint, and from efficiency of administration.

Regardless of the manner in which architects are educated—and there is no one "best" way—educators must remember that architecture is a personal experience of plain, ordinary people, not merely an architect's personal expression. People come first. Computer techniques, building systems, design methodology, and even the team concept are secondary. Architects are here to do good things for people—primarily to produce forms and spaces which possess the aura of architecture.

There are, however, many weaknesses of the "cafeteria curriculum." The major flaw is that the student's choice of courses may not fulfill his needs. It is most difficult for the student to distinguish between "wants" and "needs." It is easy for him to spread himself thin, yet still "earn" his degree in architecture without being qualified.

I recall telling my faculty when it appeared we were going in 100 directions at once that Rice may be the only school of architecture in the nation whose graduates cannot design a building. Our interests were so broad at the time, we thought only in terms of planning and social reforms. Designing buildings seemed irrelevant.

One of my young professors came up with a brilliant idea. Said he, "Let's specialize. Let's turn out students who will be honest-to-goodness architects, primarily interested in designing buildings—the project architect type." Then he added the clincher, "Rice could have a monopoly."

"Cafeteria systems" require full-time, capable counselors who are in tune with current professional practice and are familiar with research activities which anticipate new directions. Aimless roaming by students through academia is a waste of money, time, and talent.

74

Education for team must begin in the schools and be perfected in practice

It becomes more clear to those who follow closely both architectural education and architectural practice that one cannot get along without the other—that there should be no schism.

This is particularly true in the teaching of teamwork. Perhaps if team teaching would take hold, that in itself would demonstrate the effectiveness of the team idea. But team teaching does not necessarily imply teaching teamwork. In fact, team teaching was developed as a device for teaching the individuals in contrast to teaching the class.

Most certainly, at both the undergraduate and graduate level, students should participate in a few collaborative projects. It would be educationally unsound if all projects were of the group effort type. If this were to happen, development and growth of the individual would be held back, although the students unquestionably would turn out to be adept at team play. If there must be a hierarchy, there is absolutely no doubt in my mind what it should be:

The individual is first; the team is second.

A team of duds will not win any ball games. Successful team operation depends first on highly competent individuals and second on their ability to work together.

An educational program at the undergraduate level or the graduate level, therefore, must have as its prime function the growth and the development of the individual. This idea is completely in accord with education for team.

Frankly, we don't know yet how to teach teamwork once the competent individual is developed. Some ways of developing the individual are antithetical to the team concept. It certainly is when students are taught to be prima donnas.

Thus far, the most common manner to teach teamwork is simply to issue a few collaborative problems and let the students find out for themselves how to get along with each other. But that is haphazard at best. What if they don't?

For years, CRS has had a simple rule for selecting team members. We say that a person "first must know his stuff and then be a good guy." It is the "good guy" part that qualifies him for team play. How to make a person into a good guy is quite a problem. Generally, it turns out that

A **TEAM** IS ANY ASSOCIATION OF PEOPLE WHO SHARE **COMMON GOALS**, WHO ARE WILLING TO **COOPERATE**, AND WHO CAN **COMMUNICATE WITH EACH OTHER.**

as the new man learns to play on the team he becomes a "good guy." Learning to play on a team, therefore, takes practice. The schools offer a limited kind of practice of theory, but the offices are in a much better position to educate for and by team—doing real jobs. A soldier needs a battlefiield.

Education for and by team, therefore, should begin in the schools and be perfected in practice.

Perfected in practice? How? Basically an office is like a school. Most professionals are frustrated professors. They love to take over rookies fresh out of the universities. And what advantages they have over professors! For the first time the student is in a real world, not a paper one,

"Every man on the team is a specialist." In CRS we have what we call vertical specialists including people who devote their entire lives to specific building types such as schools, colleges, university planning, and hospitals. Then we have horizontal specialists, who cross the various building-type people, such as graphic designers (shown at right), programming experts, architects, engineers, building systems specialists, design developers, estimators, and specification writers. Most of these we have "educated" ourselves. The schools are beginning to assume this responsibility; however, there seems to be a deluge of programmers and only a trickling of designers coming out of schools of architecture.

and deals with real clients. He is on a pro team, mixing with seasoned pros. He is in the big league for the first time. Also for the first time, the pieces of the fragmented curriculum are falling together in one "ball of wax." He is beginning to see the totality of practice. It is easy to understand when the architect-to-be-remarks, "I've learned more in this office during the last six months than in the five years at the university." In actuality, it was not that he had learned more but that the learning was more meaningful. There was immediate, direct application. The total look begins to come into focus.

In-service education concerns two facets: There must be education for professional development of the individual—expansion of scope and continuum of accumulated knowledge and perfection of skills. And there must be education for team action—constant improvement of the art of collaboration. It is my contention that the two go together.

Everyone in CRS wants to go on the next squatters—a back-breaking, sleepless week. Why? Because it's always a great learning experience, no matter how many squatters a person has experienced. Learning takes place in two ways: through the dynamics of group action and through individuals being challenged to perform at the highest level of proficiency. A squatters stretches minds and abilities. Learning is both accelerated and extended. It is one of the best in-service devices we have—indirect and informal.

CRS has, however, more direct and formal "schools." We have classes for technologists, classes for project managers, classes for programmers, seminars for designers, seminars on cost control, lectures on a variety of subjects, and division meetings that go beyond the "pep rally" idea into intensive professional preparation. These "schools" serve the development of the individual and the perfection of group collaboration.

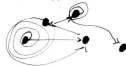

THE **SQUATTER TEAM** THRIVES ON **SPONTANEITY** AND THE **AD LIB:**

LIKE A DIXIELAND BAND.

Also there have been specific schools for specific projects. Take the case of the San Angelo School Planning Clinic, July 6–7, 1954. Thirty-eight people participated—including teachers, school administrators, school board members, curriculum specialists, city officials, a city planner, mechanical and electrical engineering consultants, structural engineers, as well as representatives of the five architectural firms with which CRS was associated. The clinic had only one purpose: to meet, pool our experiences and knowledge, develop empathy, and provide a climate for creative endeavor so as to give the children of San Angelo buildings highly conducive to learning and at a price the community could afford.

Why so many people? Let me quote from the report of that meeting:

"The approach to planning the school plant requires a panoramic concept centered around the pupil. Our problem of giving the pupil a healthful, stimulating environment economically must be approached from the eyes of many specialists. Let's face it: One man cannot design a school—and do it right. It is difficult for one man to have a panoramic point of view. What is meant by his panoramic concept?

"Consider a plowed field. What does a plowed field look like? It looks rough to the farmer who is sowing it and smooth to a pilot flying 20,000 feet above it. It looks large to the farmer and small to the pilot. Scoop up a handful and you have a third point of view. Examine some under a microscope and you have a fourth. The farmer, the pilot, the housewife, the child, the casual passer-by, the soil analyst, the artist—all see the plowed field differently, each according to his own kind of knowledge and interests. Who is to say any of them is wrong? And who could insist that his observation is the only one, his image the true one?

202

"Is not looking at a school or considering the planning for a school something like this? Here too, there are many observers, each with his own point of view—members of the building committee, the finance committee, and of the site selection committee, the superintendent, the teacher, the building custodian, the architect, the illuminating engineer, the heating and ventilating engineer, the acoustical engineer, and the sanitary engineer, not to mention the children for whom the school is to be built.

"What each of these people sees is right. Yet what each of them sees is wrong.

"The heating engineer, for example, see the ideal school with very little glass area; he is right because this would decrease the heating loss, and he is wrong because this would also reduce natural lighting. The building custodian sees the ideal school with hard-glazed walls; he is right for hard-surfaced walls facilitate cleanliness, and he is wrong for such walls generally make for poor acoustics."

The clinic allowed us to learn from each other, giving each participant a panoramic view of the total task. It also developed a stronger commitment to the team concept, paving the way to subsequent team action.

Another clinic was held in Roanoke, Virginia, April 8–9, 1958, the prime purpose of which was "to exchange philosophies, to generate ideas, and to formulate a program for new schools." This was attended not only by an interdisciplinary mix similar to the one mentioned in the San Angelo situation, but by city council members (responsible for financing the schools), local businessmen, and members of the state board of education as well. The news media were there in full force. The entire city was in-

203

terested in this group effort. How effective was it? The CRS-conducted Roanoke City School Planning Conference did what we intended it to do. The conference was the kick-off of a large school building program. Dr. E. W. Rushton, Superintendent, summed it up nicely when he said, "We are off to a fine beginning. What we have done is comparable to the best thinking and planning for school buildings in the country." While this may sound a bit ostentatious, the fact is that the conference did successfully educate members of the community to appreciate better schools and solidify its intent to have only the best, educate the school people to think in terms of education/architecture concepts, educate local architects, engineers, and consultants to operate on the leading edge of school planning and construction, and educate the CRS team in understanding of the locality and of the client's needs and values.

A third CRS-conducted "school" (made possible by a grant from Educational Facilities Laboratories) was in the form of six seminars held in January and February 1968. The seminars related to planning an 11,000-student campus on four and one half acres in the Washington Market urban renewal area of lower Manhattan. Dr. Murray H. Block, then President of Manhattan Community College, stated the purpose clearly: "The first stage in planning was to assemble groups of thoughtful people from diversified disciplines, pose the challenge to them, let them react and interact, and use the resulting mosaic of ideas as raw material for later analysis and architectural programming."

Sixty distinguished educators, business leaders, politicians, urban planners and architects attended the seminars. It was more than a "kick-off" to planning a high-rise, high-density urban campus. There was a touch of team. Dr. Block credited the seminars with "generating a body of fresh and farsighted ideas that crystallized a good many problems in a way that will force planners to respond with a theory of campus design that will accommodate itself to the denser and more restricted urban conditions."

Parenthetically, out of this "school" came some fresh thinking about two-year colleges and community involvement. Dr. Edward J. Gleazer, educator, said, "This college is the community—its people, its problems, its issues, aspirations and goals in an organized expression of learning." Dr. Milton Akers, another educator, said, "You must totally involve the neighborhood and its people. Use the neighborhood as a laboratory." One of our architects said, "We need a 'chameleon' type of college that can change with changes in the environment." Charles King, government official involved in social reform, said, "Think of it as an educational halfway house." Hon. Harmon Goldstone, then a Commissioner on the City Planning Commission, said, "Make it a wonderful mixture of town and gown with the whole emphasis on participation." Most of the ideas concerned reaching out into the neighborhood—no ivy-covered walls that separated college and community. An interesting interpretation of this prime idea was that the majority of the participants believed the college should be "a 24-hour learning center." For Manhattan this makes sense.

These three examples of formal "schools" conducted by CRS represent only a small part of total education that takes place in a firm such as ours. Professional development must be continuous on an everyday basis.

Section 8

People Who Play on Teams

Good people with special individual capabilities, working with unity of purpose, make the team go. But there is something else which contributes to the power of the team. Coaches call it team spirit, whatever that is. Certainly, team spirit is hard to define. Among other things, team spirit is the atmosphere created when people love to work together, when there is harmony of minds, a willingness to share loads, respect for every individual's capacity, belief that the team can do almost anything, and room for each team member to express his individuality. With team spirit, a team can go.

75

People come first

Any qualified administrator can design an organizational structure to help do the tasks at hand. What the administrator cannot do is to design a person. Regardless of how cleverly conceived an organization, how beautiful its organizational charts, or how thoughtfully planned and skillfully executed the day-to-day operations, whether the organization accomplishes things efficiently still depends upon its people. Frank Lloyd Wright said, "No stream rises higher than its source. Whatever man might build could never express or reflect more than he was."

The first concern of any firm is to recruit the best talent available; to see that the talent grows; to assure dedication to the task and to perfect team action. Then greatness can be approached.

PROFESSIONAL GROWTH OF ANY SPECIALIZED TEAM MEMBER: DEPENDS UPON HIS ABILITY TO BROADEN HIS LIBERAL ARTS BASE. TO GO UP ONE MUST GO WIDE.

Take the case of one of our capable leaders, Mike Trower. We spotted him as a potential member of our team when he was a junior at Oklahoma State University. A number of us had graduated from O.S.U. and had kept in touch, particularly with our former professor, Philip A. Wilber (later an associate and consultant). Wilber many times said, "Keep your eye on Mike. He's got what it takes." As expected, Mike graduated number one in his class. He came to Houston to join our CRS team. He was one of the very few new graduates who did not want to be in the design group, although he was one of the best designers in his class (now most graduates want to be in programming). "I want to learn how you put things together; so put me in working drawings." After giving Mike a thorough indoctrination in production, we saw that he had a wide exposure to other facets of architectural practice, particularly to the managerial aspects and client relationships. He was out of school less than two and one half years when he had "man-to-man" client contact with a Vice President of Harvard University. Certainly, this should dispel the notion that new graduates must serve a "three-year slave period" before being registered to practice. Before Mike was thirty, we gave him the responsibility of the Connecticut project office. Later, we gave him a professional leave, paying his tuition, expenses, and salary to attend the four-month management course in Harvard's Graduate School of Business. Now in his early thirties, he is still learning—for two reasons: he is completely dedicated to CRS and committed to professional development. And CRS is giving him every opportunity to grow.

So people come first. First you have to get them. Then you help them grow.

76

People on a team must learn to work together

Admittedly, there are some few activities within the scope of architectural practice that an individual can best do by himself. But most tasks must be related to other tasks. An artist can go off in a corner and make a rendering of a building, but if the rendering does not communicate to the client what the designers have in mind, then time has been wasted and purpose unaccomplished. A heating engineer can go into isolation to determine the size and general location of the main supply hot-water line with a high degree of engineering efficiency, but if the line is required to go through the middle of an important beam, he must collaborate with the structural engineer. So must the designers. If not, the building may fall down aesthetically (not to mention actually). Specialists who design buildings must get together in team action. The better they can collaborate, the better the chance that the building will perform as it should.

This is the way the Industry school turned out—clean and uncomplicated. It was one of the first double-loaded schools in America with "outside" corridors. Harry Ransom took the design lead.

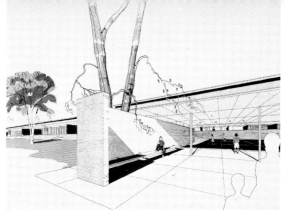

There is such a thing as rendering by team. In the fifties quite often three or four of us would work on one small sketch, complementing each other's talents. For example, the sketch above was submitted during presentation of preliminary drawings for a little elementary school in Industry, Texas. Bob Reed did the inkwork of the building itself; Cleon Bellamy did the figures; I did the trees; and John Rowlett did the color work. We developed a CRS style. Many architects would say, "The sketches are so simple and clear. Who is *the* artist in your firm? We would like to have him do a rendering for us." Even after we told them, they never believed rendering by team was possible.

To be effective in team action, the individual should have the following characteristics:

(a) ability to communicate
(b) tolerance of other opinions
(c) empathy with others
(d) willingness to associate
(e) talent and experience relating to task
(f) attitude assuring professional interchange
(g) team spirit.

Teams are usually formed to do specific tasks. Either the people on teams must already know how to work together or they must learn very quickly, for most tasks have to be done in a hurry. The success of the task depends upon the talent, the experience, and the willingness to cooperate. This "willingness" is the key. I recall the time I was a graduate student at M.I.T. The first semester was strictly doing problems on an individual

211

TO EFFECTIVELY
COMMUNICATE,

ONE MUST BE AN
INTERLOCKER —
ENGAGED, INVOLVED,
RELATED, AND
TUNED IN.

basis. Four of us, forgive the immodesty, were truly outstanding as individuals. The second semester was to be devoted to a cooperative project. The "big four" therefore decided to team up. What a combination we would make! All that talent working on one project—how could we miss?

As it turned out, our "team" effort was a disaster. We did no work to speak of. We fussed throughout the entire project. Each of us wanted to be *the* designer. This was natural. Each was taught to be a prima donna. The miracle was how we ever finished the project.

While we fussed, a less talented group worked cooperatively, bringing into full play their diversified talents and experiences. Their project turned out to be far superior to ours.

This view of the Olin Hall of Science, Colorado College, shows the peripheral utility core by the six-foot deep ravine of the windows. The double wall houses the vertical structural supports and all of the myriad of pipes and conduits needed to supply a science lab. The concept of flexibility agreed upon by the faculty committee headed by Dr. Will Wright (one of the best user clients we ever had) is reflected in this statement made by one of the professors: "Let's design a science building that can be changed as easily as an office building." We just about did it.

They had team "willingness." We did not.

To the architect who was trained to dictate rather than collaborate, team action comes hard. Even in the oldest teams there are still "I" people among the "we" people. There still prevails the "me against the rest" attitude. The only way of dissolving this attitude and solving the problem of inner conflict is:

• to instill an appreciation and empathy for the worth of others in fulfillment of team goals;
• to continually develop better ways of communication in team matters.

The first consideration requires that the individual member place team over self to a certain degree. This is hard for him to swallow. It means that the acceptance of team goals supercedes any that are purely personal. It means that the individual must be able to imagine himself filling the positions of his teammates, seeing things from their point of view. He must have full appreciation of the work of these professional associates. Without this appreciation, there is no team spirit. Without team spirit, there will be no outstanding team performance.

The second consideration—finding ways to communicate—is just as difficult to do. In the early days of CRS during a rather heated discussion in a partnership meeting, Tom Bullock said, "Our problem is that we do not communicate." Wallie Scott articulated the problem even better when he replied, "What do you mean?"

A member of a team cannot think or act in isolation. He must somehow project his thoughts to his teammates.

A few economical lines on yellow tracing paper might be just what is needed.

During the fifties, eight of us learned to fly and we had three airplanes. That was the time when we could make a living 300 to 400 miles from home. Small airplanes proved profitable. Now that we are spread all over the United States, and all over the globe, we have to use the commercial jets. Wallie Scott is shown on right.

"WE OPERATED BY
SILENT SIGNALS."

A memo might do the trick.

An informal discussion over a drafting table may be in order.

A serious, formal, verbal/graphic presentation may be required.

Or perhaps all that is needed—as Richard Neutra used to say—is a "wink of the eye—to seal common understanding."

Once there are empathy and communication among the members, the team will move and every member will benefit. Without the two, people cannot work together. Without the two, there is no team.

77

Can a strong individual play on a team?

People will argue about the gnawing problem of the individual versus the group for years to come. Some will take the stand that group activities have a downward leveling effect on the individual, that groups will deny the expression of individualism, that to play on a team will smother creativity, that teamwork will force conformity, and that groups generally nullify and limit human endeavors. And to some extent these critics will be right.

Every team needs strong men. Every strong man needs the backing of other people to do the thing he wants to do. A champion needs a team. And a championship team needs highly individualistic "all-Americans." Strong, substantive people are necessary if the team is to move. The stronger the individuals, the better the team—provided its members learn to work together.

Strong individuals, unaccustomed to working on teams, will run into trouble. It took about two years each for key people like Norman Hoover, Charles Thomsen, and Paul Kennon to be effective members of CRS. At first, each complained that team action resisted creativity. Each felt the need for self-expression and believed he was not getting it. And to a degree, they were right. Team action does have its restrictions.

Two problems existed: The CRS team has a natural tendency to reject experienced transplants. Perhaps we did not readily accept these new men who came to us with new thoughts and "strange" forms. So it was partly our fault. The other reason was that our people felt that these new men were more interested in self-expression than team-expression. As one of our people said, "He won't listen to me." And there was some truth to this. Nothing malicious. The fact was that these new people had not yet developed the art of collaboration. It takes about two years. It took

Designer-partner Charles Lawrence took a strong lead in creating the Institute of Texan Culture, San Antonio. A University of Texas graduate, Lawrence possesses a sensitivity of form and space that is rare. To him design is a philosophy covering everything from eating a meal to a discussion on architectural ecology.

THERE IS

STRENGTH IN DIVERSITY PROVIDED INDIVIDUAL DIFFERENCES ARE RECOGNIZED.

THE MERGENCE OF A DROP OF MERCURY INTO A **BLOB** IS NOT A TEAM CHARACTERISTIC.

A **TEAM** IS MORE LIKE A STRING OF PEARLS.

me ten years just to learn to communicate with Charles Lawrence. It was worth the waiting. What a great designer he is. He is particularly adept at meticulous detailing. To him composing the parts of a door jamb is as challenging as composing the parts of a city. I recall the time Lawrence purchased a sports coat at a bargain price. But he did not like the buttons. By the time he switched buttons, the new buttons cost more money than the coat. The point is that a team needs "button men"—someone to look after the little things.

Little things bother even broad brush people like Tom Bullock, who spent $200.00 removing some of the doodads on a new car he purchased. It takes all kinds of people to make a good team—particulary strong individuals.

Each member of the team retains his individuality. Individualism and team action need not be in opposition; in fact, the very strength of the team lies in the highly personal contribution of each member of the team, contributions which mold the team into a whole which is far greater and stronger than the sum of the individual components.

Architects who have not worked with the team must rethink their image of the team. I used to consider architectural teams as a blob of mercury —a blob which came into being when four or five or more components came together, merged, and were henceforth indistinguishable in the blob of the whole.

Today I know better. Architectural teams are, rather, more like a string of pearls—composed of readily distinguishable individual members, tied together in unity of purpose. Members must maintain their individuality; the team derives its strength from the individual contribution of each member.

78

Team members must learn to "fight and make up"

Our experience at CRS has taught us that team play can get rough, that the team can be a tough thing to handle. In fact, we have learned that tempers often fly, and that tension is part of the team experience, part of reconciling diverse opinions and philosophies in the process of building a better product.

FRICTION IS INEVITABLE.

Yet somehow, when there is friction, even when tempers seem to have gotten out of hand, extra energy is created, energy that helps people think more clearly, do their work more quickly, and put out that extra effort which makes a superior product. It's wrong to look at the team as just one big happy family.

There was the period when Willie Pena and Frank Lawyer would hardly speak to each other. Frank came to me after one particularly argumentative squatters and said, "Willie is the most negative person I have ever known. He says 'no' to every idea I have. I don't ever want to be with him again on a task team." Shortly after that, Pena complained, "Bill, what are we going to do with Frank? He just will not pay attention to the functional aspects. Or to cost controls. I know this job is going over the budget if Frank gets his way all the time. How can we convince him that programming is the prelude to good design? He absolutely ignores the program. All he is interested in is pretty form."

What they did not know at the time was that each needed the other. And badly. Lawyer was inclined to be too much of a formalist, Pena too much a functionalist. Because of their opposing views and talents, there existed

For me the design of the CRS building, completed in December 1969, was a headache from start to finish. We knew what we were in for. Four years before starting the plans for our first "home" the partnership was nearly broken up when we changed the design of the stationery. It was decided that there was only one hardened SOB in CRS who could pull it off—the design of our new building. I was elected and was given a relatively inexperienced team. After two miserable attempts at trying to please the worst client I ever had—thirty partner-architects-engineers-planners and forty profit-sharing associates —we finally "hid" ourselves in a U-Totem warehouse and completed the plans, away from the worried eyes of over-emotional designer types. During the height of this fiasco Wallie Scott became what I considered overly critical to my sensitive, raw nerves. Tom Bullock, in the peacemaker's role he so often played, went to Scott with this comment: "Wallie, you are too hard on Bill. He said you said that he had a bastard design." Scott replied, "Tom, I did not! I said it was a terrible design!" Team is tough. Scott, in moments of weakness, has told me he likes part of our building, particularly the view above.

a highly desirable symbiotic relationship needed to produce better buildings.

After many more fights which lasted nearly a year, Lawyer and Pena finally learned to work together. It was more than mere reconciliation. It was learning the art of give and take. Lawyer found that Pena more than anyone else in CRS (and the United States) could help give meaning to his form. Pena found too that were it not for Lawyer's great design talent, the buildings which might work with efficiency might never produce architecture.

LAWYER AND PENA FINALLY LEARNED TO WORK TOGETHER --AND VERY EFFECTIVELY.

Consider that with the involvement of many people there will necessarily be some negative reactions, some positive ones, and that from the struggle will emerge better solutions to the problems at hand. One man's idea will set off another man's idea, and a chain reaction will take place, a reaction which allows both men to rethink their ideas, to verbalize thoughts which they formerly could not have expressed.

In team action, all opinions should be valued—because each member of the team has been selected for his excellence in a specific field necessary to the successful completion of the project. We have learned, then, that the team should be a sounding board for all opinions.

Veterans of team action at CRS love to talk about the in-fighting which goes on in our "yell rooms," about how they barely got over one philosophical impasse before another came into being, about how the young Turks fought the old hands, about the labor pains they all suffered in the process of creative team endeavors. Somehow, the stories always end with a miraculous togetherness of team members after the fights—and the creation of architecture, made possible by the establishment of a situation in which group dynamics could occur.

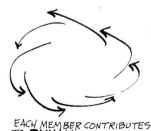

EACH MEMBER CONTRIBUTES TO DYNAMICS OF TEAM.

TEAM ACTION REQUIRES
STRONGER LEADERSHIP
THAN DICTATORSHIP.

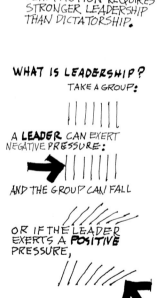

WHAT IS LEADERSHIP?

TAKE A GROUP:

A **LEADER** CAN EXERT
NEGATIVE PRESSURE:

AND THE GROUP CAN FALL

OR IF THE LEADER
EXERTS A **POSITIVE**
PRESSURE,

THE GROUP CAN BE
RAISED.

79

A team must have strong leaders

The most talented, experienced, and willing people cannot perform as a smooth-running team unless there is strong leadership. Paradoxically, it takes stronger leadership to run a team—a democratic social group—than it does to guide people performing in a dictatorial situation, where there is no opportunity for personal opinion.

The best team for the creation of architecture is one in which authoritative management has given way to free-form team cooperation where team participation has replaced simple fulfillment of orders. The result is that the traditional pyramidal organization is superceded by a new management substructure—those members of the team who do not actually manage, but who, because of their strong professional skills and experiences, have a strong voice in decision making.

Leaders thus have a tough time, because they are leaders, and not bosses. They allow for differences of opinion, and do not impose their prejudices. They persuade, rather than command. The word "team" does not imply that decisions are made by vote or that all the leaders of the team are mere tabulators of group opinion. Rather, team leaders must be strong enough to go against the current of prevailing opinion when necessary.

The leader need not be a popular person, but he must be highly capable, possess strength of conviction, and have the ability to meld a variety of sometimes conflicting viewpoints and opinions into a unified and efficient course of action. Thus, the strong team leader might possess qualities which the popularly elected team leader, the man liked by all, might not possess.

Leading a team is an art. Sometimes this takes gentle persuasion. Sometimes it takes the Machiavellian touch. Sometimes it takes a hands-off attitude. Sometimes praise. The leader must see that every member of the team is pulling his share of the load—and pulling it in the right direction.

Two of the best leaders CRS has ever had were Willie Pena, a master at gentle persuasion, and Tom Bullock, more dictatorial in a sense, but with charismatic qualities. Pena might have been termed a "quiet leader" (his own term) and Bullock a "loud leader" (more like me in the early days). When Bullock blew his top, things happened. I recall Tom's saying, "Every time I smile, we lose money!" Not true. Tom had a way of kidding us into action. He relied heavily on his humor to make CRS move as a group. Willie took an entirely different approach—soft, intellectual, logical, and on a man-to-man basis.

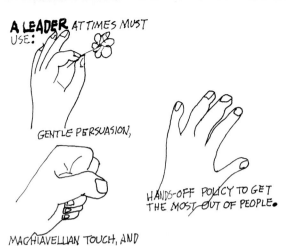

A LEADER AT TIMES MUST USE: GENTLE PERSUASION, MACHIAVELLIAN TOUCH, AND HANDS-OFF POLICY TO GET THE MOST OUT OF PEOPLE.

Tom Bullock, with one of the best native minds in CRS, is active in all phases of CRS operations. His complete dedication to making the profession viable and relevant to this day and tomorrow carries him all over the country giving speeches and working with other architects toward improving architectural practice; yet he still has the energy and enthusiasm to be one of the driving forces for making the CRS team go. He serves as president of the CRS corporation. This is a 1970 photograph taken during one of the CRS juries. Rice University's Professor Jack Mitchell, an invited juror, is shown in the background.

The leader must be less interested in personal power than in creating an environment which maximizes human resources. He should encourage many kinds of interaction and should set the stage so that group dynamics may take place. He should maintain an openness of communication, giving every idea a hearing, and every member a chance to voice his opinions to the group.

The leader must also be one who—at times—is willing to relinquish his position of leadership to another with expertise in a certain necessary area. A true leader can lead from any position. And one of the great beauties of the team is that any member, depending upon the circumstances at hand, can "lead" at different times.

80

Each member plays a role in the democracy of the team

Opinions count. But democratic action in team play is not a matter of voting on every question that comes up; in fact, such a method would be disastrous when creative architectural solutions are at stake.

Rather, the successful team is a democratic structure in that:

• Each member has his say.
• Each member has unique experience and competencies which help the other members to complete the task at hand.
• Each team member has specific jobs to do in which his performance will largely determine how effectively the other members will do their jobs.

- Each member is respected for how well he does his job rather than what he does because all tasks in team operation depend upon the completion of other tasks.
- Each member of the team is insured of his freedom because his worth depends upon freedom to act creatively, and criticize objectively.

The team must never be regarded as a free-for-all, however. Like a democracy, the team must operate within an ordered framework so that individual input may produce maximum benefits.

81

The team member—participant or pencil sharpener?

The prima donna usually gives a degree of credit to the people working under him by referring to them as "my team"—with heavy emphasis on the "my." But in essence, his teammates are mere lackeys in the Beaux Arts sense. They are there strictly to serve him, drawing up his ideas (or sharpening his pencils so he can do the drawings), not to cope with the task. Such a "team" is more like a one-man gang. The key to holding together a group like this is dictatorship. A few years ago, architects could get by with this sort of thing, but not today. No team member wants to be a full-time pencil sharpener.

At CRS, we try to start our green newcomers on a team by instilling in them a team consciousness, then by teaming them with highly experienced people. Sure some of the green ones have to do menial tasks— even sharpen a few pencils. But they are not lackeys. They are there to learn.

Frank Lawyer and I were too dependent upon each other for years. The partners finally broke up our combination because they thought I might be holding him back. Now I feel they may have been right. Olin Hall (right) is a product of the Lawyer/Caudill design effort. When Frank did the first sketch of the greenhouse, a difficult composition in constricting forms and materials, I yelled in delight, "Frank, that's wonderful. It's like pouring hot fudge on ice cream." To this day I think Lawyer is the most talented architectural composer in the business.

The faculty committee for planning Olin Hall of Science, Colorado College—a few of the thirty-member group are shown here—actually was part of the CRS team. During the squatters, six worked all night with us. The woman in the foreground, a science professor, conceived the name "exoskeletal structure" applied to the peripheral utility core. She said that the building was built like a grasshopper with all the "bones and guts in the skin."

For many years, Frank Lawyer was my understudy. But the first day he came into the office, I knew that there was much to be learned from this rookie. He had more talent to "think through his hands" than anyone I had ever come across. He was a highly talented artist right out of school. Frank was never a flunky on the CRS team. If anything, as a wise leader, I was his pencil sharpener.

Frank and I, through the years, learned how to work together, and we helped design such prize-winning buildings as the Olin Hall of Science, Colorado College; San Angelo High School in Texas; and Larsen Hall at Harvard. Since then he has designed many beautiful, functional buildings without Caudill looking over his shoulder.

The understudies are not the only ones who have their frustrations. Our partner, Paul Kennon, has had as his understudy a most sensitive, talented, deeply intellectual young man, Eddy Bejar. Kennon worked with Eddy for months, teaching him new skills and new methods of architectural practice. If given the right guidance and opportunity, Eddy could be a great designer. There was a beautiful teacher-pupil relationship going. Then Eddy came to Paul and said he wanted to go back to school to get his Ph.D. in Spanish literature, and become a professor. That is frustration of the highest order.

From the beginning CRS has always considered the client as a member of the team. I recall Tom Bullock's comment after we jubilantly received the news from Harvard University that we had been chosen to design the Graduate School of Education Building. It sobered us up a bit. He said, "They didn't hire us. They hired themselves." He was right. The members of the building committee knew that we would respect and value their judgment. We did. The client proved to be a major team participant.

THE CLIENT IS ON THE TEAM.

82

Two types of thinkers make the team

IDEA PEOPLE AND DEVELOPERS
NEED EACH OTHER.

There seem to be two kinds of thinkers—the idea people and the developers. Idea people come up with the ideas. Developers see that those ideas reach fruition. Idea people are not usually organizers (but there are exceptions). They often lack the necessary follow-through, and would rather explore other, newer, ideas than develop the older ones. The developer has a single-mindedness and determination to carry out the ideas. He likes to "wrap up packages." Developers are rather more rigid and often are quite dogmatic. They give stability to the team.

A team needs both kinds of people—developers and idea people. The developers should not be undervalued; often dedication to the development of an idea is more important than the creation of the idea.

We have been most fortunate in having completely dedicated developers—Bob Walters, Ed Nye, Bill Perry, Don Wines, Bill Steely, and Jim Hughes—whose talents allow them to get things done. We would not be where we are today without their ability to build from ideas. They are the great stabilizers of CRS. Don't misunderstand. The idea people hold no monopoly on creativity. The developers, too, must be creative, but at a different level.

THE **CREATIVE** PERSON
ENERGIZES THE TEAM.

We have also been very fortunate to have idea people at the top leadership level. For the first ten years or so, I led the total CRS team. Most certainly, I am not a developer. I like to start things, but lack follow-through. That's why I have the utmost appreciation for the developers. Ideas come fast to me, but I know more than anyone else that ideas are useless without dedication and developmental talent to bring such ideas into reality.

Tom Bullock, who succeeded me as head of CRS, was even more creative. He designed administrative structures. The man was full of ideas for making CRS operate better, which, in turn, helped us to produce better buildings. If Tom did not actually design buildings himself, he designed the creative climate to get the buildings designed.

Herb Paseur, who took over after Bullock, is another idea person. At one time, he was chief designer of the Oklahoma City office, responsible for some superb pioneering school plants. But as the managerial director of the total CRS operation, his creativity flourished even more. Like Bullock, his ideas relate to improving the process. Herb would say, "When we improve the process, we automatically improve the product." His innovations relating to organizational and operational procedures have unquestionably improved the CRS product. His reorganization of CRS into separate profit centers and spheres of responsibilities has particularly improved operations of this firm. While most of us think *things,* Paseur thinks *people*— how they can best work together in the interest of creating architecture.

How to get highly creative people to work together in efficient team play is the most pressing problem of architectural management. The very survival of the architectural profession may depend upon how this problem is solved.

Creative people energize the team. Developers get the job done.

Here is a view of Tom Bullock's AIA Regional Award winning home. The young people in CRS were completely surprised that our highly capable administrator could also design. Tom enjoys getting back on the board. In the early days of CRS, working under Scott, he proved to be one of the best design development architects we ever had. The exquisitely detailed schools in Port Arthur were the result of Bullock's sensitivity to the "little things." But today Bullock's ability to switch roles makes him the best "big things" man we have.

83

Democratic action recognizes people differences

There is no equality of talent and experience. Some designers in CRS can go six times as fast as others and the results are of better quality.

There is no equal degree of creativity. Some people are creative in everything they do.

To get equal pay and have equal vote has no validity. If a good leader were responsible for a group in the woods and the group was lost, most certainly there would be no vote. The leader would seek and accept the opinion of those in the group who had the most experience and knowledge in getting out of such predicaments, trusting their judgment over his own.

When we were planning the San Angelo High School, we got "lost in the woods" four or five times. One time the problem concerned the selection of the most economical and functional structural system. As the partner-in-charge, I certainly did not call for a show of hands. I told Ed Nye, our structural engineer, to take a cold professional look at the situation and present his proposal. Thank goodness I was wise enough to take his opinion over my own. Had we gone the way I thought best, we would really have run into trouble. I wished, however, I had overruled the suggestion of using a folded plate roof shape over the circular auditorium form because we got caught in the bottom of the cliché barrel. That was the only faddish form on the campus. The other ten buildings were strictly bullseyes, resulting in fresh, meaningful forms.

Voting in team action simply won't do. Being smart enough to know whom to trust—recognizing people's differences—is the key to team leadership.

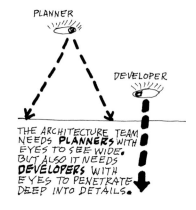

PLANNER

DEVELOPER

THE ARCHITECTURE TEAM NEEDS **PLANNERS** WITH EYES TO SEE WIDE. BUT ALSO IT NEEDS **DEVELOPERS** WITH EYES TO PENETRATE DEEP INTO DETAILS.

The San Angelo High School above was our structural-engineer partner Ed Nye's first job with CRS. He was a major participant and contributor of the team which designed this pioneering high school. I recall during the hectic days of meeting with the school board weekly, sometimes twice a week for what seemed months, arguing about the design proposals, the superintendent, G. B. Wadzeck, said, "Bill, you are getting a terrible beating these days by the board. Next time why don't you bring Ed Nye to help you win a few battles?" Excellent advice. Ed, who is not as emotional as I, calmed the board down and lifted me into a higher position of negotiation. Team leaders need line backing too.

84

Team members may be in one of three stages of professional life

The first stage is the *adolescent* stage. In a way, it is a glorious period. The young architect-to-be is just out of school or soon will graduate. He has great ambitions to save the world through architecture. He thinks he is capable of doing anything. He has enthusiasm. He loves to pioneer. He tries to be original, and is generally confused with misplaced values. He is usually more interested in beautiful models and sexy renderings than in actual construction. When the buildings are built, he likes to see and feel the spaces without people who "get in the way of architecture." He prefers not to revisit a building after the users have moved in, marring the spaces with furniture and scarring the forms with use. His self-expression preponderates over user satisfaction. But these freewheeling young professionals have vitality that only youth can provide. Every team needs these rookies, but it is wise to mix these adolescent professionals with the experienced pros. It is a two-way rub-off.

The second stage is *maturity.* It has nothing to do with the age of the person. Some middle-aged architects are simply retarded adolescents in terms of professional development. A mature professional possesses an inner, often quiet enthusiasm. He still has originality, but tempered with the experience to make a source of originality. Now he is grown up and can make wise decisions. He has reexamined his values and has established clearer goals. He has developed an open mind for the deserving young members of the team and is willing to teach them to assume roles of leadership. He is receptive to new ideas and is instrumental in giving them form. He builds upon experience. He has taken advantage of the opportunities of professional growth through research and education. He has a social consciousness that makes him want to go back to see how the spaces and forms help people go about their daily tasks. He is much more interested in actual buildings and their spaces than in renderings and models. Pleasing the users of buildings has become more important than self-expression. Experience, confidence, and competence replace outward display of enthusiasm.

The third stage for some architects is that of *old age*—the period of "over the hill." It is characterized by extreme conservatism, concentration on details, and an overemphasis on organizational procedures and the tendency to hold to old but "proven techniques." Innovation becomes too risky. Professional senility starts setting in.

"Old age" professionals quite often cause an organizational crust which will not allow the young people to rise to the top. These over-the hill professionals become either too disinterested to revisit buildings after the users have moved in, or they wish to avoid the complaints. There is often an emphasis on economic security over the desire to create artecture.

THE SADDEST CASE IS WHEN A PROMISING YOUNGSTER NEVER DEVELOPS PROFESSIONALLY.

The saddest case is when a promising youngster never develops professionally and goes directly from the adolescent period into the old age stage. It happens quite often. There is nothing so sad as to see a thirty-year-old architect with good potential get caught in this stage of extreme conservatism with more desire to make money than to make architecture happen. "Old age" need not be.

As has been pointed out, not all people go through these stages of the usual progression. Some skip the period of professional maturity all together. Some never get out of the adolescent age, regardless of how old

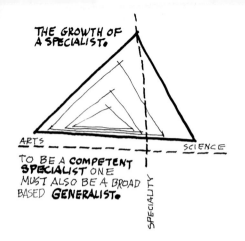

THE GROWTH OF A SPECIALIST.

ARTS — — — — — — SCIENCE

SPECIALTY

TO BE A **COMPETENT SPECIALIST** ONE MUST ALSO BE A BROAD BASED **GENERALIST.**

IF A TEAM MEMBER OR A **TEAM** OPERATES ON A NARROW BASE, NOT ONLY ARE THERE LIMITS TO THE HEIGHTS OF DEVELOPED COMPETENCY,

BUT THERE EXISTS THE DANGER OF THE SPECIALTY BECOMING **OBSOLETE.** WITH THE BROAD BASE A **NEW** SPECIALTY CAN BE DEVELOPED.

COMPETENCE LEVEL

they are. The good ones, however, extend the life by staying "mature" for years through profiting by the accumulative experience and constant renewal. The really good ones never reach "old age." The great masters, Wright, Corbusier, Mies van der Rohe, and Gropius, were doing creative, pioneering work in their eighties.

85

Beware of overspecialization

Researchers are so prolific that information in most fields doubles every ten years. In any specific field the amount of highly relevant information is so immense it cannot be retrieved even with sophisticated computer methods. A biology professor, a client, once said that it was cheaper in the long run to start a research project from scratch than to try to find out what has been done. The only way out is to narrow the field to areas of specialties where each is manageable and where depth can be assured.

Yet one can become overspecialized and get trapped in his own foxhole. A firm can also get caught in the same kind of trap. This has been the strongest argument against the hyphenated architects—the church-architect, the school-architect, the house-architect and so on.

Only through specialization can professional depth be achieved. So it is worth the risk—both for firms and for individuals. Specialization must grow from a broad, multidisciplinary base.

CRS started out specializing in schools. We found that even a building-type specialization such as a schoolhouse requires an unusually broad

base. Planning a school, for example, includes everything from educational psychology to computerized programming. And in an educational plant there are many different building types. A high school in a small city generally has the largest restaurant in town, the largest theater, the largest recreation center, and some of the best industrial shops.

The scope of specialization is not so narrow as one might think. The specialized architect has to be an unusually broad person. When the "architect" is a team, and most are these days, the team must first be a good generalist.

A team (or a person) aspiring to reach the top in any specialty must have a very large interdisciplinary base of operation—from abstract art to business to engineering. The broader the base the higher one can go.

At one time CRS was dangerously close to specializing in only little elementary schoolhouses like this. We dearly loved to do them, and did them quite well. This pleasant (to both students and teachers) small school in Liberty, Texas was one of our best. Designed in 1956 for a rainy, hot climate, Charles Lawrence led the design effort with Pena on programming and Scott as project manager. The Lawrence/Pena combination worked together on many projects. The chemistry of team action is still a mystery. All we know is that it's there.

233

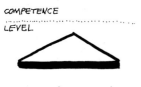

COMPETENCE
LEVEL

A PERSON (OR A FIRM) CAN
SPREAD HIMSELF TOO THIN.

SPECIALIZATION IS...

...LIKE STACKING CANS OF
TOMATOES--TO GO UP
HIGHER CANS MUST BE
ADDED AT THE **BOTTOM**.
THERE MUST BE A BROAD
LIBERAL ARTS BASE.

Both large and small firms (or individuals) get caught spreading themselves too thin. With fewer team members the small firms must limit their specialties. If a project requires high competence in more than what the firm can offer, then there is the necessity to bring in outside consultants to "balance the team." This is why there has been an increasing number of consultants—hospital consultants, educational consultants, acoustical consultants, many varieties of engineering consultants, and computer technology consultants.

Large firms working on larger and more complex projects generally have these specialists as permanent members of their teams. If not, they seek them out as needed. During the past few years the CRS firm has been hiring an increasing number of nonarchitects, particularly in the behavioral sciences and computer technology to help give balance to the team. It also has added building-type specialists so as to have more than one peak rising from the multidisciplinary base—providing specialization in hospitals, civic centers, office buildings, university and college education, as well as the elementary and secondary schools which were the original specialty. The total CRS team has at least one national leader in each of these areas of specialization.

86

Team members play different roles

Every member of a team has strengths and weaknesses. A team functions best when the strengths are brought into full play and the weaknesses are kept in the background.

The challenge of successful team action is for each person to play roles he is most qualified to play. To assign the role properly one must know the qualification profiles of different people as related to management, design, and technology.

Take Frank Lawyer for example: A qualification profile of this great artistic architect would show that he is very strong in design, just so-so in management, and very light in technology. During our Corning, New York, days, we tried to make an administrator out of him. Ridiculous! Why should this great design talent be smothered to death in management routines?

Consider Jack Smith's qualification profile. He is very strong in management and technology, but light in design, at least in comparison with Lawyer. On the other hand, Bob Reed's strength is in management and design; however, I would judge him to be relatively weak in technology (except in natural light and ventilation in which he excels). Ed Nye's qualification profile would still be completely different, since he is very strong in technology, particularly the structural and estimating aspects of buildings.

I'll probably be criticized for making these comparisons. My out is this: qualification profiles change from year to year, depending upon how a person develops.

A highly competent architectural specialist is always a good generalist. He has to be. The notion that all good designers are poor managers and poor technologists is not valid.

Generally, however, each professional does have his long suit. He should play the roles he is best qualified to play.

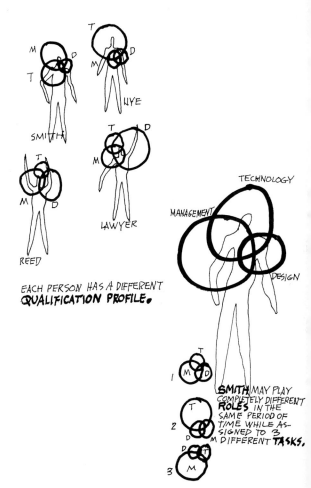

EACH PERSON HAS A DIFFERENT **QUALIFICATION PROFILE.**

SMITH MAY PLAY COMPLETELY DIFFERENT ROLES IN THE SAME PERIOD OF TIME WHILE ASSIGNED TO 3 DIFFERENT TASKS.

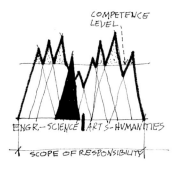

COMPETENCE LEVEL

ENGR.–SCIENCE | ARTS–HUMANITIES

SCOPE OF RESPONSIBILITY

THIS IS WHAT A **TEAM** LOOKS LIKE. THE SCOPE OF RESPONSIBILITY IS TOO GREAT FOR A SINGLE ARCHITECT TO HANDLE.

What would a team profile look like? Triangular profiles of competence might well be made of each member of the team, so that at a glance one could see how extensively broad is the base of the member and how high is the competency of his specialization. The team profile would consist of all members' profiles superimposed.

87
Who gets the credit?

One of the most perplexing problems of team operation is how credit can be given to the individual. Every architect wants credit whether he operates alone or plays on a team. Every team member wants to be a hero. But when fifty people design a building, crediting effort and performance becomes quite a problem.

In the early days of CRS when two firms were selected to work on projects, it was found that during the negotiation between the firms the greatest arguments were not about the division of fee but the division of credit. There was a fierce pride about who would get first billing between the associating firms. An arrangement which seemed to work in most cases was for the local architect's name to appear first in the local situation and CRS to come first in the national situation. More recently this problem has been less acute.

All architects vie for credit. As mentioned, the trouble lies on the outside as well as on the inside. If outsiders—the press, critics, writers, and others —continue to identify creative achievement with single individuals instead of with the combined effort of many creative individuals helping each other toward one common goal, the idea of the team will never be understood.

The press wants to know what *one* person designed the building. It had a reporter call me aside after a public presentation which emphasized team effort and say, "Now, Mr. Caudill, who really did design this building? It was your idea, wasn't it?" I answered, "Hell no! I did not design it. We did. If you must name names put in as many as you can, certainly no less than three—the manager, the designer, and the technologist."

When Jones Hall for the Performing Arts won an AIA National Award of Merit, I got into a lot of trouble with the AIA Headquarters by insisting that three of our people's names be included on the plaque instead of the one which was already engraved. As it finally turned out, Tom Bullock's name was included in management, Charles Lawrence in design, and James Gatton in technology. However, many other people should have been credited. But the plaque simply was not big enough.

The 1967 AIA award winning plaque for Jones Hall gave these credits: Tom Bullock on management, Charles Lawrence on design, and James Gatton on technology. And rightly so if only three names are to be mentioned. However, many other highly talented people participated, including Wallie Scott, Frank Lawyer, Willie Pena, Ed Nye, James Thomas, and (yes!) Bill Caudill.

Some of our people in CRS prefer to give no credit to the individual, just to the team. I am against this. Individual credit is needed for professional growth. When a person writes an article or gives a speech, it is difficult not to give him credit.

I contend that where credit is due, credit should be given—but not to the detriment of team spirit.

88

People can combine their talents to make the team a genius

In his time, five centuries ago, Leonardo da Vinci was a generalist—a combined designer, technologist, and manager. He could do most anything and do it well—the original jack-of-all-trades. As a plumber he fixed the drains of Italy's palaces. As a military engineer he was a wizard at draining lakes. His findings in geology are still valid. He left us excellent models of flying machines. He was an architect of great renown. In between all these endeavors da Vinci painted and sculpted a bit. He first came up with the idea of the contact lens, too. He was a generalist genius.

There are not many geniuses like da Vinci around these days. If there were, they would be hard pressed to cope with all of today's technology which demands specialization. One could argue that there are generalist specialists who probe in certain areas. A twentieth-century da Vinci would probably be heading a space exploring team or leading an organ transplant team of surgeons or some other exotic pioneering endeavor. Whatever he would be doing, the chances are he would do it with a team.

LEONARDO DA VINCI QUALIFICATION PROFILE MIGHT LOOK SOMETHING LIKE THIS:

TODAY STANDARDS

ARTS   SCIENCE

HE WAS QUITE A **GENERALIST GENIUS**—IN HIS DAY. IN THIS DAY HE WOULD NOT FARE SO WELL. IT TAKES A TEAM TO SOLVE THE MANY INTERRELATED PROBLEMS OF BUILDING. **THE TEAM IS A GENIUS.**

ARTS   SCIENCE

A MIES OR CORBU TYPE ARCHITECT

And if he chose to do something relating to making the world a better place in which to live, architecturally speaking, he most certainly would do this in team action. There would be no other choice.

The fact is, however, that if the makeup of the group is right, a team can be a genius—more of a genius than da Vinci ever was. Its intellectually creative capacity covers a broader scope and possesses greater depth within each area included in the scope than one genius could ever master. All it takes then is the ability to learn to work together.

People who play on teams cherish this thought: The team is a genius.

A team needs people who can paint with the broad brush, squint their eyes to see only the big things, as in this case—to see that "new" Harvard's Graduate School of Education honors the "old" Georgian setting.

Section 9

The Team and Building Systems

One of the great mysteries of this century is how the building industry, particularly builders themselves, escaped the Industrial Revolution. We have superb methods for producing clothes, cars, furniture, TV's, stoves, washing machines, loaves of bread, and bags of peanuts, but methods of building have changed little in one hundred years. The last five years, however, show signs of radical change. And when the new momentum is achieved, the building industry will never be the same, nor will architects. Systems building is at last taking hold. An old fragmented industry is being replaced by a new, young, and unified industry demanding greater collaboration among architects, engineers, builders, and manufacturers of building materials and building components. Private architects operating in isolation, creating private architecture will be a thing of the past. The change to systems building will give impetus to architecture by team.

89

The three sectors of the building industry are getting together

Consider the overall look of the building industry, particulary what happens at the site. It is a piecemeal operation at its best with too many pieces to put together and too many crafts involved. Workers step on each other's toes or have to wait until the other workers do their work before they can start their own. Added to this confusion at the site, where most of the money is spent, are the traditional three sectors of the building industry: manufacturers, designers, and builders who haven't yet learned the art of collaboration.

The radical change in the building industry is causing a unification of these three sectors. Let's examine the situation. We have the manufacturers of the materials and components for the building. Then we have the design profession including architects, engineers and their consultants who program and prepare the plans for the buildings. And then we have the general and subcontractors who erect the building.

These three groups in the past never seem to have gotten together effectively. In fact, it is difficult for those in any one group to communicate and cooperate among themselves. The manufacturer seems to have had no other interest than in his own product. The architect appears to do everything he can to maintain his role of the prima donna. And the general contractor has held tight to his position of construction broker. Under these conditions, trying to complete a building or a group of buildings is too complex when people are crying for new dwellings, new schools, and new hospitals.

The low-income and minority groups particularly are becoming very impatient. They are taking a hard look at the dyed-in-the-wool industry and asking why. Why does it take five to ten years to plan and build a school for New York City or six years to build a public housing project in Cleveland? Why does it take two or three years after the decision is made to build a community college for the ground breaking to begin and then two to three years more to move in? Why are there three segments of the building industry? What's wrong with the "package dealer"? What's so bad about architects constructing as well as designing? Why can't financial planners and builders get together? Why can't financial planners and social planners get into the act?

Anything to get action—that's what these people want. "We want schools. We want hospitals. We want houses. And we don't care how we get them just so we won't have to wait." These are pressures on the three sections of the building industry. Social reforms are making the three groups get together whether they like it or not. Industrialized methods of the building process—an obvious answer to the need for quick delivery—require close cooperation of manufacturers, designers, and builders—perhaps even a merger (a team of many specialists, including the behavior people).

It's a new ball game. Manufacturers, designers, and builders now have an entirely new set of rules.

90

We built a house of 30,000 pieces

Permit me to trace the evolution of building systems through teaching and the CRS experience. Since the time CRS has been in business only a few architects in this country have been interested in systems building (a process) or building systems (a product). Notable exceptions are Carl Koch and Ezra Ehrenkrantz. Most of us talked about it. These two and a few others did something about it.

I was a talker. In 1940, while teaching at Texas A&M, I had my students count the number of pieces which went into a typical small house. As I recall, there were something like 30,000 pieces, involving a dozen or so different trades. Then, as now, if Rip Van Winkle, carpenter, woke up after a fifty-year sleep, he would be perfectly qualified to do his job. Worse yet, he would not be the least surprised at what he saw. He would find that a typical suburban home and apartment had changed very little. There still are the thousands of little pieces that he could put together.

In an attempt to be a doer, I had my class design a house trying to use the fewest number of pieces. It was not a very imaginative attempt; nevertheless, we cut the number of pieces down to about half. Instead of placing little sticks of two-by-fours upright for studs 16" on centers, we used four-by-fours on center with a sandwiched panel cement-asbestos board with insulation between. We thought we were pretty smart—using advanced technology, but doing our bit to advance it .

For the ceiling and roof deck instead of the usual 2" × 8" joists, 16" on center, with 1" × 6" shiplap decking and with taped-joint gypsum board ceiling, we used what we thought was a far-out "system"—a factory-made glued-up box girder roof panel 4' × 8' by the thickness of 1" × 6" "struts" 16" on centers with 3/8" plywood on each side. Our buzz word then was "skin stress" and we looked to the manufacturers of wood airplanes for inspiration.

But nothing was built. Just more talk.

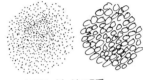

LESS IS MORE

Later, around 1947, my students with Professor Jason Moore and me did build a house, but we were not sure enough of ourselves to use either the skin-stress plywood roof panels or the sandwiched cement-asbestos wall panels. It was a conventional house of 30,000 pieces.

91

Anyone for a prefabricated, demountable, portable, automatic laundry?

IN 1941 AT TEXAS A&M WE TAUGHT BUILDING SYSTEMS AND **INTEGRATED TEAM EFFORT** OF ARCHITECTS, ENGINEERS, MANUFACTURERS AND BUILDERS; WHAT ELSE IS NEW!

I once had my sophomore students at Texas A&M work together as one architect-engineer-manufacturer-builder team. At that time, prefabrication was a nasty word; nevertheless we designed and "manufactured" every component for a "prefabricated, demountable, portable, automatic laundry." That was in 1941. I remember it well because that was the year I went into the service. Apparently, I left A&M in a financial bind, because six months later, I received a letter from that great guy, Ernest Langford, head of the Department of Architecture, saying that he had an unpaid bill for plywood used in the project and that he would pay half of it if I would. So I sent him a check for $37.50.

I've often wondered what A&M did with the one-fifth size, terrible-looking prefab, so big that it occupied two-thirds of one of the large drafting rooms. The model was about four feet high, large enough for me to crawl through to count the pieces (which I dearly loved doing). It was the biggest thing I had had a part in building. As I recall, our "manufacturers" cut down the number of pieces to around 200 and the types to five or six. The walls, floors, and roof panels were manufactured on a mass-produced basis, using carefully designed jigs to allow a fast assembly and gluing method.

What a mess that "drafting" room was! And I certainly did not win the popularity contest among the faculty, not to mention Mr. Langford, who had to cough up $37.50 out of his own pocket and then get rid of the mess to boot.

But I learned something about building systems and I think my students did. I've often wondered, however, what happened to those students. One, I know, was an elementary school teacher for a while; another went into the ministry; another took over his dad's business, and still another went into politics. Maybe a prefabricated, demountable, portable, automatic laundry was just not for them.

92

Mass production on the site is one way to go

Perhaps my later experience with the U.S. Engineer's Office in Nebraska and Wyoming prior to enlistment in the Navy dulled my enthusiasm for mass-produced buildings. During 1942–1944, I served as the Chief Engineer (architects' reputation was for "doing nothing constructive, just making pretty pictures") for three air bases and two internment camps. I became quite an expert—known in those days as "T. O." Caudill—on Theater of Operation buildings, those light, stock-plan, five-year life buildings which could be erected in a hurry. I began to associate prefabricated buildings with stock plans.

Parenthetically, I should add that prefabricated buildings do not necessarily have to have stock plans. There appear to be three basic building systems. The first might be classified under the stock plan category. More appropriately, it is called the *closed system*—since the components are so tailored to a specific system like the T. O. buildings, like stock plan temporary classroom buildings, or like mobile homes, that these components cannot be interchangeable with other systems. Consequently, the results can only be preestablished forms, generally relating to a specific building type. The *open system* on the other hand has much more flexibility and options of choice by architects who use the system. Although generally the components are not interchangeable with other systems, they offer many varieties of forms which relate to similar kinds of building types. There is a third generation of building system classified *universal system,* which theoretically provides an "erector-set" building system capable of building anything a variety of ways, offering unlimited design options, but it is a long way from reality. These will be explained in more detail later.

Although the products were deadening from the standpoint of design and completely void of architecture, I found the process of construction most exciting. The barracks-type buildings were essentially mass produced on the site. To pour the 20' × 100' floor slabs, we brought in the most up-to-date highway paving machines. I can't recall how fast we poured and finished a slab, but it was a matter of minutes.

Prior to the pouring obviously we had to prepare the soil. This too was done using the best and some of the largest earth-moving machinery available. It was pure joy to see the giant Le Tourneau digger-scrapers, like great praying mantises, moving about constructing the fills, followed by tremendously large sheep-foot rollers massaging and compacting the soil. An army of laborers could not have beat those machines in either speed or quality. That was the first time I had ever seen great machines used on the building site as a young professional. Today, however, huge climbing tower cranes and gantry cranes are commonplace.

Using mass-production methods, we built the superstructure of these simple buildings. Our "assembly line" stood still, however, while the workers moved. We would have one crew trained and geared to build only one large component on the slab such as one entire side; another crew to tilt it up and secure it in place. The end walls we would do the same way. We manufactured all of the 20' wood trusses at a central shop making use of jigs for cutting, assembling, and fabricating; hauled the truss components in a specially rigged trailer; and installed them with a crew that did nothing but erect the trusses. No wonder we turned over these air bases three months ahead of schedule.

I should add, however, that all was not up to the best technology. The only material we could get for the roof deck was 1″ × 6″ boards. Our carpenters had to do what their great granddads did—put each little piece in place, one by one. That slowed up things considerably. To make the situation worse—in the interest of economy of both time and money—we tried to space the trusses 4' on center. The span was so great and the deck so weak, that it was hardly strong enough to hold the carpenters working on it. I found out the hard way. I fell through!

If we had used the previously mentioned skin-stressed plywood roof panels, we would not have had this trouble and we could have done a better job faster.

The use of heavy equipment affording industrialized methods on the building site should be given serious consideration. To do the tasks that need be done in providing buildings for an ever-growing population will require industrialized methods, both on the site and at the factories.

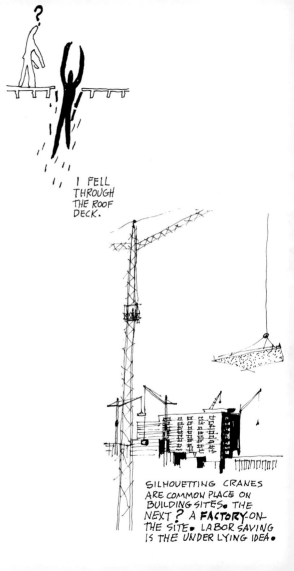

I FELL THROUGH THE ROOF DECK.

SILHOUETTING CRANES ARE COMMON PLACE ON BUILDING SITES. THE NEXT ? A FACTORY ON THE SITE. LABOR SAVING IS THE UNDER LYING IDEA.

93

CRS' first school commission was a "building system"

In late 1948, CRS was given its first school commission, that of designing two elementary schools for Blackwell, Oklahoma. At the time of signing the contracts, Wallie Scott had not yet received his registration in Oklahoma, so the first contract was in the name of Caudill and Rowlett, although Scott actually did more work than either Rowlett or myself. He was more adept at putting the pieces together. The classroom unit was developed by Willie Pena when he was a student. After graduation, he had the rare experience of helping bring reality to a student project.

Looking back, we apparently were a bit ahead of our times. We developed a systems approach, making use of repetitive structural bays for economy and fast erection. There was nothing superfluous or pretentious about those two little schools. Every component was put to work doing one or more function. For example, the steel tie beams were also the fascias; the steel window sills were horizontal braces for wind stresses. Every piece counted more than once. Although built from the same erector set, the schools looked different. The little schools might well be the first steel frame schools in Oklahoma.

Walter McQuade, *Fortune Magazine* editor, "discovered" those schools when he was a young freelance writer. He wrote about them in an article called "The Little Red Schoolhouse Goes Modern" which appeared in *Colliers* 9 September 1950, using colored photographs of the completed schools. That article immediately put CRS on the national scene.

Moore Junior High School, Tyler, Texas, was ready for occupancy in the fall of 1955. This was one of the last of the light exposed steel structures designed by the CRS team. State officials about this time passed regulations which force most school boards to use concrete because of high insurance premium rates. Note the extensive use of interior glass. We wanted the children to have no feeling of confinement. We wanted the teachers to feel they were in a family of teachers. This school is transitional between the self-contained classroom and the open plan school with team teaching. The firm of Bruce and Russell was our associate architect.

I remember how concerned Scott was that other architects would crib this school. Those were the days when our competitors would guard their precious favorite cross section like an expensive piece of jewelry. Every so often when one would feel he could trust someone else, he would look both ways, then sneak the sketch from his inner coat pocket and show it to his trusted friend. Thank goodness the profession is more open today and architects now realize all can benefit by sharing.

Two or three years after the Blackwell schools were completed, however, something happened which shocked even me. What flagrant display of architectural plagiarism! One of our architect acquaintances apparently obtained a set of the Blackwell plans from a bidding contractor. He aped the school right to the details. We had carefully engineered a device—a slot in the roof of the covered walk—after experimentation in a wind tunnel, which would allow the prevailing breeze to enter the clerestory windows. He did not know this and he put the slot on the wrong side of the building. Not only that, he repeated some of the bloopers we had made.

IT TAKES A SMART
ARCHITECT TO KNOW
WHAT TO CRIB — ST. BASIL
OR CRS HEN-HOUSE MODERN.

To see "our" building copied so blatantly shook us up a bit, but then we began to realize that for the first time, CRS was having an influence on the profession. We decided that imitation is indeed the most sincere form of flattery and was permissible in this business. Another thing we learned was that we had "to stay ahead of the pack" and we should be grateful to the people who copied us because they forced us to come up with other ideas.

As far as the light steel frame system was concerned, it certainly was not our idea. As a matter of fact, if anything, we copied some of the ideas of the Fairfax School in California designed by a great friend and MIT teacher of mine, Architect John Lyon Reid of San Francisco. It takes a smart architect to know what to crib.

When building systems become more prevalent, I am afraid many of the buildings by various architects will look alike. But, is this so bad? At least perhaps the number of those terrible buildings which scream for attention will be reduced.

94

A bucket of paint makes the difference

After the Blackwell experience, CRS tried to improve the system, if that's what it was, by using a similar steel building frame system for three schools in Stillwater, Oklahoma, and two in Port Arthur, Texas. These early "systems" were crude; nevertheless the schools were designed for quantity buying, fast erection and economy.

We were very proud of the fact that none of our schools was alike. "Ours are tailor-made to meet the situation." This was not quite true. It was true the schools were not alike in plan, but the basic subsystems were essentially standardized. The two Blackwell schools used the same heating and lighting systems, the same structural systems, the same ceiling and roof systems, and the same materials. So it was with the three Stillwater schools and the two Port Arthur schools. Each city had its own system. In today's terms, they would be halfway between the closed system and open system.

Standardization of materials and of some form—like the clasrooms of a particular set of schools—forced us to go strong on color. We believed that each classroom should have its own individuality. In other words, we thought the students and the teachers would want their classroom to be

CRS has had to change its thinking about "tailor-made" buildings like this little Peter Pan School in Andrews, Texas (the first carpeted classroom in America), designed in 1955. We cared only for what the children and teachers thought about their spaces. Product was relevant, process irrelevant. It mattered little how much time it took to plan and construct—the main thing was to do it right. After all, we were taught that time to the true artist and architect meant nothing. "Mies van der Rohe took ten years to design a small house." If we were to be "masters" we too must have

plenty of time to make our masterpieces. This is all changed now. Saving time is of the essence. People are demanding better buildings, delivered fast. Now the main thing is to do it in a hurry. Some standardization of materials is inherent in systems but individuality is expressed through the size, color, and texture of storage and space divider elements, children's artwork, and the clothes children wear. This is the interior of Birch School, Merrick, Long Island, completed in 1970.

different, yet because of standardization of parts in form they were basically the same. The materials were the same. We were boxed in except for color.

This was when Willie Pena rose to national prominence as an expert on color in schoolhouses. He wrote several articles and made many speeches explaining how, through color, the designer can achieve this individuality. Pena often referred to CRS-designed classrooms as the "blue room" or the "gray room." While visiting one of our schools, I asked a little second grader where he lived. I had in mind his home because I thought I knew his parents. His answer was, "I live in the room with the orange door." He went to school in Pena's orange room.

A bucket of paint can take the sting out of standardization.

95
Lifting the lift-slab

In September 1951, CRS was commissioned to design some schools for Laredo, Texas. At the time there was much hullabaloo about the lift-slab system—a method of pouring concrete slabs on the ground and lifting them into place with hydraulic jacks.

Outrageous claims of saving up to $2.00 per square foot on the structure alone were made. We knew differently. How can $2.00 be saved over structure of conventional structure—steel and wood—when conventional structure was costing about this same amount? Nevertheless, on clients' insistence and "to keep up with the time" we went the lift-slab route. And it cost more (but not much more) than what we had been doing. We found this out by making two sets of plans—one for the lift-slab system and the other for the conventional structural system of steel columns and beams with wood joists. On $500,000 total construction cost, the lift-slab bids were $25,000 to $80,000 more. The school board decided to pay the extra $25,000 over conventional construction because of the lower insurance premiums. We were "in." Strangely enough, we neglected to find out if the lift-slab went up faster—a very important consideration today. Then everyone accepted that it took two to three years to design and build a school—even in an all-year construction country like South Texas.

It can be said CRS built in Laredo one of the first lift-slab public schools in the country. Architect O'Neil Ford, however, was the pioneer in this field.

About this time, our Oklahoma City office started by John Rowlett and Tom Bullock was trying to make a reputation for itself. We thought the popular lift-slab system could help focus attention on CRS-Oklahoma. We persuaded the school board in Bartlesville, Oklahoma to try out the system on a small four-room addition. Our plans were to have a lot of fanfare. We decided that on the day of the lifting we would invite school board members and their superintendent to see this "marvelous new way of building schoolhouses." Let them be in on the lifting—what a great idea that was!

Just before we sent out invitations (sometime in 1954) there appeared on the front page of the Oklahoma City Times a picture of a not-so-successful lifting in California. In fact, it was a real fiasco. The steel columns had buckled and two floors of slabs which had been lifted in place smashed a truck underneath. We "ate" our invitations and quietly had our lifting without fanfare and without special guests. It's a good thing, too, because our lifting was not clean.

Slab-lifting for a school addition in Bartlesville, Oklahoma, in 1954, was carried out without fanfare.

In any case, the lift-slab system represented one of the first highly mechanized systems for cutting down labor and time on the site. And for the period was successful. It never quite lived up to its press notices. Someone needs to take a fresh look at the concept of lifting floors "by their bootstraps." If developed further such a site-mechanized method may help solve the problem of speedy erection.

CRS wanted to use the lift-slab system for A&M Consolidated High School, College Station, Texas, but the "conventional system" was cheaper. *Cost* then was everything. It's a guess that in the future *time* will be everything. System building will have a better chance to come to the front to save *time*—to meet physical demands of social immmediacy and offset the high cost of money. At this writing, if we can cut six months from planning and construction, we can save the client the cost of our fee. In the future, the building industry will be more time-conscious.

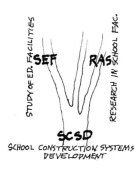

STUDY OF ED. FACILITIES
SEF
RAS
RESEARCH IN SCHOOL FAC.
SCSD
SCHOOL CONSTRUCTION SYSTEMS
DEVELOPMENT

96

CRS was in on the start of SCSD

The most exciting program in building system development was initiated by a grant from Educational Facilities Laboratories (EFL) in the sixties. Harold Gores and Jonathan King of EFL (who joined the CRS team in 1970) unquestionably started a movement which has affected not only architects who do schools but also those who do houses and hospitals. And what they (Gores and King) did to the total building industry!

The project, *School Construction Systems Development* (SCSD) grew out of the School Planning Laboratory at Stanford University and the University of California, Department of Architecture, Berkeley. The driving force behind the project was Architect Ezra Ehrenkrantz. During 1961–1968, through his dynamic leadership, SCSD became an influential force in shaping schoolhouses in this country. (Architects at the time were rather alarmed at what he was doing. And with good reason.)

CRS got in on the beginning of the project through Charles Lawrence, who served on the advisory board. In addition, we "loaned" SCSD one of our people, Bert Ray, for a two-year period to help develop the ceiling system.

A prototype structure was built on the Stanford campus and was visited by thousands of school planners, including architects, engineers, and educators. It was a beautiful little building which articulated the structural and mechanical and electrical systems. Unfortunately, none of the scores of SCSD schools that followed ever equaled the prototype.

I have never been quite sure why. Was it because the architects did not have the imagination to take a given system and work within its constraints to create architecture? Was it because they simply were not interested in designing buildings from an "erector set"? Whatever the reason, architects and their teammates must now learn to work within the constraints of building systems. It is a guess the architects involved in designing SCSD did not know how to do this. Perhaps the system was too "closed" in nature. Hopefully, new systems will be the "open" type to allow architects the creativity necessary to make human-occupied spaces possess that quality which we call architecture.

The SCSD system—the integration of design, fabrication, and erection—is attracting the attention and participation of space age industries. Industry is coming out with various proposals of the erector set idea—

MANUFACTURING CONCRETE WALL PANELS AT THE FACTORY SAVES EXPENSIVE FORMWORK ON SITE. SEF USES CONCRETE WALL PANELS ATTACHED TO LIGHT STEEL STRUCTURAL FRAME.

an open system which permits many forms and spaces in contrast to the closed system such as a prefabricated house of a certain size and shape. Some are taking hold. Unquestionably SCSD has had great influence. To see thirteen California school districts taking advantage of mass buying power for the various components which can be assembled in a number of arrangements to satisfy the functional requirements of each of the districts is a convincing argument for industrialized building.

A second-generation SCSD, the RAS system in Montreal, Canada, and the SEF system being used in Toronto, Canada, carry the "kit of parts" a step further. Where SCSD covered no more than 45% of the total cost of construction, SEF goes up to 85%.

97
We missed a good opportunity

I am afraid CRS did not fully capitalize on the SCSD experience. Either we were never given the opportunity to design a SCSD school, or we failed to make the opportunity. At the time, we were one of the nation's pioneering school architects; yet the CRS team seemed content to sit on the sidelines instead of playing in the game—although we did have two strong individuals playing on someone else's team.

I suspect the reason for this was that we had become bored with little schoolhouses and wanted to do something bigger and more significant. And we wanted to produce the masterpiece—write the great American novel, so to speak. We wanted to compete with Mies, Corbusier, and

Saarinen. We were tired of doing little schools that looked like chicken-houses.

It is a matter of record that during the sixties CRS, in its attempt to produce "a better architecture," lost ground in system building. Like so many other firms, we got caught in the bottom of the cliché barrel in the temple-building era. We got on the one-material, monolithic concrete jag—the idea of making a building like a hollow piece of sculpture. And it was not a bad idea from the standpoint of achieving architectural unity. The trouble with most of the SCSD schools and its offsprings such as SEF (Toronto's Study of Educational Facilities), RAS (Montreal's Recherches en Aménagements Scolaires), or SSP (Florida's Schoolhouse Systems Project) is that they lack the architectural qualities. Some have very little unity. They are too loosely jointed—they look too nervous. I might add however that there are some building systems in England, France, and the Scandinavian countries from which architects can design beautiful, functionally adaptable buildings that have the architectural unity lacking in the early SCSD Schools.

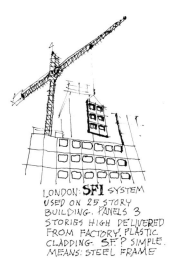

LONDON: SF1 SYSTEM
USED ON 25 STORY
BUILDING. PANELS 3
STORIES HIGH DELIVERED
FROM FACTORY. PLASTIC
CLADDING. SF.? SIMPLE.
MEANS: STEEL FRAME

There have always been attempts by CRS to capitalize on the economies of mass buying and standardization of components. In July 1964, CRS was hired to coordinate Minneapolis' Phase I five-year $28-million building program. Our contract required us to have a man in residence for two and one half years and then follow with minimum coordination for the next two and one half years. We had great hopes of getting the thirteen Minneapolis architectural firms involved to standardize details, if not subsystems. It was most difficult, and not always the architects' fault. For example, we designed and prepared specifications for a standard two-by-four 40-watt, rapid-start light fixture and attempted to volume purchase these in a quantity of 10,000 which would have been sufficient to equip eleven schools. For political reasons, the light fixture proposal was not even presented to the school board for their approval.

All told there were thirty-five school projects—eighteen of which were major. On seven of the projects, CRS performed schematic design services only, in association with seven local Minneapolis firms.

We aided the administration in establishing budgeting procedures and scheduling of projects; prepared sets of construction standards pertaining largely to mechanical, electrical, and plumbing items within a building to achieve standardization; and developed a "boiler plate" to assure consistency in all bidding specifications.

The program was successful. However, we were not able to do as much coordination among local architectural firms as we would have liked. Originally we had wanted to take Minneapolis on "the SCSD route," but neither climate (physical and psychological) nor the school board was ready.

98

Texarkana gave us a chance to try out the SCSD experience

Bert Ray's reentry into CRS after two years with SCSD was not programmed as well as it should have been. We were not quite sure what to do with him or him with us. All we knew was that we wanted to profit by his experience. We wanted a more systematic approach for designing and building a schoolhouse which we could use on other building types.

About that time, we had a typical school project which turned up in Texarkana, Texas—a high school. After conferences with our client and with our own people interested in building systems, it was agreed that Texarkana should be processed on the system route, using Bert Ray's experience. Naturally, he was chosen as one of the lead people with Don Wines. The project also had a strong backup from Charles Lawrence, who had served on the SCSD Advisory Board.

The underlying idea of SCSD was to get manufacturers to work together to design and produce subsystems which would make up a substantial portion of the construction—to keep on-site work to a minimum.

Since Inland Steel was the successful bidder for the structure-lighting-ceiling subsystem, CRS first contacted this company. Cost analysis, however, showed that Inland's price was $2.00 a square foot too high. We had

The Texarkana High School in Texas, completed in 1968, was CRS' first attempt in the development of a building system based on the SCSD experience. As a school it was highly successful. As a building system there was much to be desired. Moore and Thomas associated with us on this project.

a proposal for cutting this down to within the budget, but the company was not interested. The reason for this was that we did not have a big enough carrot to dangle—not enough mass buying power. We also dangled a junior high school in front of them, but still they refused to run. A couple of schools in an isolated northeast Texas town simply were not enough; they were accustomed to a batch of twenty schools in booming California. I could not blame them.

We then went to Mosher Steel of Houston and their engineers and research people were most cooperative. They helped us develop the concept of the "star columns," an ingenious (by our own admission) device for glass, walls, partitions, and ceilings. Yet when the "moment of truth"—the letting—arrived, Mosher Steel did not choose to bid.

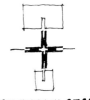

THE TEXARKANA **STAR COLUMN** OFFERS A DEVICE FOR JOINING GLASS, BRICK, PARTITIONS, AND CEILINGS

As it turned out, the Texarkana High School was built and it was a very successful schoolhouse—having the amenities which most building systems schools lacked, at the same time being a good educational tool. And it was built at a reasonable cost. Only one hitch: It was bid and built the traditional way. Although the approach was preanalysis, preselection of subsystems, it simply did not turn out that way. We failed to bring the manufacturers into the act.

We fully understood that the strength of SCSD was in the process, not in the product. We had a good product. What we did not have was the new process—the original intent. What we had hoped for was to "copy" the process, and with our years of experience and design talent, improve the usual dreary product, resulting from the building systems approach.

Although Texarkana was given a good high school, we made no contribution whatsoever in advancing systems development. We did quite well in the *design* category of the practice disciplines, but not so well in either *technology* or *management.* It was a one-shot project. We never used the system again. Like SCSD, it lacked universality, particularly relating to fire protection. The beautiful ingenious stair columns simply would be lost and the aesthetic and engineering endeavors would be in vain if the columns were wrapped in fireproofing. When wrapped, the logic would be lost.

99

Fast-track scheduling is a management technique to save time

In 1969, the term "fast-track" came into our vocabulary. CRS can't claim the name, but we certainly had a hand in promoting it. Tom Bullock, as Chairman of the National AIA School and College Architecture Committee, became concerned that in a city like New York, it took ten years to build a high school. Smaller cities did not do much better. There had to be faster ways. CRS spent a lot of money trying to devise ways to cut time, and subsequent savings in total construction cost, through having lower interest on borrowed money, lower insurance premiums, and trying to outrun inflation. "Fast-track" was the 1969 buzz word.

In November of that year, Tom Bullock, Willie Pena, and John Focke completed a study called "Fast-Track Scheduling." The purpose of the study was to find a managing device to speed up design and construction time. Our clients, with good reasons, were crying for faster project delivery. For years we had maintained that architects should not be expediters. Like it or not, we got caught in the speed war. Something had to be done. Although in one sense we found nothing new, we did find new adaptations.

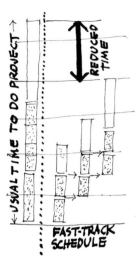

USUAL TIME TO DO PROJECT →

REDUCED TIME

FAST-TRACK
SCHEDULE

THE FAST-TRACK IDEA IS
A MEANS OF OVERLAPPING
DESIGN AND CONSTRUCTION
ACTIVITIES WHICH USUALLY
ARE SCHEDULED IN SEQUENCE.

Briefly, fast-track scheduling is a means of overlapping design and construction activities which are normally scheduled in sequence. Instead of waiting until programming, when plans and specifications are delivered in one big package, fast-track breaks it up into three packages—to allow construction to start ahead of the usual schedule. For example, the separation of a project into three bid packages allows early start in the construction of (1) site work and foundations, followed by the construction of (2) the building shell, and finally, the installation of (3) interiors systems.

A building consists of many subsystems each consisting of many components. This is a 1969 photo of construction of William Rainey Harper College, Palatine, Illinois, designed by the CRS team in association with Fridstein, Fitch, and partners.

Substantial reductions in project delivery time (up to 20%) can be achieved with fast-track scheduling. Additional savings in time (up to 45%) are possible if a preselected industrialized building systems approach is integrated into the process. In other words, without radically changing either design or technology, and centering only on management, the reduction in time—from decision to build to moving in—is significant.

Following are advantages of fast-track:

- Fast-track can be used in the public sectors, particularly schools and housing.
- Fast-track is adapted to the complex client—school boards, city and county governing boards, and the like.
- There is opportunity for professional concern of the user.
- Competitive bidding is encouraged.
- And the architect retains his role as a major contributor.

The study helped move CRS a step closer to solving the nagging time/money problem. There will be no overall solution, however, until the same kind of innovations are used in the aspects of design and technology, for the three disciplines of practice—management, design, and technology—must be considered as one.

The young new breed of CRS loved to think of fast-track as strictly new stuff, the panacea of the construction industry. Not quite true. Eight years before CRS set a speed record on the old slow track. A new school district out of Saginaw, Michigan, was formed and we got the job with Prine Toshach and Spears as associates to do two middle schools. The pressure for getting the plans out and the schools up was tremendous. Superintendent George Mills and his board had to have the building ready

In 1961 CRS set a speed record on the old slow track. This middle school in Saginaw, Michigan, and another one like it, relating to subsystems but completely different in plan (one a decentralized plant and the other a compact centralized plant), were designed and built in only one year between signing of the architect-owner contract and moving in. Prine, Toshach, and Spears were our associates.

for their children and teachers to occupy in an unbelievably short time—from master planning and programming to the move-in within a year. *Only one year.* That stunned us. But CRS responded. Twelve months after the signing of our contract for the two schools, the children moved in. The contractor went like sixty after taking our record-setting produced plans. And this was cold-country construction.

That was the last of the fast cats on the slow track. We needed faster tracks, and we are getting them. Herb Paseur was the project manager. No wonder he is now running the firm.

In November 1969, the CRS team completed a study for the State University Construction Fund, State of New York, called "Fast-track and Other Procedures—A General Study of Design and Construction Management." This report stemmed from state officials recognizing the need to make design-construction changes to cope with escalation in construction cost and rapidly growing space needs for higher education. The report revealed these three techniques, more evolutionary than revolutionary, which could accelerate design-construction:

Fast-Track Scheduling—a procedural device for saving time. By overlapping phases (by scheduling a second activity at an appropriate stage during the first, for example) time is reduced.

Preselected Systems—a reservoir from which to draw material as required to speed up the design-construction sequence. This reservoir of already approved software (programs, building geometries, standard details, design criteria, etc.) and hardware (prepackaged building components, manufactured subsystems, prefabricated elements, etc.) reduces time in almost every stage.

Continual Delivery—a process which considers the design-construction sequence not as a series of discrete packages, but rather as a continual process with repetitive cycles. This is based on the premise that a campus is organic—it never stops growing.

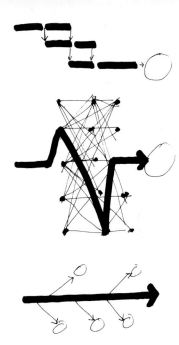

At the time we pointed out to the client that the first proposal, fast-track scheduling, required the least amount of change from traditional processes; the second, preselected systems, required more change and greater commitment; and the third, continual delivery, required the greatest effort to implement. Today we still believe it.

For history's sake, the conclusion of the report is included here:

"Substantial reductions in project delivery time (25%)can be achieved with fast track scheduling.

"Remarkable savings (45%) if a pre-selected systems approach is integrated into the process.

"If the continual delivery process were fully operative, the whole notion of project time would need to be re-thought since, as classically defined, the project delivery time could be reduced to less than a year. Construction could operate in cycle with the university's annual incremental growth."

To save 25% delivery time with fast-track, and 45% if preselected systems (the SCSD idea) is superimposed, this process appears a bit on the optimistic side. Nevertheless, because of slowups from labor shortages, strikes on the site, at the factory, and between factory and site (hauling), we shall need many timesaving devices to accommodate the demands of social change (which require "building in a hurry") and the escalation of construction cost.

100

We brought the contractors in as members of the team

In early 1970, through the efforts of our New York office under the leadership of Chuck Thomsen, Steve Kliment, Norman Hoover, and Peter Piven, line-backed by Al Pierce and Perry Martin of the Houston office, CRS finally made a serious attempt to build some schoolhouses on the SCSD pattern.

It was a relatively small contract for us, but a most important one at the time. It introduced to the CRS team a new approach—basically managerial —which presages great changes in the method of designing and constructing buildings.

We had a bit of fun by giving it the computerized name of FAST-I—most significant because the project had to be exceedingly fast, both in getting out of the CRS drafting rooms and in getting the building constructed.

Our job was to design three relatively small additions to existing elementary schools in Merrick, Long Island, New York, and see that they were built ready for the children and teachers to move in by the start of school in September. We had only ten months to do it, from the time of our first involvement to moving in.

Fortunately the additions were fairly simple, including typical classrooms and multipurpose rooms. The task team quickly arrived at a pavilion design, which was an open shell with a core of service elements surrounded by flexible space for the inevitable changing of the educational program.

Again our carrot was small—too small to interest a lot of bidders. Again we had relatively little buying power—and hardly any time. We had to make the building simple—permit preengineered subsystems of proven character and compatibility. So in order to get any bidders at all under the circumstances, we relied heavily upon the groundwork laid by SCSD. In fact we adapted some of the performance specifications from earlier SCSD projects to insure compatibility among the subsystems. We tried to make sure that the subsystems would successfully interlock according to what Roderick Robbie of Toronto's SEF called the concept of "mandatory interface"—another favorite buzz word with the building system people.

Prebidding on four subsystems—structural support, integrated ceiling, heating and air conditioning, and roof allowed us closer control of the final building cost by reducing the unknown elements. This accounted for 30% of the construction budget. It enabled the successful bidders to

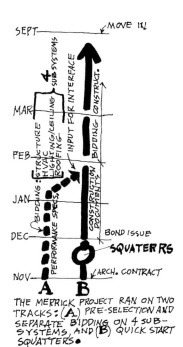

THE MERRICK PROJECT RAN ON TWO TRACKS: (A) PRE-SELECTION AND SEPARATE BIDDING ON 4 SUB-SYSTEMS, AND (B) QUICK START SQUATTERS.

place orders for materials earlier, thus assuring on-time delivery and prices free of the escalation factor during the planning and construction period. It also allowed the general contractor advance knowledge of whom he would be working with and eliminated "shopping"—that bugaboo to sub-contractors.

As it turned out, all four subsystems were bid at under our estimate. After the Texas failure, this victory was sweet. It looked as if CRS was finally on its way to becoming involved in the building system approach.

Bids on the subsystem components were taken January 12, 1970—six weeks after the design contract was given to CRS. On March 4, 1970 the school board awarded final construction contracts for the remaining non-system work.

The September move-in deadline, however, was not met. We missed it by two months. One month of the delay was caused by the school attorney's reluctance to approve signing of the four subsystems contracts. Another two weeks' delay was from a truckers' strike affecting structural steel delivery to site. And the other two weeks' delay was caused by slow delivery of windows, which resulted in a holdup on interior partitions and ceiling. Lesson? Lawyers and truck drivers are important, too.

According to *Building Systems Information Clearinghouse Newsletter* of 30 March 1970, the Merrick project is the first use of fast-track scheduling and building systems together. The newsletter quoted Chuck Thomsen as follows:

"Merrick was seen by CRS as a project which would give the office a chance to combine several innovative time and cost saving procedures in a concerted effort to meet an 'impossible' deadline within a limited budget.

Pre-bidding of sub-systems, use of performance-type specifications, pre-integration of certain key sub-systems would essentially ease some of the burden of the design phase by allowing the manufacturers to interject their own technical expertise before design decisions were frozen. At the same time, the manufacturers would acquire greater freedom to specify the most economical systems to meet specified performance requirements and sufficient time to gear their manufacturing processes to faster delivery of components."

We believe that combining fast-track with building systems will give time savings beyond those normally expected from building systems alone. The Merrick project may have greater significance in that for the first time building systems techniques—performance specifications, subsystem pre-bidding, and fast-track scheduling—generally associated with large-scale projects—are applied to more typical-sized programs.

A point of interest, however, is this: When a jury of the Quality Panel evaluated this project it gave the *economy* leg an unbelievably high score of 9 with only a relatively low 6 given to *function* and *form,* with this directive to the task team: "(1) The strength of the process is evident; keep it, and improve it. (2) At the same time improve the product specifically in terms of better design."

What happened was this: We beat Texarkana by a mile on *process* primarily because we successfully persuaded the manufacturers to join our team. In essence, they helped design the little additions. And they designed them from the standpoint of economy both at the factory and on the site. In doing so, since time is money, they fulfilled the "fast" condition as well as the performance specifications. But as the jury discovered, somehow in emphasizing process, the product suffered somewhat; as regards functional adequacy and aesthetics, Texarkana was better. Al Pierce,

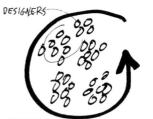

BUILDINGS ARE PRODUCED BY A TEAMS OF MANY **SPECIALISTS,** NOT JUST DESIGNERS. IF THOSE BUILDINGS ARE INTENDED TO HAVE ARCHITECTURE, THEN IT IS LOGICAL TO CALL SUCH GROUPS **ARCHITECTURE TEAMS.**

who was on top of this project as much as anyone said, "From the standpoint of the architectural process, this project has been highly successful. The process gave a true sense of accomplishment and revealed a clarity and purpose in the roles of management and technology." He did not say it, but could have: "What happened to design?"

Most of us do not feel that the architect need sacrifice design in this kind of an approach. We are convinced that a task team having strong, sensitive designs can produce beautiful, functional schools and other building types using this same approach—involving the manufacturers as an important member of the architecture team.

101

The "design team" idea must give way to the "architecture team" idea

It has been very hard for us in CRS to keep from referring to the team as a design team. We have referred to CRS as a "design firm" for years. The practice of architecture has been labeled as a segment of the "design profession." So "design team" fits naturally into the picture.

Perhaps the team is still valuable as a sub-team, a part of a larger architecture team. On the same basis then, there should be managing teams and technology teams, if not programming teams, engineering teams, design development teams, manufacturing teams, erection teams (and I could go on indefinitely)—even include the user's team. Each of these is after the same thing—the creation of architecture. If all disciplines work in concert, it seems more logical that the total team be called the *architecture team.*

102

Construction time is a major design determinant

The element of time cannot be overemphasized. Time is becoming increasingly important—the time that it takes to get a building up. At this writing, CRS is working on an office building. Interest rates are terribly high, the highest in history, and interim financing rates are exhorbitant. Inflation prevails. Our problem is not so much designing a building with a very low unit cost. For the first time in CRS history, the problem is not square foot cost. Our problem is to design a building that can be erected in the shortest amount of time.

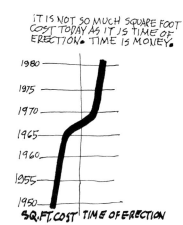

IT IS NOT SO MUCH SQUARE FOOT COST TODAY AS IT IS TIME OF ERECTION. TIME IS MONEY.

SQ. FT. COST   TIME OF ERECTION

Time is money. Industrialization of the building process saves time. That's what counts. If the buildings look different, fine. What's wrong with that? What matters is that the people who use them experience architecture. This photo shows construction of the library of Southern Colorado State College. The "puckered" windows offer the same desirable transitional area as the early pueblo buildings—to control lighting from extreme outside brightness to low interior intensity. The photo was taken in 1965.

THERE ARE THREE BASIC TYPES OF **BUILDING SYSTEMS.** EACH CONSISTS OF FACTORY-BUILT COMPONENTS WITH DESIRED MINIMUM SITE LABOR. EACH TAKES ADVANTAGE OF INDUSTRIALIZED BUILDING METHODS RELATING TO PLANNING, DESIGN, MANUFACTURING, ERECTION, AND MANAGEMENT.

PIECES

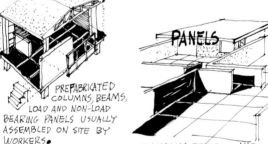

PREFABRICATED COLUMNS, BEAMS, LOAD AND NON-LOAD BEARING PANELS USUALLY ASSEMBLED ON SITE BY WORKERS.

PANELS

USUALLY PRECAST AND LOAD BEARING AND PRE-FINISHED INCLUDING WINDOWS.

BOXES

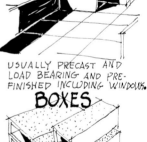

PREFABRICATED **3D** COMPONENTS USUALLY PRECAST CONCRETE BUT SOMETIMES "STACKED MOBILE HOMES."

Every month of construction time saved will save our client $100,000.

We have selected a structural system which costs a little more, but which can cut construction time by three months. This is money in the bank for our client.

Where the CRS team fought the "low square foot" battle during the past decade, we shall have to fight the "fast delivery time" battle in this next decade. So will everyone else in the building industry.

103

Boxes, big panels, and pieces will be designed to go up quickly and economically

It is increasingly clear that industrialization of building will be required to provide the large volume of building, particularly in housing, to meet the social needs of this country and others. This will put architects, contractors, and labor in another period, so to speak. As pointed out, time of construction will have as much influence on the building as any other design determinant. At every stage of design development the question "How fast will it go up?" will be asked. This will affect not only the economy of a building but the form and function as well. It may be that most architectural teams must design their products in the very near future within the constraints of certain kits of parts or erector sets which give assurance that the building can go up quickly. The so-called "traditional" methods of building construction are gradually being replaced by "industrialization," which generally implies the classes of systems: factory-built *boxes*—completed and finished room-sized enclosures; *big panels*—wall-sized slabs and floor units; or *pieces*—the smaller components, all designed to be assembled on the site in the shortest time with the least labor. Industrialization also implies that factory-type equipment and procedures are used at the site. Minimization of construction time is of the essence.

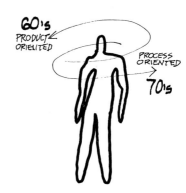

104

There has been a switch of attitude from "product-oriented" to "process-oriented"

Architectural practice during the last three decades has been product-oriented. The so-called design profession simply was not very interested in process. Most significant buildings were single structure, highly individualized, custom designed, and custom built. The entire construction industry, from unionized hod carriers to prima donna architects, was tooled to provide the custom product. And the architect did the tailoring. Industrialization was a bad word. Team was worse.

A look-back unfolds the fallacy and failure of the product-oriented approach. The single building—however grand in form or concept—has had little effect on the total urban environment. When a large and increasing percentage of families is buying or renting trailer homes, architects must surely realize where they have failed and acknowledge industrialized housing is here. Architects' singularly designed tailor-made homes are hard to find on the scene. The confusion and waste of manpower of all different trades converging on one single building, stepping on each other's toes and waiting until the "other guy gets done and gets out" is destroying the construction industry as we know it today. The lack of teamwork is causing the trouble. Not only is construction scandalously inadequate, but to make matters worse, the material manufacturers and the design professions are hardly on speaking terms. Strikes of relatively minor trade unions causing stoppage of work in all major trades adds to the difficulties of getting a building up.

CRS advocates, with good reasons, that the concept of the team include the manufacturers, contractors, and suppliers as well as the architects and engineers. The pendulum has swung. Now we are more interested in process than product. History tells us it will swing too far. When it starts to come back, we may be in a wonderful age of construction—total teams planning and constructing buildings having architectural quality, having space people can afford and buildings which can be speedily fabricated and erected through industrialized methods at factory and site.

105

Prefabrication becomes respectable throughout the world

During the last five years there has been considerable progress in industrialized building in this country and in the United Kingdom, France, Sweden, Finland, and particularly in Russia, where high-rise apartments are being built on the assembly lines as cars are in this country. Phrases like "factory-built buildings" and "package dealers," still dirty words to most architects and engineers, are now being cleaned up with synonymous terms such as "system building," "kit of parts," "closed systems," "open systems," "design-and-build contractors," "turnkey contractors," "client-sponsored systems," and the like. Even the word "prefabrication," very dirty only a few years ago, is being accepted. However, it is rather difficult to pin down just what is meant by "prefabrication." At the present if the definition had to be quantified, prefabrication would mean that from 40% to 50% of total construction cost is factory-built as building subsystems.

Tailor-made housing and schools as we know them today look as if they are on their way out—at least until the time the computer joins with automation to make everything tailor-made including ladies shoes and a man's lunch. In any case, industrialization now is playing old Ned with the traditional architectural practice. The mass-produced factory-made buildings have arrived and are being accepted. Mobile homes now have a well-established beachhead having in 1968 consisted of 85% of the homes built in the United States under $15,000. In this country, Canada, and England "building systems" for schoolhouses have particularly advanced the art of prefabrication and professional acceptance. In fact, whole cities are being produced in factories.

As mentioned, there are two ways to industrialize the building process. One is to produce everything in a factory. The other is to use factory-like methods and equipment on the site—in essence a "factory at the site" idea. Portable factories have worked to varying degrees, but generally the permanent factory seems to be preferred at this time. In either case, the objective is to do as many things with machines as possible. Where there is a shortage of skilled labor—and throughout the world there seems to be one—building with machines may be the only way to solve the problem of housing the masses. Machine building is necessary to compensate for the labor shortage. Perhaps even more important is the time shortage. Machines are needed to get the dwellings, the schools, the hospitals, factories, churches, and stores up in a hurry.

Russia has been particularly effective in using industrialized methods for solving its housing shortage. The war destroyed millions of its dwellings.

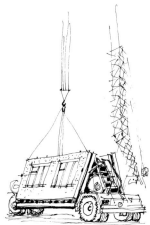

PANEL CARRIER AT SITE...
COMPONENTS HAULED FROM
FACTORY COMPLETE WITH
FACING TILE, WINDOW SASH
AND GLASS _ LENINGRAD.

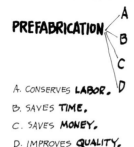

PREFABRICATION

A. CONSERVES **LABOR**.
B. SAVES **TIME**.
C. SAVES **MONEY**.
D. IMPROVES **QUALITY**.

The Soviets had to go the prefabrication route for time's sake. About 70% of housing in Moscow is prefab—37% for the total country. Apparently Russia's target is to build all prefabs. Officials give reasons of time, weather, and cost. One official told the writer during a recent trip to Russia that prefabrication is used for four reasons:

(1) to conserve *labor,* since 50% of labor is saved over traditional methods;
(2) to save *time,* since there are 45% savings in length of time to build;
(3) to save *money,* since prefabs cost six to seven percent less than traditional construction;
(4) to improve *quality* since factory-built "houses" are better.

Other nations think and act along the same lines. The United States has approached its problem a bit differently, but there is a change in the wind at this writing and by the time this goes to press, we may be in the middle of a revolution in the building industry in which prefabrication is looked upon as a solution, not a threat.

106

A factory builds a city

England, particularly, looks upon prefabrication as a solution to the housing problem. A crystal-clear example of how industrialized building differs from the traditional way is found in the study of the new town of Thamesmead, which flanks the river between Woolwich and Erith. This project, under the Greater London Council, will eventually accommodate 60,000 Londoners on a 1600-acre site.

SPEEDY
ERECTION
TECHNIQUES
SAVE TIME
AND MONEY.

The traditional crafts/trade approach was abandoned. The idea was to industrialize the building process, keeping the on-site labor to an absolute minimum. In other words, do as much in a factory as possible. So in simple terms: *London built a factory to build itself a new town.*

There has been some misconception about the temporary aspect of that particular factory. It is certainly not temporary. It will be there for fifteen years, the time it will take Thamesmead to reach its 60,000 population target. The large overhead cranes, for example, will be amortized and probably replaced in twelve years. The steel mold and machines for manufacturing the concrete components are heavily industrialized type units and will last indefinitely. They can be moved, but certainly with considerable expense.

There is another misconception—that the Thamesmead project is a pure form of a factory-on-site idea. Not quite so—not like the kind in France where huge concrete molding machines—"the house-laying" idea—are set up at the site and then moved away after the building is completed. Although the factory is close to the building sites, nonetheless concrete components must be loaded on trailers, hauled to the site, and unloaded as if the site were 200 miles away. Most certainly the factory is neither temporary nor a strictly on-the-site operation. It is in the trucking business too, but it benefits greatly from the short hauls.

The equipment used is the French-German system of making precast concrete panels called Balency-Shuhk. Six hundred fifty-five different components or "units" are being manufactured. The Thamesmead "house-building" factory is a specifically designed fifteen-year factory to build the main structural elements—floors, walls, and cladding—for a small city

VARIETY OF
FORM AT
THAMESMEAD
HELPS ELIMINATE
MONOTONY OF FACTORY
BUILT "HOUSES."

which will take fifteen years to build. The factory has only one customer—Thamesmead. The factory does not manufacture parts for plumbing, heating, electrical wiring and equipment, brick, tile, and other finishing materials, but by definition it does turn out prefabricated buildings since the building system it manufactures amounts to about 50% of the total cost of construction. At present, the Greater London Council not only owns and operates the factory but does its own erecting. The output is about 1000 flats a year. To meet the timetable, the Londoners will have to expand the factory and increase production to as much as 2000 flats a year in order to reach the 17,000 target for Thamesmead. Or, it could do as the Russians do and put the factory on two and three shifts and make do with the equipment already there.

The thought of building a factory to build a city would have shocked architects five years ago by its sheer scale and by the use of advanced industrialization to build. More significant is that such a thought would have been repugnant to even the most forward-thinking architects. Only a few years ago, prefabrication meant anti-architecture and anti-architects.

107
Someone must be concerned with architecture

Any vital, viable profession not only adapts itself to change, but causes change. But change is not the threat many think. Refusal to change is the danger. Whether professionals concerned with architecture will meet the challenge will determine their survival. They had better be up to the change, because people need architecture.

Architects and architecture-conscious engineers, planners, and designers concerned with the physical environment are needed now more than ever before. The Russians learned this the hard way. Twenty years ago when the Soviets initiated their intense industrialized building program to solve the housing problems created by World War II destruction, they either allowed the architects to take a back seat or deliberately pushed them back where they would be ineffective. Architecture did not seem important. Shelter—architecture or not—was the first and foremost.

Russians now know they erred. High officials are beginning to realize that along with quantity, in which they excel, there must be quality. If architects and their collaborators, who are sensitive to human needs and human values of form and space, had been involved then, the chances are the "architectureless, dreary, monotonous houses," which dominate the Moscow, Leningrad, and Kiev scenes would not exist. The lesson is learned.

Architects, the only trained sponsors of architecture, are regaining their popularity in Russia, which, incidentally, is blessed with a splendid architectural heritage. The U.S.S.R. is putting pressure on its schools to produce more architects.

The "lost profession" has been rediscovered and revitalized. Russian architects are now charged with seeing that the people are not deprived of amenities. The new breed of social-minded architects know that they must take building a step further, that just "putting a roof over their heads" is not enough. That buildings, particularly housing, must possess the aura which is architecture. It makes no difference whether a building is built in a factory by machines or built at the site by skilled hands. It still must have architecture.

THESE "HOUSES" ON THE MOSKA - MOSCOW ARE PREFABRICATED. SOME RISE OVER 20 STORIES. RUSSIA'S PROCESS IS BETTER THAN THE PRODUCT. OFFICIALS ARE AWARE OF THIS AND ARCHITECTS ARE BEING TRAINED TO HUMANIZE HOUSING THE MASSES.

CONCERN WITH PROCESS IS NOT ENOUGH. THERE MUST BE ARCHITECTS' CONCERN WITH THE ARCHITECTURE OF THE PRODUCT.

In Russia, hope lies in the so-called "catalog system"—a super kit-of-parts which permits the components of many building systems to be interchangeable. If and when this happens, the every-one-alike, factory-built "houses" will be unnecessary, because the "kit" permits variety. As it is now, the architects have very little to say about either the function or the form, except those few architects who got in on the development of the model or "series" as the Russians call it. If the catalog system takes hold, the Soviet architects can get off the bench where they have been sitting for fifteen years and start playing the game. When they do this, they can flex their design muscles and develop the skills they seem to lack at this time. They might even still be quarterbacks and call the signals again.

In this country, the architect had better join the team before he is opted out. No longer can he have professionals around him serving as caddies. He must learn to work with not only other members of the expanded design profession which includes sociologists, psychologists, urban anthropologists, economists, and the like, but he must also form a working relationship with the manufacturers and the builders. All members must be concerned with architecture.

Process is not enough. There must be concern, too, with the product.

108

Building systems need examining to clarify the architects' position

Building systems were going strong as early as the 1850s, exemplified by the Crystal Palace, which might be classified as a "closed system." It took another 100 years, however, to reach the development stage which might be classified as an "open system," in essence a second-generation building system. There is a third generation, the "universal system," in the offing. The three generations of building systems are described as follows:

Closed systems are those which result in a standardized, complete building such as the sectionalized house, where several boxes are put together with only one option—to vary the length of the building. A more pure form of the closed system is the portable classroom or the mobile home. Essentially, the products of closed systems are stock buildings. If one wants to buy such a building, he chooses the model that seems best to fill his needs as he would in buying a car. It might well be he would even select the "model" from a showroom. There may be several models to choose from, but certainly the buyer or the user has very little choice.

Closed systems are prevalent in Russia. The Soviets have "trusts" and "combines" which manufacture huge stock buildings. For example, in Leningrad there are six housing combines which manufacture and erect large apartment houses. These combines are like auto manufacturers. Each one makes a different model. One manufactures the structural concrete components—walls, floors, and cladding—and erects five-story "houses" to a turnkey situation. Another combine does the same thing for a nine-story "house," and still another for a sixteen-story "house." The models are different and the parts are not interchangeable. Each model has its own stock plan, its own assembly line for manufacturing the parts, and its own established erection techniques including equipment to put the component in place. Only the lengths can be varied. Closed systems have the advantages of economy and speed of manufacturing and erecting; and the disadvantages of the products being monotonous. The "box system" or "3-D System," as it is called in Russia, is a classical example of the closed

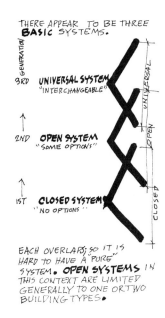

THERE APPEAR TO BE THREE **BASIC** SYSTEMS.

3RD GENERATION

UNIVERSAL SYSTEM "INTERCHANGEABLE"

2ND **OPEN SYSTEM** "SOME OPTIONS"

1ST **CLOSED SYSTEM** "NO OPTIONS"

UNIVERSAL / OPEN / CLOSED

EACH OVERLAPS; SO IT IS HARD TO HAVE A "PURE" SYSTEM. **OPEN SYSTEMS** IN THIS CONTEXT ARE LIMITED GENERALLY TO ONE OR TWO BUILDING TYPES.

system for large-scale housing projects. It's fast and relatively cheap, but carries with it the outlandish restrictions that since the boxes are the same size, all the rooms in the apartments must be the same size. There is monotony inside and out. Even the Russians are aware of this but say "It's a good way to put roofs over the masses."

Architects have no use for "closed systems." They are too restraining in the design effort. They breed monotony. And frankly, they eliminate the need for architects except in the developmental stages.

Open systems are defined as those which permit some options of choice relating to form, function, and economy of the final product. In other words, an open system would allow designers a reasonable range of choices of form, say the opportunity to have either a three-story building or a nine-story building. It would also be sufficiently flexible so that the "kit of parts" might be used to build either an apartment block, an office building, or perhaps a school. And the open system also would permit choices in materials and finishes which affect the quality of the fabric and subsequently the total cost. One is the Balency system used at Thamesmead. Another example of the open system is one called the "Bison wall frame," a system for housing manufactured by Concrete Limited of London. It can be used for offices, wings of hospitals, university buildings, dormitories, and townhouses. The system is of precast concrete and can go up from two to thirty stories using the same size transverse loadbearing wall panels. There is a wide choice of finishes, exterior and interior. The components are transported to the site and are erected by a small but skilled construction team which makes use of mobile and tower cranes. The architects have choices within a limited range, enough so that the buildings do not look or function alike; however, this particular open system is not "open" enough to permit building a schoolhouse. The same company has another system for that. The various so-called open systems do not have interchangeable parts with other systems. The main reason for this is the lack of communication among the manufacturers and strong resistance by the design profession.

Architects are still reluctant to accept fully the "open systems" because they think the systems are not "open" enough—too restrictive, with little room for creativity. The first Toronto SEF system school, which some classify as "open system," most certainly is "closed" as regards exterior cladding—heavy concrete wall panels, anchored on the light steel structure. But it would have been "open" in concept if the low bids had included three or four choices of materials and panel designs.

Universal systems, with a much higher degree of universality, are defined as those systems in which there are interrelationships among the various systems, specifically where the parts are interchangeable. The intersystem represents an advanced stage of evolution of building systems, but is far from reality. What such a system would do is this: Designers would have an infinite variety of choices. They would have at their disposal a super "erector set" which would allow them to build any building type, any size and shape, yet reap the benefits of the economies of standardization and mass production. It would be a kind of Sweets catalog erector set that works. The Soviet architects have such a system in mind when they look forward to the day the catalog system is put into full operation. It too is far from reality. In essence, this type of system calls for manufacturing prefabricated building elements according to specially prepared catalogs and standards mandatory for both designing and mass industrialized manufacturing. Theoretically any type, size, and shape of building can be designed and erected from standardized parts. In this country, the architects look forward to the day when computers serving as brains can be combined with automation to mass produce total tailor-made buildings.

The universal system is considered a Uptopian scheme by most authorities, but it must come about. It might well be the answer to giving assurance that mass housing has the aura of architecture. But if this truly universal intersystem does come about, the design-type architect will have the opportunity to exercise his full design talents.

109

Let the team—designers, manufacturers, and builders—be the architect

Let the process be industrialization.

What has been said in this section is this: Out of our chaos of construction confusion, there appear these clearly recognizable trends of building processes and procedures:

• The incredible gap between design and construction is gradually being closed by architects' willingness to design within the restrictions of construction systems.
• The confusion and fragmentation of on-the-site construction is decreasing and there is more at-the-factory erection using the systems approach.
• The design professions, the materials and components suppliers, and the erectors are beginning to see that they must get together in teamwork.

Industrialization of the building industry—on the site as well as in the factories—is necessary to conserve money and time. But there is danger in industrialization if it leads to complete standardization and if architects are left out of the process.

This is the Quincy, Massachusetts Vocational/Technical School designed by the CRS team with Kenneth F. Parry and Associates in 1964. Architecture is not so precious that it is only for the elite. It should be for everyone to enjoy. Someone must be concerned about architecture, even for factory-type buildings.

Jonathan King, who took charge of CRS' building system program in 1970, has some definite ideas concerning industrialized building:

"Economic and population demands are increasingly going to force us to deal with building problems in a generic rather than on a project basis. This means pulling manufacturers, builders, and planners together to solve social problems. And this means building systems as well as the systems approach—dealing with social, economic, industrial, and architectural factors all at once.

"It requires different kinds of people with a great variety of skills working together on a set of common objectives; not a hierarchy, but a team. Real industrialization of the building industry doesn't just imply making more of the building in a factory. It means a whole new set of relationships and long-range commitments."

King argues further that "manufacturers, builders, and designers, if not completely unified in the future, certainly must know a lot more about each other."

Regardless of how extensive and well-developed the industrialized process is, there will be mass-produced sameness and dullness unless architects fight for architecture. Architecture can come about only when manufacturers, builders, and designers join together in concert to create architecture by team. Let the team be the architect.

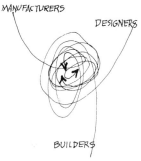

MANUFACTURERS
DESIGNERS
BUILDERS

THE DIVIDED TRISECTOR OF THE **BUILDING INDUSTRY** MUST BECOME INVOLVED WITH EACH OTHERS PROBLEMS.

Section 10

The
Expanded
Team

Small teams do simple, small projects. Large teams do large, complex ones. Some teams consist mostly of architects. Some, engineers only. Other teams are highly interdisciplinary in character. The latter, particularly the large, interdisciplinary team, is our concern in this section. The trend is toward the expanded team—the team that can perform mammoth tasks, such as providing housing, transportation, harbors and waterways, shopping centers, schools, churches, colleges, recreational facilities, and cultural centers as integral parts of a unified, living, beautiful city. Problems of urbanization can be solved, provided that the many specialists within government, private enterprise, the building industry, and the service professions join in team action.

110
The CRS team expands

When Rowlett and I started the firm, all we needed was a two-man team. And that was all we wanted. It was just the right size to do the small houses that came into the office. But we still worked as a team—a tiny team, but a team nevertheless.

The small houses were so simple that with our training we could do the mechanical and structural ourselves. But when we got a small elementary school, we had to acquire a mechanical engineer and a structural engineer to complete the job. And when large projects were given to the firm, we had to increase the size of the firm simply because there was more work to do in the same amount of time. To do the more complex jobs, it also became necessary to enlarge the team with people of varied talents and experience.

Later, as still larger projects, such as the thirteen-building San Angelo High School, began to come into the office, we felt the need to add a planner to our team—a person with skill and experience in large-scale planning, one who knew how to deal with pedestrian and vehicular traffic, solve the landscaping problems relating to the "outdoor rooms," and design outside spaces such as promenades, plazas, courts, walks, and drives. So by necessity, the CRS team had to grow, and keep growing.

My professional friends who claim they deliberately control the growth of their firms do so by restricting the scope and type of projects they are capable of doing. If they wish to do only small houses on an individual basis then they can keep the size of their firms to small numbers. Some

Desert Samaritan Hospital and Health Center in Phoenix, Arizona is designed for expansion. Year-long programming and design process brought the whole community into the action. Drover, Welch and Lindlan were associate architects.

294

do. This is great. The profession needs all kinds of firms. When CRS chose to do larger and more complicated schools, then colleges and universities, then urban redevelopment, civic centers, and large hospital complexes, we committed ourselves to a much larger firm.

So throughout the years, we have added specialists in all facets of engineering, including civil engineering. We have also added specialists in programming, estimating, computerized specifications and estimating, interior design, architectural graphics, publication graphics, and landscaping, as well as specialists in the various building types, such as hospitals, community colleges, civic centers, and convention centers. And last but not least, we have brought in trained business people to keep us out of the red. They were not always successful, I should add, but over the long haul, CRS has been a money maker. We don't think it is sinful to make money— to give our people decent houses and their children educational opportunities.

The team to design a highly complicated hospital complex must be quite different from the task team which designed the Carlsbad High School (below). Kern Smith was our associated architect.

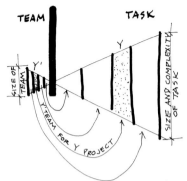

TEAM   TASK

SIZE OF TEAM
Y'
Y
Y-TEAM FOR Y PROJECT
SIZE AND COMPLEXITY OF TASK

THE **LARGER,** MORE COMPLEX
PROJECTS (OR TASKS) REQUIRE
LARGER, MORE SOPHISTICATED
TEAMS.

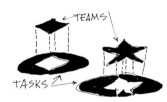

TEAMS
TASKS

TEAMS MUST MATCH TASKS.
THE CONSISTENCY AND MAKE-UP
OF THE **ARCHITECTURAL
TEAM** CONSTANTLY CHANGE.
SOME SPECIALTIES BECOME
OBSOLETE; OTHERS JUST
BEGIN. MORE BASIC IS THE
FACT THAT MOST EVERY TASK
OR PROJECT REQUIRES A
DIFFERENT KIND OF TEAM.

In any case, CRS grew in volume of work produced and in number of people required to do it. The CRS team became larger and larger—deliberately. To do the size jobs we wanted to do, we had to grow. From a talent point of view, we had to have more coverage. From the sheer numbers aspect, we had to have more people to get out the work. We committed ourselves to the large team. And we shall have to be larger if we are to tackle the giant, complicated projects of urbanization which we would like to do.

111

Teams are made for certain types and sizes of projects

Architectural firms are like general contractors in a way. Some contractors do "heavy construction"; some do 'light construction." During CRS' first five years, whether we knew it or not we were limited in what we were capable of producing. We could do small houses, stores, and apartments with a fair degree of competence. And we could do elementary schools up to $500,000 with a high degree of competence. When we were ten years old, it was necessary to establish a minimum construction cost limit. It seemed that we could do nothing under $500,000 without a financial loss. In fact, one-third of our buildings were in the red and the majority of them could be classified in the below $500,000 class. We were geared to do large work. We became "heavies." This lower limit was increased every year until at this writing, Scott, Rowlett, and Bullock, our chief job getters, don't try very hard to land jobs under $3,000,000—simply because we are geared to do even bigger jobs and cannot seem to make a profit on the small ones. We do the small ones either for fun or in the hope that they will lead to larger ones.

At this writing we have initiated a program with great promise for recapturing the small schoolhouse market which we enjoyed and which made a substantial contribution during CRS' first ten years. We are beginning to retool (pardon the expression) for industrialized building systems which hopefully will provide high-quality schools at mass-produced prices. The next step, then, is to reach down to see what we can do with small dwelling units.

My wife Edith and I had already designed and built two homes for our family: the first in Bryan, Texas in 1946 and the second in neighboring College Station in 1952. So if there was a burning desire to design my own house, this should have been satisfied.

When we moved to Houston in 1959, I honestly wanted the CRS team to do our next house. I had envisioned Frank Lawyer on the overall massing and proportions—there is none better than Frank at this. I wanted Charles Lawrence on design development—there is none better. And I wanted to bring in our landscape people, our interior designers, our best engineers, and many others, each of whom had surpassed me in certain aspects of design.

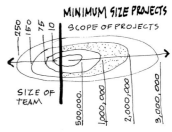

WE BECAME **HEAVIES.** WE HAD GEARED OURSELVES TO DO ONLY THE LARGE, COMPLICATED PROJECTS.

I wanted this all-star team for two reasons: First, as a team, it could produce a better house than I could by myself. And second, I was, by this time, committed to the team concept, certainly more so than during the design of our first two houses. I wanted my third home to be CRS-designed, not Caudill-designed.

The sad truth was that I could not afford my own firm.

To do that house, either CRS would have had to take Caudill on as a charity case or I would have had to pay an enoromous fee to keep the project in the black. We are "heavies," so by necessity I did it with my own lily white hands. The preliminary plans were done on the circular breakfast room table and the working drawings on a small drafting board in the living room. My son Bill would ask me every weekend, "Dad, when are you going to get that drafting board out of the living room?" No wonder he decided not to be an architect.

THE YOUNG MEN IN THE FIRM WERE AMAZED THAT **THE OLD MAN** COULD EVEN USE A T-SQUARE AND TRIANGLE--NOT TO MENTION A **CIRCULAR DRAFTING BOARD.**

The house story points out the ridiculous state of affairs for people who want tailor-made homes. The situation is this: Most architects are not geared to do small houses. There are very few architects who are able, willing , and in a financial position to enjoy the luxury of designing individual houses. And there are very few contractors geared to bidding and building architect-designed houses. So both architects and contractors have lost the house market by default. To regain it will require drastic changes in professional attitudes and construction procedures. Attitude? Architects must be willing to design within constraints of "kits of parts." Procedures? Contractors must have closer liaison with manufacturers. But doesn't this rule out the tailor-made house? Not necessarily.

If designers, manufacturers, and builders can get together—think and do in team action—a new kind of tailor-made house (as well as small schools, churches, and stores) is within the realm of possibility. Automated mass production with computers serving as brains could produce special individual houses on an assembly-line basis. This idea, according to Gary K. Stonebraker, President, Advanced Planning Research Group, Inc. (closely associated with CRS2 and CRS) is far past the dream stage. To do this will not require a giant interdisciplinary team. After the system is established, then the small architectural firm and the small contractor can come back into play.

112

Who is an architect?

If architects fear infringement of other disciplines on our territory, and we do, what do the other disciplines think when architects move into their territory—if it really is "theirs" or if it is "our territory"? Jim Falick of the CRS team, in May 1970, spoke at Columbia University College of Physicians and Surgeons to a group of doctors who were in for post-graduate training in community psychiatry. His lecture concerned how one pulls together into a team a group of people who are of very high status and competitive attitudes; how one gets the dynamic group on a CRS programming squatters going; and how the CRS design squatters can involve the community.

At the end of the session, one of the physicians turned to the professor and said that what he could not understand is why an architect, even one trained in community psychiatry as Jim was, should know about implementing community action programs, and added, "This architect knows more than three quarters of the sociologists and psychiatrists who have lectured to us."

Highly qualified professionals like Jim Falick are eradicating superficial borders separating the disciplines. Is it "their" territory or is it "ours"? Really! Competence must always overrule territorial rights.

CRS has moved into other territories. In early 1969 we found ourselves with three other firms in the finals competing for a commission with the Baltimore City Public Schools to develop "a management system for facilities planning." There was no building design involved in the traditional

WHO IS AN ARCHITECT?

AN ARCHITECT IS A PROFESSIONAL WHO CONTRIBUTES THROUGH TEAM EFFORT TO PLANNING, DESIGNING, AND BUILDING FORMS AND SPACES THAT POSSESS THE AURA OF ARCHITECTURE, FULFILLING PUBLIC RESPONSIBILITY.

WHAT IS AN ARCHITECTURAL TEAM?

IT IS A TEAM OF PROFESSIONALS WHOSE PRIME CONCERN IS TO PRODUCE FORMS AND SPACES WHICH POSSESS ARCHITECTURE.

architectural practice sense. Competitors? Two were nationally known management consultants, a third was one of the world's largest accounting firms. We were the only architectural firm in the running. We got the job.

Our prime task was to "assist in establishing an orderly and efficient approach to meeting its (Baltimore's) school facility needs." This strictly concerned process—nothing directly to do with architectural product. A CRS team led by Don Wines spent from March 1969 to June 30, 1970 in Baltimore. Bob Brooks and Dave Thorman remained for another year as a follow-through. Wines expressed it well in a memo dated 25 June 70: "In Baltimore we have no *direct* responsbility or control of the end result; in fact, the traditional services of the architect are expressly omitted. We are, in effect, an agent or extension of the client/owner." The team's main activities covered problem identification, development and approach, implementation and training, support and documentation. In the CRS team's report to the Superintendent of Public Instruction, Dr. Thomas D. Shelton, Wines stated that future activity of the Board of School Commissioners "will require the dedicated effort of a larger team to ultimately involve the total city in a creative partnership." Without a doubt the Baltimore experience expanded the concept of team for CRS, if not the team itself. For the first time Wines and his group of architects were involved in solving problems unrelated to design.

In the summer of 1967, CRS sent an arm of its team, led by Mike Trower, to Hartford, Connecticut, to manage the design-making process necessary to plan and construct six schools with community facilities for a total of $53,000,000. CRS had direct control or influence on the design as well as a responsibility for overall management. Within three months after being hired, CRS had initiated or completed the following studies: construction market analysis, study and refinement of educational program and translation into a space program, budget analysis, site analysis/climate analysis, coordination with City of Hartford Master Plan, review of existing City and State educational plans, and code research.

In June 1967 an intensive work session "pre-squatters" was held in Houston. Research data previously collected were discussed, alternatives presented, and basic decisions taken affecting the firm's approach to the school building program. Hartford officials were flown to Houston to take part in the session; design and management personnel—in fact, everyone who would have responsibility for seeing the work carried out—were brought in at this early stage. As a result, educational priorities were established and principal building systems selected.

Decision to establish a satellite office in Hartford was based on the premises that (1) the scope of the project would require day-to-day management; (2) continuous study of the local situation was needed to keep up with fast-changing social attitudes; (3) the characteristic of the multi-headed client/user—City Council, City Engineering Department, School Board, City Welfare Department, and City School Administration, not to mention the various civic groups—required daily on-the-spot attention; and (4) "being there" insured good communication with the associate architectural firms, Russell, Gibson and von Dohlen; Jeter and Cook; Richard Butterfield and Associates.

Both Baltimore and Hartford expanded the scope and accelerated the experience of the CRS team. To do this, attitudes, particularly "design is everything," had to be changed. Designers had to be converted to management consultants and programming experts. But it was not as drastic a change as it might appear. For years CRS was gradually conditioning itself for the expanded team—obtaining commissions that had nothing to do with individual buildings. Certainly this was true with the Brazos Area Plan.

In August 1957, officials of the two cities of College Station and Bryan, Texas, and Brazos County began to discuss the idea of coordinated planning among their agencies. They found that Texas law had no provisions for joint planning between two cities or a city and a county. They went on to develop a new kind of planning team. The Brazos Area Planning Corporation was established in 1958 as a nonprofit corporation with representatives from Brazos County, Bryan, College Station, and Texas A&M. CRS joined the team as consultants in 1958. The CRS team included planners, architects, and engineers. Phil Williams and Ed Finlay represented CRS. It was decided not to seek state or federal funds, and financing was accomplished through contributions from the agencies involved, in the forms of money and services.

The BAPC met each month to review and coordinate the consultants' work. Day-to-day support and data were supplied by officials of the public agencies involved. Traffic engineering and computer processing of an origin and destination survey of campus traffic were furnished by the Texas Transportation Institute at A&M. At appropriate times, volunteer citizen committees studied CRS reports on specific elements of the plan. The planning study process covered over two years and must have directly involved nearly 200 people.

The study developed through a series of preliminary reports and culminated in a comprehensive plan for the entire county. The final summary report was published in April 1961. The study was thorough, with effective citizen participation and support. An important result was a far better understanding by everyone of each agency's particular problem and needs.

This led to a plan which incorporated effective coordination of land use, circulation, and services, without sacrificing differing basic philosophies

302

and traditions. For example, College Station retained and revised its zoning ordinance, while Bryan remained unzoned.

The basic concept of the plan was a connected system of complementary centers. This meant that instead of each city's competing in every area of endeavor, Bryan would concentrate on commercial services, College Station on supporting the educational center, while the total group cooperated on development of a cultural center.

What lessons did we learn from this study? Phil Williams states it: "For the first time CRS was confronted with problems relating to an entire county. The planning approach is exactly the same as it is for a small neighborhood. There is no reason why we are not qualified to do the same thing at the state scale." (We did it for higher education in New Jersey and Connecticut.) Another lesson: "The planning process itself can be an effective catalyst for communications. It requires a team. Where the law or custom does not encourage it, determined people can form the right team and do an effective job."

Williams, however, points out that without law or custom, implementation may run into difficulties. He continues, "There's one problem with this. In the case where the planning study is on a voluntary 'quasi-public' basis, it is difficult to develop effective (legal) tools for implementation. To a large extent the Brazos Area Plan has been a useful guideline. In some cases, however, there have been sharp departures by certain agencies, for example in school site selection."

Throughout CRS' history, there has been an increasing number of "management-only" projects; not only planning projects, but surveys and feasibility studies as well. We have gradually overcome the notion that design is everything (in the product sense). On the other hand, we are becoming more convinced every day that creative, highly artistic designers must be strong participants on almost every team, particularly planning projects like the one we did for Brazos County.

113
The computer joins the CRS team

Bob Mattox learned early the value of the computer in architectural practice—and did something about it. For one thing he convinced the CRS board of directors to put him into business as president of CRS2, Computing Research Systems. He was only thirty years old.

This is a rather remarkable story because at the time Bob was plugging for a separate division for computers, board member designers, including Caudill, had real doubts. Why should we buy a computer when we could use the money better buying designers? Actually it was Chuck Thomsen, another computer addict, who convinced the CRS Board to get a computer. He and Bob deserve credit with a strong assist from Paseur and Bullock for creating CRS2.

As for me, I did not exactly fight it, but I certainly did not push it. I shall never forget the day in our Houston office on Richmond Avenue when, feeling rather insecure, I spent some time in the computer section, trying to figure out how computerized specifications were being produced, how Phil Williams and his group were programming Duke University with the computer as the main tool, and how to justify what seemed to be an exorbitant

Architects fought the computer at first. Now they know they need it. They need it to help program jobs and the way people move about, as well as to make estimates, design structures, figure heat loads, and write specifications. They now look toward the day when the computer can serve as the brains for a highly mechanized assembly line which can turn out components for "tailor-made" buildings. CRS has always been in the forefront of computer use in architectural practice. CRS2 (Computing Research Systems) is a separate corporation to serve other architectural firms and compete in a more open market, unhampered by outmoded professional ethics.

expense to maintain our roaring monster that disturbed my tranquility and vomited the tons of numbers which I could not understand. I looked at Bob and he appeared to be in ecstacy. Not me. I was in a state of cultural shock.

Leaving the carpeted computer "home" (we designers did not have carpets), I went around the corner to our interior design section and immediately felt better. There I saw Janis Jones (who later married Bob) working away on a sewing machine. It seems she was making a portion of an 8' × 20' fabric mural for the Texas Children's Hospital. I did not care in the least what she was making, but I understood what she was doing with that machine and that made me feel better. What Bob was doing with his machine was beyond my comprehension, then.

Architects pride themselves on their ability to probe for original ideas, new approaches, inventive solutions to problems of their clients' environment. Paradoxically, architects are often the most reluctant to accept changes in their processes of achieving these solutions. If we accept progress as desirable and necessary, we should make use of every tool, device, method, and procedure to enhance the possibility of attaining the most contemporary solutions.

The electronic computer is about as old as CRS. Twenty-five years ago this most remarkable invention became a reality. According to Bob Mattox, already we are in the third generation of computer complexity. Staggering advances lie just ahead. We want to be ready, if not to be one of those firms to cause the progress.

Bob is convinced, and most of us in CRS agree, that the computer as an information processing device has liberated man's approach to thinking in many problem areas. New sciences and industries have developed around the computer industry, creating new professions and jobs which could not have been defined a few years ago. Architects, engineers, and planners are finally beginning to take notice.

CRS approached this new and mystical science of computing with curiosity and trepidation at first, but later with an eagerness to learn, primarily because of Thomsen, Williams and Mattox. As with any ventures into new fields, the experiences have been helpful, productive, and sobering.

In the summer of 1966 Educational Facilities Laboratories, Duke University, and CRS entered into the first phase of a study which was to last two and one-half years. The objective of the study was to develop and demonstrate ways in which computing technology could assist planners and administrators in managing and planning campus facilities. Application of systems analysis and computing had already begun to be used in administrative operations; this study focused upon the demands for different kinds of facilities based upon changes in activities of students, faculty, and staff.

The study was divided into three major tasks: (1) room inventory data collection and analysis, (2) student activity data collection and analysis, and (3) Campus Planning Model. Charles Thomsen, Phil Williams, and Bob Mattox took the lead for CRS. Robert Holz and Richard Willard, data processing consultants, were brought in to help.

The room inventory procedures captured data on each room in the university and included dimensions, utilities, number of occupants, use and type of space and other pertinent information useful in assigning space to users, such as departments and administrative functions, studying utilization of space, repairs and maintenance.

Scheduled student activities were well documented; however, unscheduled student activities such as study, recreation, and eating were more difficult to quantify and locate. A "diary" was developed and tested at Duke. A sample of undergraduate students kept records of their activities twenty-four hours a day for seven consecutive days. Each student recorded the time, location, and nature of his activity. These diaries were optically scanned and computer programs were written to analyze the resulting data. Analysis shows facility utilization, student circulation patterns, frequency and duration of activities. This technique for collecting data provided more continuous and comprehensive data and permitted analysis of subsamples of the data by characteristics of students. These two aspects of the study have since proved useful in managing and planning facilities.

The third task was to develop a mathematical model of the university. This model was not successful in being applied in an actual planning context but may be useful in generating ideas for more practical planning tools. The model accepted descriptions in terms of space and activities. Changes in both activities and space were simulated over time as a result of changes in other variables such as number of students, desirability for activities to be near one another, and utilization goals.

During the course of the study, seminars were held to include sociologists, educators, planners, and architects. The initial seminars helped define the relative roles which these people should play in the planning process. Designs of student diaries and questionnaires were shaped as a result of these seminars.

The conclusions of the study were that systematic approaches to planning are valuable because of the rigorous discipline imposed in the definition of objectives, collection of data, and interpretation of analysis. A major benefit is the ability to ask questions and study alternative strategies.

CRS leased its computer in 1966 and began developing applications in management and architectural production. The goal from the beginning has been to integrate the computer and the people and disciplines surrounding it into the CRS team. The operation grew. In July 1969 CRS2 was formed as an affiliate company, taking as its nucleus CRS people, machines, and programs. We now rely upon CRS2 for computer services. To separate the operation might seem to weaken the effort to make computing part of the team. Not so. CRS2, under the CRS umbrella, is another team of specializing architects and information specialists who have as their basic concern to improve and refine the procedures and the content of information processing for decision making.

The excursion into computing is a logical extension of the basic CRS approach of problem seeking/solving. Computers are used because problems are larger and more complex, the amount of data and their interrelatedness often overwhelming, and the number of alternative approaches more numerous. The purpose of processing data by any means is first to provide information to define problems more clearly and solutions more meaningfully. Secondly, processed data should provide information to make better judgments about alternative solutions.

Often the greatest benefit of using the computer is the discipline it imposes to order and structure the problem. It has made us think straight. It helps eliminate the fuzz. One must state very clearly the problem that is to be solved and the method for evaluating alternative solutions. The uniqueness of CRS2 is the combination of information processing and the problems of architecture. There simply are not many companies treating these problems in this manner.

114

Use the users

Involving the users in the planning process cannot be overemphasized. And it is not impractical to do. We have done it with schools—actually bringing in the children as well as their teachers; with hospitals—involving the nurses as well as the doctors and administrators (and each of us has been a patient at one time or another); and with university buildings—bringing in the student leaders as well as the professors and administrators.

A rather unique method of user involvement is connected with programming and planning the Albert Thomas Convention Center, Houston. James Gatton, Truitt Garrison, and Norman Hoover led our portion of the team. We were dealing with the city as a client, with Francis Deering as Director of the Civic Center Properties as our immediate city contact. Chester A. Wilkins, Executive Secretary of the Greater Houston Convention and Visitors Council, guided our early work.

This was the first major convention center that we had done. It was a joint venture with Bernard Johnson Engineers, who provided the mechanical, electrical, and structural services for the exhibit end and underground garage. Deering and Wilkins suggested that we visit a number of existing successful convention centers to find out what they were doing

This view is from one of the longest buildings in Houston with one of the longest names: The Albert Thomas National Space Hall of Fame Convention and Exhibit Center. It is a part of a four-unit segment of the Civic Center including the concert hall (background) adaptable to seating 1800 to 3000, the plaza occupying a downtown city square block, underground parking for 1800 cars, and the Convention Hall, which has 300,000 square feet. To plan this large complex required not only terribly large CRS teams, but also large teams of consultants outside of CRS—a team-of-teams situation.

309

right and where mistakes could be avoided. Gatton toured exhibit halls in Miami Beach, Baltimore, Philadelphia, Cleveland, Detroit, Chicago, and Tulsa during the programming phase (gathering as much information on what *not* to do as on what to do).

Wilkins and Deering suggested a series of "users panels" to be held in Houston, sponsored jointly by the Convention and Visitors Council and the City of Houston. The first panel was held the week of May 4, 1964, and involved the following participants: W. D. Lewis, Executive Secretary, Canning Machinery & Supplies Associates; Robert Burkhart, Assistant Executive Director, Texas Hospital Association; T. J. Hull, Executive Secretary, National Association of Corrosion Engineers; Ron Warren, Convention Manager, American Chemical Society; W. Price, Jr., Executive Vice President, Texas Restaurant Association.

They contributed to the late stages of the programming phase. The panel was timed just prior to the squatters.

The second users panel was invited to analyze the relative merits of the alternative designs that came out of the squatters session. These people helped us with that evaluation: William A. Belanger, Convention Manager, Air Force Association; Robert P. Kenworthy, President, American Welding Society, Inc., Robert Butts, Executive Director, Southern Medical Association; Robert Pore, Show Manager, Southern Automotive Association; "Buck" Freeman, President, Freeman Decorating Company.

The user panel idea has two merits: (1) A more functional building will result; and (2) unquestionably bringing the "users" in during the programming and planning stages arouses the interest of those participating organizations who contemplate conventions.

310

115

The "squatters" expands CRS' team

The CRS squatters was invented to solve a communication problem.

It came early. We were working on our first school project—two elementary schools for Blackwell, Oklahoma, 525 miles away from our office over the grocery store in College Station, Texas. We were having a most difficult time getting the preliminary plans approved. It seemed that we made at least four round trips trying to get the board to say "yes." It was always "no." Patience, enthusiasm, and money were running short. Finally I said (at least I'll take credit for it) to Wallie Scott, "Wallie, we are going to lose our shirts if we don't do something quick. How about you and me loading the drafting boards in your car (my car was so old it wouldn't stand the trip), driving to Blackwell, and squatting like Steinbeck's okies in the board room until we get the damn plans approved?" So we did.

We drove in on a Sunday night and early Monday morning we had our office open for business—in the board room. We never dreamed that fourteen years later we would be doing the same thing in the Harvard Faculty Club with a team of nine architects/engineers working with twelve distinguished professors. Back to Blackwell: Frankly, all we were interested in was to "get the damn plans approved." And come Friday night at a meeting with the board and the administration in the same room, the plans were "approved with unanimous enthusiasm." But a lot happened between Monday morning and Friday night. That could be another book. Part of it was written up in *Colliers* magazine. The main thing that happened was this: In trying to find a way to lick the distance problem, we happened upon a truth that should have been obvious to us all the time—the client/users want to get into the act of planning, and when they do there is no reason to get approval because then that is automatic. The communication problem is solved.

Throughout the years of our practice we have learned that client/users' involvement generally assures better facilities. This was hard to prove. Our friends in the profession thought that the squatters was the worst device that could possibly be. There were at least two articles written condemning the system. The chief argument was that to bring clients in would "nip good ideas in the bud." And there is some truth to that. That's the chance you take with the squatters. But we think it's worth it.

Not too long ago we received a brochure from another firm which included this sentence: "Our firm uses the new squatters method of design." It was a supreme and elegant compliment for such a "terrible" name to be included in the nomenclature of architectural practice.

Every so often CRS needs to be reminded of the advantages of client involvement. In 1953 we had a task to design the Florence Black Elementary School for Mesquite, Texas. We thought we could get along without a squatters. There was relatively no board members' involvement although the administration did participate heavily on the programming. Because of Pena's consistent insistence throughout the years, programming has always been a main strength of CRS. During the school board meeting in which we presented the preliminary plans, I found myself refereeing a fist fight between two board members. One liked the plans; the other violently disliked them. After we calmed them down a bit, the guy with the black hat (the bad guy) turned on me and said, "Damn it, it doesn't look like a school." "What does it look like?" I retorted. Then came the shocker. "It

"Talking out the bugs" during a squatters must go on continuously. Here Russell T. Tutt, Board of Trustees, Colorado College, is shown with me evaluating the output of the squatters for Olin Hall of Science. He was as much a part of the planning team as I.

looks like a bawdyhouse." Taken aback, I finally mustered up all the quiet indignation I could and said, "Sir, I wouldn't know."

Although I scored a few self-satisfying brownie points on that reply, it is a very poor way to communicate with clients. This would not have happened had we had a squatters with this man involved.

Compare the aforementioned fiasco with the squatters held in June 1968 for the Baltimore Comprehensive Mental Health and Retardation Center. Paul Kennon, Jim Falick, and Andy Wolfe led the CRS team. Fenton and Lichtig were the associate architects.

We established a work base at a walk-in Mental Health Center in the heart of the Negro ghetto area. This was a most stimulating squatters experience—a real advocacy planning effort. The squatters team set up a projector showing slides at five-second intervals of community images.

313

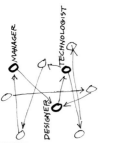

BEING A MEMBER OF A
CRS SQUATTERSTEAM
CARRIES RESPONSIBILITY
AND REQUIRES **TEAM-
WORK** WHICH HAS TAKEN
YEARS TO DEVELOP.

This was in the main work space and going at least twenty hours a day, involving the team continuously in the existing life style and providing an immediate involvement on the part of the hundreds of visitors and participants during that week. Participants included university staff, black leaders, agency heads and department heads, and other community representatives. Each person became stimulated by the work environment, expressed himself, and was very carefully listened to. Our response to each individual was sincere, and at the completion of the squatters, each of the leaders was presented a complete set of slides documenting the program and design process. These leaders went out into the community of 250,000 people and presented the process to all who would listen. The involvement was gratifying to all as an expanded team concept.

A year later, development of the project was stopped by a new state official. The community, the psychiatric and retardation staff, and various agencies felt so closely identified with the project that they initiated a program of people power, gained the support of the local press, and had the project reactivated. Talk about team action, this was on a combined community and professional scale—"epitomizing the concept of the expanded team" as Kennon so aptly put it.

The squatters, originally a freewheeling operation, every so often loses its intent by becoming overstructured. Periodically the squatters must be secularized, rejecting inherited rituals and phoney taboos so that open-mindedness prevails. Nothing will age a firm more than its own self-imposed rigidity.

I recall the time after a two-year absence from any CRS squatters, how shocked I was at the congealed attitude. The CRS squatters had been a free-wheeling, free-of-rules affair, in which there was only one purpose—to conceptualize with the client at the site the best solution with no worries about procedures. We worried only about finding the best solution in the most direct way. But now I was confronted with such outrageous talk as, "Mr. Caudill, we don't make our drawings in pencil anymore; we make them in ink." "Mr. Caudill, it is against our current policy to have fewer than twenty-five analysis cards." "Mr. Caudill, what you are doing is usually done at the end of the week since we have certain procedures which we must follow during squatters." Hogwash! Such overembellishment, overstructured procedures and methods can only lead to premature hardening of the arteries. The next squatters allowed for much more freedom of action, be assured.

Make no mistakes. The squatters is not easy to pull off. Tempers fly. Every day can be a crisis. Take the case of the February 1968 squatters in Bethlehem, Pennsylvania, to conceptualize the Northampton County Community College. Paul Kennon was the CRS design leader, Ralph Carroll the project manager, Joe Thomas the technologist, who formed the task troika. Coston, Wallace and Watson were our associated architects.

The CRS squatters team members who participated in this Abington, Pennsylvania, high school will never forget that event. We had set up office in the basement of the Administration building free from distractions—except one. It was during that week that Alan Sheppard made the first space flight. The excitement of designing this school and bending our ears to the little radio was nearly too much. Both projects proved successful.

During the squatters a real crisis appeared Tuesday night as a concept began to emerge in response to the college's educational program and goals. This was an extremely innovative program, producing an innovative architectural diagram for the community college. The president, while dynamic in educational conceptualizing, reacted very strongly when the design concept was not what he had imagined it would be. He stated that his image of a college was one of dispersed buildings with ivy on the walls and was shocked to find a contiguous kind of growth diagram emerging. The president was asked if the diagram was in direct response to his program and did the architectural organization fail to meet his objectives. He said it did, indeed, meet the objectives, but that it wasn't "looking like" what he had anticipated it to "look like" and perhaps the program should be changed. At that, Kennon, Carroll, and Thomas recommended the team pack its gear and return to Houston until the program was firmed up. The president made the very intelligent remark that he had learned never to make a major decision after midnight—it was then 2:00 A.M. He suggested that the group reconvene the next morning to decide what action should be taken.

Our CRS people went back to the motel quite disappointed. They conceived a plan to wear Northampton County Area Community College sweat shirts that the students were wearing to let the president know that "we are all on the same team." So, first thing in the morning Ralph Carroll secured six of the sweat shirts from the campus store—dark blue with bold white letters—which the CRS men quickly donned, then began working away. When the president arrived, the scene had him in stitches. Goodwill was established and the message was clear that the CRS gang and the client/user were indeed all on the same team. The president became more confident that the concept was correct and was reassured by visits from the Chairman of the Board.

I guess the message here is that a little humor helps smooth over some of the rough spots and gives a clear perspective. Even though there are times of conflict, as there will be in human interaction, we should somehow maintain the awareness that team members work toward common goals.

Squatters are becoming more complex and more sophisticated. One held in Galveston, Texas, the week of March 28, 1969, bears recording (March 1970 issue, *Progressive Architecture*, "Beating the System Game"). This time it was more of a team of teams. A. T. Kearney Company, a Chicago management consulting firm, served as the "prime contractor," CRS as the team of architects and programmers. The job was to program/plan a new Public Health Service hospital for merchant seamen. On Monday morning the squatters team met with the client to turn a "long and nearly impenetrable maze of tasks, sub-tasks, and sub-sub-tasks into a hospital program." Representing CRS at the leadership level was Bob Douglass, Jim Falick, and Bill Cannady.

Our people created a simple game to try to resolve complexity into simplicity. Bob Douglass spelled it out this way:

"The game we devised was not a sophisticated theory-of-games game. It was more like a real kid's game with a game board, simple rules, pieces to move, and different positions or roles for various players. The game was scored by all the information in the Functional Packages, but mainly by the Master Cross Relationship Diagram. This diagram had been developed as an abstract, quantitative expression of the idealized proximities and reasons for the desired proximity for the total hospital. The more relationships on the game board that agreed with the Master Cross Relationship Diagram, the more points that particular scheme received. The areas that lost points were identified, the scheme was modified if possible or abandoned if not. The game board rules were based on the idea that the thing that makes a building different from a totally abstract system is that people and things get into it and move around. These concepts—access and movement—were the ordering elements around which the squares of colored paper began to organize themselves. By simplifying our process into the most elementary terms that anyone could understand, and into a format that didn't intimidate by looking like DESIGN, anyone could play and become a designer."

Everyone did get into the act on this one. Not only the programming team (ATK/CRS) and the PHS Hospital staff, but the president of the University of Texas Medical Branch in Galveston, members of this staff, PHS headquarters personnel, the mayor of Galveston, and the congressman from the district. Bob related the experience of group dynamics this way:

"The way the gameboard catalyzed communication, the spontaneous and furious ricochetting of ideas around the gaming table, was fascinating."

The squatters resulted in the winning solution our CRS people liked best (that's always nice) but the decision was not uncontested. Final decision came about after the squatters team constructed a three-dimensional flow chart (started 3 A.M. Friday) which was presented to the Public Health Service and the University of Texas Medical Branch officials just after lunch.

The next step in programming the increasingly complex projects our firm and others like ours are getting is to make use of the gaming method with the computer. But most likely this will not be as much fun as the game at Galveston.

116

Outsiders add strength to our firm

In 1963 CRS experimented with bringing professors in to stimulate our designers. Wearing two hats at the time—being Director of the School of Architecture as well as being an active partner in our firm—I conceived a plan which would help Rice University as well as CRS. The professors at Rice needed practical experience and the designers in CRS needed more theory. "Why not get the professors and the CRS designers together in team action, but not in the usual sense as summertime employees in the case of the professors? Let the professors come in and do their 'thing' which our people could not do. Dream. Philosophize. Be uninhibited. And then, let our people do the things the professors were less qualified to do because of the lack of experience, like functionalizing the buildings and hitting the budget." Since up to this time CRS had been such a close-knit, even fraternal organization, the thought of bringing in outside designers was repugnant to many of our people. But when chosen with Rogers and Nagel of Denver to design a completely new campus for Southern Colorado State College, we tried an experiment.

The prime purpose of the experiment was to stimulate our design team. We hired two professors from Rice University—Anderson Todd and Bill Lacy—and gave them these instructions: "Go to Pueblo. Literally live on the site. Talk to the town's people. Forget program. And budget. Just think. Just dream. Make a few sketches if you wish. Decide the spirit. Then come back and give our design team a shot in the arm. Inspire. Challenge. Suggest. Do anything to stimulate the designers to do a great job." Todd and Lacy, after spending a week in Pueblo, came back to

FOUR YEARS PRIOR TO THE **TODD/LACY** REPORT, THE CRS TEAM IN CORNING, N.Y. DEVISED A PROGRAMMING DOCUMENT, SIMILAR IN CONCEPT, CALLED **SPECIFICATIONS FOR ARCHITECTURE.** I HAVE ALWAYS BEEN **SCHIZOPHRENIC** ABOUT TEACHING AND PRACTICING. I WAS INTRODUCED ONCE AS "A MAN WHO RAN HIS SCHOOL AS A FIRM AND HIS FIRM AS A SCHOOL".

Houston with beautiful words and suggestive sketches. They reported their ideas to us. They brought back slogans like "let's be bolder than Boulder," which they said would rid the inferiority complex which Pueblo had for thinking itself only a mill town. They made beautiful but vague sketches of suggested form. We were stimulated, particularly Charles Lawrence, the chief designer; Herb Paseur, the project manager; Jim Hughes, who helped put the package together. Lawrence and his design group came very close to capturing the spirit advocated by the Todd-Lacy report.

In 1966 and 1967, the college received three awards—honor awards in both the Western Mountain Region and Texas Region of AIA, plus an award of merit for the library in a national competition. The experiment apparently paid off. The professors did something the pros could not—dream. Our people were too tied down to the realities of program and budget. In our desire to serve the client by putting every penny to "practical use" we had forgotten the amenities. It took two outside professor-architects to jar us loose so we too could dream.

WE BROUGHT IN
OUTSIDE TALENT.

Even more important, this experiment changed our attitude about bringing in outside talent. Up to then, we considered design too precious to be tampered with by people other than our CRS designers. We were too possessive of our product. This experience took us a step closer to the expanded team.

Expanding the team to include outsiders may prove difficult to most architects. It was at first with us. At least two different times the CRS team informally decided that we would discontinue our practice of associating with other architects. We were blaming all our troubles on our associates—like poor client relationship, design interference, over-the-budget lettings, excessive number of change orders, and poor construction administration. And unjustly so in the far majority of cases. The trouble was this: We had not yet learned to appreciate and work with other firms. Now it is a lot easier for those of us in CRS to work with outsiders because we have put the expanded team concept into practice. We are convinced that associations can produce better buildings and services.

Consider CRS involvement in an Illinois community college program. Some thirty-five districts were created throughout the state and are now in various stages of planning new campuses. CRS is doing nine of these new campuses from scratch. All but two are being done in association with local architects. The planning process here calls for top-flight team action because of the number of state agencies involved, each having different responsibilities.

Jim Hughes, one of our community college specialists who with Bob Reed has assumed leadership in our behalf, particularly values the important role of the local associate. Jim states, "Having local architects on the project team is most natural for us in CRS. In fact it is a lot easier for CRS to accept him, than for him to accept us. We are probably more committed to the team idea and have had more experience bringing in outsiders, and making them a part of the team."

During 1968, 1969, and 1970 our experience in Illinois proved that planning colleges calls for high-level team action: (1) with representatives from the college administration and faculty who are responsible for determining space needs for the functional aspect of planning, (2) with the local college board which controls policy direction and approves (what could be more important to an architectural team), and (3) with representatives from the Illinois Junior College Board since this group reviews the master plans and applications for the building programs before submitting them to the Board of Higher Education for its approval. For all practical purposes each of these groups could be considered on the team.

One of the most important outsiders (really an insider) is the Illinois Building Authority, responsible for funding the state share of the project cost and for the construction phase of the project. The IBA, who become the owner of the project when construction begins, has its own requirements which the project must meet; therefore it is especially important to have its staff represented on the task team from concept to completion.

Familiarity with the requirements of the various agencies is, of course, essential to the architect. But achieving planning solutions which satisfy all parties concerned requires much more than getting to know people and their requirements. Compromises have to be made, and sometimes variances to the established guidelines have to be requested and approval granted. This is where team action is an absolute must—to generate consensus. CRS, with our associates, has in most instances taken the lead in coordinating these efforts. Conferences were held in Springfield with the IJCB staff and in Chicago with the IBA resulting in reports and recommendations to the local college board. The process involved many people, each of whom had responsibility for a particular segment of the project—team effort with an expanded team.

To carry the expanded team idea to more current and more complex projects, consider the proposed Governors State University which we were commissioned to do with Evans Associates of Bloomington. This new university is one of two to be built in Illinois in this century. The State of Illinois decided to create the new institutions primarily to serve graduates of the community college system. This meant a new kind of university; a three-year senior institution starting at the junior year and offering bachelors and masters degrees. It offered a chance to start fresh, without tradition, in creating an innovative and experimenting element in higher education.

Phil Williams, Ralph Carroll, and Frank Lawyer headed our portion of the planning team. The team began to form when the Board of Governors selected Dr. William E. Engbretson as president. He brought Dr. Keith Smith of the Illinois Board of Higher Education aboard as vice president and Dr. Ted Andrews, formerly Director of Science, Educational Research Council of America. In August of 1969, Dr. Engbretson held a large weekend seminar in Chicago to brainstorm educational concepts and begin additional selection of faculty and administrative personnel.

From that time the team has rapidly grown to include: three key administrative persons—Dr. Tillman Cothran, Dr. Clay Johnson, Dr. Edward Dodson; key staff including Mr. Tom Laysell; fourteen prospective faculty (most of whom participated in the squatters); Johnson Johnson & Roy, planning consultants in charge of developing the master plan; Evans Associates, Architects (J. Orme Evans—Richard Mills) with whom we associated for Phase 1; Davis McConnell Ralston, Educational Consultants (Dr. Paul Wisch); Brown-Davis-Mullins and M. Dean Wurth, Consulting Engineers; Dean Robert B. Downs, University of Illinois, library consultants; Instructional Dynamics, Inc. (Phil Lewis, Media Consultants); McKee, Berger, Mansueto Management Consultants; Illinois Building Authority; Educational Testing Service, Dan Hotton; and of course the Board of Governors.

Seven months of educational programming by DMR and site analysis by JJR culminated in a planning squatters involving virtually the entire team. Monthly meetings had been held for coordination and information. The squatters was overwhelming in some respects, and tremendously successful. Skillful management by Keith Smith was important. Prospective faculty and administration were divided into task forces to study various aspects of the program and made periodic reports to the design team (JJR, Evans,

323

CRS). The various consultants were interviewed. JJR, as planners, took the design lead, and the architects accompanied this with program interpretation and basic architectural concepts. DMR was represented full time by Paul Wisch.

Phil Williams made this curt post-mortem on the squatters: "An inspiring week of team dynamics. An approved campus plan and pre-schematic architectural concept, supported by a participating team of over 30 people. Education of various team members in each others' skills and responsibilities. Involvement. A careful balance of organization and latitude, plus extensive preparation, plus creative people dedicated to a task, can produce a hell of a squatters! Even in large numbers. It was also a highly successful builder of involvement and spirit for the fledgling staff, and should reap management rewards for the administration."

When a project is downtown it becomes even more complex. Urban redevelopment is complex even in its most simple state; nevertheless, a problem-solving team consisting of membership which crosses political as well as disciplinary boundaries can and has revitalized tired, worn-out downtown areas. But it is not an easy task.

A good way to restore life to the downtown is to build a new college in the area. A wonderful opportunity opened up to the CRS team early in 1968 when we were commissioned with others to plan the Delaware Technical and Community College to be built in the heart of the old decayed "south center city" area of Wilmington. Bob Reed, Paul Kennon, and Fred Matthews took the lead on this one for the CRS portion of the total planning effort and became members of a close-knit combination of an urban planning team including President Paul Weatherly, Bill Norton and Bill Faucett of the administration, together with the Board of Trustees. All participated heavily in the conceptual design squatters. In early 1970 we were given the assignment to plan Brandywine Educational Park, also located in the downtown area. This second contract related to the secondary segment of Wilmington Public School and is somewhat of an innovative experiment from the sociological point of view.

The user/client portion of the educational park planning team in addition to the school board included Dr. Gene A. Geisert, Superintendent; Dr. Samuel A. Scaranato, Assistant Superintendent; and Dr. LeRoy Christophe, Project Coordinator, along with many others.

CRS history tells us to expect even larger and more complex teams during the next decade. We shall need more sophisticated methods to help us work together—outsiders as well as insiders.

117

Giant projects require giant teams

It might well be that the single-building projects from which most of today's architects make their living will be a thing of the past. Land is becoming precious. A neighborhood is becoming too complicated to deal with building singly.

We have on our boards (and on our computers) many multifunction, multiform projects—ranging from civic centers, including everything from convention facilities to sports arenas, to highly complex centers, including not only an assortment of hospitals and clinics, but office blocks and huge parking garages as well.

But these are only small segments of the larger urban scene which require the attention of the architectural team. The CRS team wants to deal with larger pieces of the city.

Recently CRS turned over to client/users a carpeted segment of an underground system for pedestrian circulation in downtown Houston. This tunnel network has evolved through cooperative efforts among private and public builders. The Ten Ten Travis Corporation had commissioned CRS to plan the extension of this tunnel system from the basement (lower level) of the Tenneco Gas Building, two blocks south to block 268. Construction of this south nerve end of the system is now being completed. We are involved in extended team action; joint-venture architects working for joint-venture clients. Houston National Co., realty arm of Tenneco, joined with PIC Realty Co. (of Prudential Insurance) and retained a team of three Houston-based firms, Koetter, Tharp and Cowell, Neuhaus and Taylor, and CRS, to develop plans for a downtown 1000-room convention hotel and office building complex.

Bellows Construction Company has been an integral part of the team since we began in December 1969. Charles Lawrence and Jim Gatton played the leadership role for CRS with Lawrence assuming the design leadership for the three associated firms, called JV3 (Joint Venture Three). We anticipate more of these arrangements—teams of teams.

We would like to tackle the entire transportation problem of New Orleans or Omaha or Houston. We would like to see if we can find better ways to deal with the cars, trucks, and buses, which must move efficiently throughout the city to give it life. We would like to devise a unique rapid transportation system which will help to alleviate the clogging of the life-giving streets and thoroughfares. We would like to tackle air travel in its totality, not deal with just one main airport at a time, but with a system of airports and heliports which solve the intra-urban problems of general aviation as well as the inter-urban problems involving air transports. We would like to plan an expansion and improvement of the Houston ship channel and its turning basin and try to extend the finger-like water transportation systems deep into the city through the bayous so that family boats can have access to all parts of the city. A beautiful city has to have water. And we would want to make sure that these sub-transportation systems of the city work together as a system of systems and reach out to help the regional systems. Even more important, we want to do these things with an architectural approach. We want to help create architecture for the masses. We want people to experience architecture when they go from one place to another whether by car, train, boat or plane. To do these things we'll have to expand our team even more. Among many other specialists, we will need water pollution experts to take care of domestic and industrial waste. We'll need all types of planners, of specialized architects and engineers who know how to handle the problems of waterfronts. We'll need highway engineers, airport planners, and rapid-transport experts. And, obviously, we shall have to include a few sociologists, economists, and project managers with the political astuteness to get the job done. It's a giant project and we'll need a giant team.

The next ten years will offer the greatest challenge architects, engineers, planners, manufacturers, and builders have ever been faced with. The government's involvement in ecology, conservation, air and water pollution, housing, schools, and hospitals for all people will stimulate unbelievable large-scale, multibuilding-type projects. The country will either see one of its biggest building booms or face a revolution. In either case the architectural profession had better be prepared.

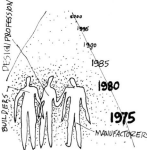

THE BUILDING INDUSTRY MUST RETOOL FOR AN UNPRECEDENTED AGE OF BUILDING AND RENEWAL. THIS **BUILDING BOOM** WILL BE ONE OF A COMPLETELY DIFFERENT **SCALE** AND CONSTRUCTION MANAGEMENT **PROCEDURES.** THE **CHALLENGE** OF THE PROFESSION OF **ARCHITECTURE** IS TO SEE THAT THE NEW SPACES AND FORMS AND THE REVITALIZED CITIES POSSESS THAT AURA WHICH IS:
ARCHITECTURE.

This is the home of Caudill Rowlett Scott, Architects Engineers Planners. Mr. Caudill, Mr. Rowlett, and Mr. Scott are logos, in a sense—symbols of a team whose main goal is to create architecture. In the early days of the limited team, the three name partners were expected to nurse every job. Not now. This is the day of the expanded team. Clients are more interested in working with the various specialists selected specifically to do their job. The names of the three original partners have less meaning each year. The partnership is losing its importance. The CRS team is basically a corporation. Some of us believe that when we are completely free of the vestiges of the false pride of partnership and have to rely on our ability to perform as individuals in an extended-team situation, CRS will be in a better position to assume national leadership.

118

Conglomerates may take over the giant tasks

It is common these days to pick up a *Wall Street Journal* and read that large companies are negotiating with architectural and engineering firms that would give these companies "the ability to redesign entire urban areas such as downtown Los Angeles." CRS has been approached by three such conglomerates. All three wanted to buy us, lock, stock, and barrel, on a stock-exchange basis. They made pretty fair offers, too. All of us on the CRS team did get—and still can get—excited at the prospects of redesigning downtown Los Angeles, replanning and rebuilding lower Manhattan, or building a new city in the foothills of the Rocky Mountains.

One conglomerate just about convinced us it would be fun to be a participating team on a team of teams. It sounded great to have as colleague teams an engineering firm specializing in the structural aspects of large high-rise buildings and elevated highways through metropolitan areas, another engineering firm which does mostly waterfront development, a third engineering firm which is experienced in airport planning, sewage disposals, and water treatment plants, plus other firms in the conglomerate which specialize in human behavior as influenced by environmental design, the economies of urbanization, and in the computerized approach to planning annd management related to large-scale operations. What the conglomerate needed was a highly organized group of architects, engineers, and planners who could successfully deal in large-building group reports. We seemed to fill the bill. Their people and our people have had lengthy discussions concerning CRS' joining the larger team. But we have rejected the offers. Our enthusiasm dulls when we think of losing control of our own firm that has been nurtured with love and tender care these many

THE **CONGLOMERATES** ARE GATHERING MANY FIRMS OF DIFFERENT SPECIALITIES TO MAKE **GIANT TEAMS** TO DO GIANT PROJECTS.

years. We like CRS the way it is. This may be our greatest weakness, because it seems almost certain that during the next few years great corporations such as General Electric, Westinghouse, and other space-age firms will be our competition. If we survive it will be because we will do a better job than they can. But to do this we will have to be a bit larger, perhaps buy out a few companies ourselves. We may need more companies like CRS2.

An architect friend of mine who has a small firm in a small city is currently trying to get other small firms throughout his state to combine to go after the large jobs. It is not quite that simple. Ten small firms do not necessarily add up to one large firm.

A firm geared to do small work has difficulties in grasping and coping with the complexities of large projects. My professors used to tell us, "If you can design a small house, you can design a small city." That is a simplism. I will admit the approach to both design problems is the same, because I believe in the triad theory—integrating and maximizing of the forces of function, form, and economy for every project. Nevertheless, because the scope is so different, the problems of house and city are so divergent, and the talent-experience necessary to solve these problems so disparate, there is very little similarity between designing a house and planning a city. There are not many house architects who can successfully plan cities nor many city planners who can design beautiful, functional houses.

The numbers come into the picture. You might say one person could design a small house, while a large team—even a conglomerate of many specialized teams—would be required to design a small city.

119

Corporate practice has certain advantages over the traditional partnership arrangement

When John Rowlett and I first hung out our shingle, we formed a partnership. That was the thing to do in those days.

We both were so anxious to do the right thing, the right way, we obtained the advice of the country's most experienced lawyer. We wanted him to draw up an airtight partnership agreement. What he recommended shook us up a bit.

The wise old judge said, "Boys, forming a partnership is like getting married. All the carefully selected words put on a piece of paper are meaningless unless you trust each other. And both of you better behave, because each is responsible for the other's actions and debts." We took his advice. For many years CRS operated without a legal partnership document.

I recall the time we first set up an agreement by memorandum when Willie Pena came into the firm. It was agreed that he would own 5% of the firm. We did not discover until the end of the year, when we added up the four partner's percentages of ownership, that it came out to be 105%! But there was no problem of distributing profit shares. That year there were no profits!

Later on, the partnership was based on a very sophisticated legal document relating to deaths, withdrawals, liabilities, and benefits. We had to. With thirty-seven partners, such a document was necessary.

Today, forming a corporation seems the thing to do. At least everyone is doing it. CRS jumped the gun by going the corporation route in 1957, eleven years after its founding. The partnership, however, was not abandoned. For the next thirteen years, we operated on a double standard. Legally and ethically we had to retain the partnership. Also because "partner" was such a precious word, we felt that we had to preserve the name. Then, everyone wanted to be a partner. Today most of our people would rather be vice-presidents in charge of something or somebody.

In the beginning there were only two partners; then four more, and at the time of forming the corporation, there were eight partners. The total firm then was forty-two. About one in every five were partners. in 1970 it was a little less than one out of every six. We have always had a lot of chiefs.

In 1970 Tom Bullock, president-elect of the Texas Society of Architects, was called upon on many occasions to speak at various AIA functions in Texas and throughout the country, on the corporate practice of architecture, since we pioneered the corporate way of practice in this section of the country. I believe Fehr and Granger of Austin, Texas, beat us to the draw by a few months.

Tom Bullock listed the following benefits of using the corporate framework, but always pointed out to his colleagues that "successful organizations did not get to the top by doing things the way they are doing them now," and pointed out the risk in getting on the corporate bandwagon. Bullock's reasons for corporate practice are:

• Corporations protect the individuals from liability suits relating to errors, omissions, and accidents.
• Generally, (but not always) there are tax advantages.

332

- There is a greater chance of good client relations because corporations (architects) can best deal with corporations(clients) through understanding of common problems.
- Corporations respect corporations; so job procurement is made easier.
- Partnerships, particularly those with family ties, seem innately to build a crust at the management top, while the corporation framework encourages professional development at all levels.
- Corporations have greater chances of staying in business longer than partnerships, most of which die when the principals die.
- The team concept has a better chance to flourish within the corporate framework than within a partnership arrangement, primarily because of the distinct gap between a partner and a nonpartner.
- The expanded team is more manageable in the corporate framework.
- There are opportunities for ownership which encourage incentives at all levels because the employee "owns a piece of the business."

During the summer of 1969, the CRS partners decided to enlarge the ownership of stock. We changed stock ownership from ten stockholders to thirty-seven, the first step to erasing the partnership altogether as an organization.

On 1 July 1970 the partnership was abandoned for all practical purposes. The corporation, Caudill Rowlett Scott, Inc., purchased the partnership, including the name. Whereas before the partnership owned the corporation, now the corporation owns the partnership. To facilitate better management, the firm was split up into eight profit center divisions with each division fairly autonomous.

The return to decentralization was timely because we had become a bit crust-hardened at the top. The young members were beginning to wonder if they could ever make it in CRS. One particularly ambitious young man said, "It's like trying to set a 100-yard dash record running in molasses." The new arrangement is giving them a smooth track with the wind at their backs. For example, we put a twenty-four-year-old youngster in charge of a very important, established division.

If titles are important, and apparently they are, the new corporate divisional structure provides for thirty-nine vice presidents.

Time will be the only real proof, but we are convinced that the corporate practice of architecture facilitates architecture by team. At least the hard line between a partner and a nonpartner will be erased, and team members will be called by their functional corporate titles.

120

To understand the concept of the expanded team there must be a new professional attitude

The expanded-team concept allows specialists in an unlimited number of disciplines to become involved in projects. Those in architecture or in professions related to design should be joined by the developer, the contractor, the manufacturer, the lawyer, and the financial planner. Even more significant is the inclusion of the user as a member of the team—whether the project be slum clearance or a new transportation system. And this may bring the project into politics, in which case the team should have some members adept at political action.

The unprecedented scale of forthcoming projects places the architect, who was the dominant professional and sole agent of the client, in a completely different role. He may not be so dominant. If he is leading the total team, he'll have to prove himself. Most certainly he will have to widen the scope of his capabilities. The "new professionals"—the systems analysts, construction management consultants, operational management consultants, space planners, environmental experts, psychologists, sociologists, economists, and consultants in building utilization—are becoming more and more active in planning buildings and viewing themselves on a par with not only the architects and engineers, but also with lawyers, doctors, and accountants. The architects will either have to bring these new professionals in as permanent members of the team or be willing to work with them as outside consultants.

Added to the rapidly expanding list of new professionals concerning building planning, construction, and operation, there is another strong force which will affect the kinds of organization architects will have. Many giant corporations are entering the professional service business. So are the "systems firms." The architects now are in competition with not only the old enemy, the package dealer, but also with more formidable rivals.

Just how the architecture profession will meet the challenge remains to be seen. There will be change.

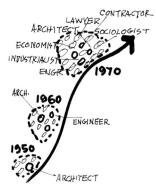

JUXTAPOSITIONAL WITH THE EXPANDED TEAM IDEA MAY REQUIRE THE CONCEPT OF THE **EXPANDED PROFESSION.** THE AIA MAY HAVE TO OPEN ITS GATES TO NON-ARCHITECTS. I CONTEND, HOWEVER, THAT IF OTHER PROFESSIONALS CONTRIBUTE TO CREATING THE PHENOMENON OF **ARCHITECTURE** THEN THEY SHOULD BE CALLED ARCHITECT.

121
The profession needs changing

There is a public obligation that goes along with being a member of the profession of architecture. We seem to have forgotten this. Somewhere down the line many of us have picked up the notion that we are artists and have all the privileges and freedoms of a painter or sculptor. We flounder in the sea of self-importance. Personal expression is more important than public responsibility.

Steve Kliment, who heads CRS' research efforts, feels that the architect has too often made major decisions based on hunches: "This worked in the days of few and well-tried options—in structural systems, heating and ventilating, enclosure, plumbing, as well as project management concepts; so the architect was able to pour his energies into the creation of forms in the role of artist-designer."

"Today, the options are too many, the turnover in techniques is too swift, and the nature of these techniques too sophisticated and exacting for architecture by hunch to be any longer valid. The new client expects from his architect the latest in technical and management expertise."

For the profession to survive, personal expression must give way to the realization that architectural forms and spaces are public domain, dependent upon public acceptance. Architects must grasp the fact that sharing the accomplishment of the completed project is an adjunct of the special calling of the profession of architecture.

There must be a change of attitude from "I" to "we." The architect and the architectural teacher must learn to work with other disciplines, but first they must learn to work with other architects—all kinds of architects. Now there are many kinds of architects and there will be many more kinds —those who specialize in programming, in the psychology of architectural space, in the sociology of buildings, in conceptual design, in design development, in technology of materials, in building types such as hospitals and schools, in urban design, in construction management, in building systems, and many others. It may be necessary for the boards of architectural examiners to revise completely the definition of architect. Certainly the scope will have to be broadened.

There are also limits. "Architect" cannot be spread all over the dictionary or the architect will end up trying to be everything, doing nothing well. The most important role that the architect must play, and this should never be forgotten, is his role as the professional liaison between arts/humanities and science/engineering. In one sense, he is the most general of the generalists. What other profession demands that its members be part artist and part scientist? Like the beach where water overlaps land, the practice of architecture flourishes where two worlds join, where science/engineering overlaps the arts/humanities. The survival of the profession depends upon how well architects manage to preserve and clarify this uniqueness. Redefining of the profession is imperative because there needs to be change.

One thing, however, must certainly be left unchanged: Architects are and should always be amphibians. No matter what kind of architects we are, we are still architects—professional sponsors of architecture—who must cope with both worlds. Within the spectrum of architectural practice, we need to know what is happening in and to contribute to both art and science. The future demands that architects increase their sensitivity to protecting and enriching human endeavor through both science and art and be able to communicate with specialists from all disciplines—from psychology to solid physics. Just how those concerned with architecture meet the challenge remains to be seen.

The change is upon us.

The professional architects must adapt to change, yet retain their identity as amphibians who practice on the beach—knowing how to run and swim. Professional architects must join hands with those of other disciplines to meet the challenge of creating a new kind of architectural practice leading to new kinds of forms and spaces—Architecture by Team.

THE **PRACTICE** OF ARCHITECTURE IS WHERE **TWO WORLDS** JOIN——

LIKE ON THE **BEACH** WHERE WATER OVERLAPS LAND—— WHERE ARTS/ HUMANITIES AND SCIENCE/ ENGINEERING COME TO- GETHER. **ARCHITECTURE** IS A RESPONSE TO THE **PSYCHOLOGICAL** AND **PHYSICAL** NEEDS OF MAN.

Photograph Credits

Aggieland Studio: p. 213
Architectural Camera, Ltd.: p. 266
John Bintliff: pp. 27, 101, 288
Bert Brandt: pp. 78, 237
James Brett: pp. 40, 77, 255
Roland Chatham: pp. 5 (lower
    right), 55, 99, 135
Robert Damora: p. 79 (lower)
Gordon Dinsmore: p. 13
Bill Engdahl (Hedrich-Blessing):
    p. 100
Rick Gardner: pp. 53, 117, 158
Griggs Studio: p. 257
Bob Hawks: p. 14
Hedrich-Blessing: p. 76
Rush J. McCoy: p. 146
McKoon Photography: pp. 84,
    118, 188
Mears Photography: pp. 97, 254
Ulric Meisel—Dallas: pp. 58, 122,
    229, 233, 251, 313
Monsanto Company, Textiles Divi-
    sion: p. 119
Jay Oistad: p. 52
Rondal Partridge: p. 224 (upper)
Ben Schnall: pp. 5 (left), 15, 106
    (right), 155, 185, 197, 200, 218,
    304, 328
Julius Shulman: pp. 10, 62, 162
Ed Stewart: pp. 5 (upper right),
    227
Studio de Lari: p. 169
Lawrence S. Williams, Inc.: p. 315
Myron Wood: pp. 87, 212, 224
    (lower)

Index